The man who
burned the
White House

The man who burned the White House

ADMIRAL SIR GEORGE COCKBURN
1772-1853

by James Pack

KENNETH MASON

For Eloïse

Published by Kenneth Mason
The old harbourmasters, Emsworth, Hampshire PO10 7DD

British Library Cataloguing in Publication Data
Pack, A J
    The man who burned the White House:
    Admiral Sir George Cockburn, 1772-1853
    1. Cockburn, Sir George
    2. Great Britain. Royal Navy – Biography
    3. Admirals – Great Britain – Biography
    I. Title
    359.3'31'0924 DA88.1.C5/

ISBN 0-85937-332-0

Printed in Great Britain by Redwood Burn Limited, Wiltshire.
Typesetting and artwork production by Articulate Studio, Hampshire

Contents

Illustrations

MAPS

9

Foreword

IT WAS A MATTER for some surprise to find that no full length biography had ever been written of Admiral of the Fleet Sir George Cockburn. As his story unfolds I hope that readers will agree, in all justice, that it is appropriate for his life to be more widely known. There will be those who will recollect his name as the man who attacked Washington during Britain's unfortunate 1812-1815 war with America, and others who will recall his awesome responsibility for seeing Napoleon into exile in the fortress of St Helena.

Less well known may be his achievements as a young frigate captain alongside Horatio Nelson who thought so highly of him; or of his later life when he displayed outstanding diplomatic and statesmanlike skills to match the courage and leadership of his earlier days.

Perhaps his legend was not passed down to later generations for the simple reason that he had no son and heir, and hence no direct descendants; the Langton baronetcy which he inherited became extinct with the death of his nephew Sir Alexander Cockburn, the Lord Chief Justice of England. Whatever the reason, the failure to record his accomplishments more widely can only be an oversight.

Sadly – despite an exhaustive search – it has not been possible to discover the existence of any family papers. In all likelihood they have long since been destroyed. While, therefore, the narrative may lack the deeply personal feeling which such papers create, the 82 volumes of Sir George Cockburn's manuscripts on his service life held in the Library of Congress, Washington, have gone a long way to compensate.

I am deeply grateful to the staff of the Library and to William S Dudley, Head of the Historical Research Branch in the Washington

Navy Yard Centre, for their assistance and encouragement; and to the Hampshire Library Service in Winchester, England, who so readily agreed to acquire the mirofilm of these volumes. The Portsmouth City Library now has the custody of these reels and I am indebted for their loan and other help. The Royal Naval Museum, Portsmouth has provided, as always, unstinted advice on illustrations and other matters.

There are many other sources and individuals too many to enumerate, who have made valuable contributions, but I cannot escape a special word of thanks to Joan Hoseason for her assistance with the genealogy of the Cockburn family; her ancestor, John Hoseason, married Augusta, the daughter of Sir George. Also to Graham Hunt for the unfailing help provided from his collection of rare books.

Visits to a number of places associated with Admiral Cockburn have helped to create a feeling for the man. Included in these have been the site of the castle at Cockburn's Law near Duns in the Border country, where the family had its origins, and the estate of Langton nearby; Havre-de-Grace, St Michael's, Benedict and the Patuxent River all in Maryland and on the shores of the Chesapeake Bay, so redolent of Sir George's activities in 1813 and 1814; and to the remote island of St Helena in the south Atlantic where little has changed since Napoleon was incarcerated there. Brief expeditions to Weobley in Herefordshire, High Beech in Epping Forest, Essex and Leamington Spa were equally rewarding. Cockburn's house, Wallsgrove, still stands in its ample grounds at High Beech and the Clarendon Hotel at Leamington where he died, remains there today.

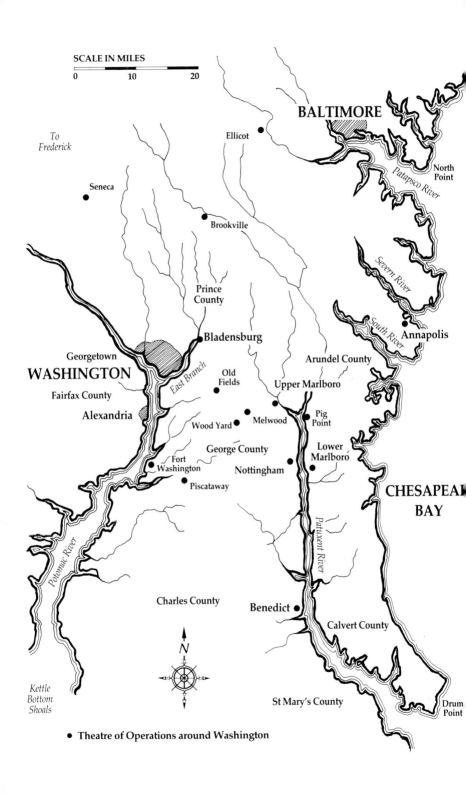

SCALE IN MILES

0   10   20

To Frederick

BALTIMORE

Patapsco River

North Point

Ellicot

Seneca

Brookville

Severn River

Prince County

South River

Annapolis

Bladensburg

Georgetown

WASHINGTON

Arundel County

Old Fields

Upper Marlboro

East Branch

Fairfax County

Alexandria

Wood Yard

Melwood

Pig Point

George County

Lower Marlboro

Fort Washington

Nottingham

Piscataway

CHESAPEAKE BAY

Potomac River

Patuxent River

Charles County

Benedict

Calvert County

Kettle Bottom Shoals

N

St Mary's County

Drum Point

●   Theatre of Operations around Washington

CHAPTER ONE

Twenty-four hours to remember 1814

IN THE TWILIGHT SHADOWS of August 24, 1814, Rear-Admiral George Cockburn caught his first glimpse of Washington, Here before him, the moving spirit behind the British advance so far, was the reward for his planning and persistence. With him was Major-General Robert Ross, commanding the three hastily formed brigades of infantrymen, marines, and seamen. In the brief period since the landing at Benedict in Maryland the two men had developed a friendly and co-operative relationship all the more remarkable in view of their contrasting attitudes.

Cockburn had been convinced for some time that Washington was there for the taking; Ross, with his small force of 3,000 regular soldiers, had marched some 25 miles from Benedict to Upper Marlborough to try out the land, ready to re-embark at a moment's notice. His highly trained veterans, flushed with the success of the Peninsular War against Napoleon's generals, had come straight from Bordeaux with no supporting artillery or cavalry and ill-equipped for battle. It was far from his mind to risk them on the whim of his naval companion in arms, and on more than one occasion he had rejected the idea of advancing on the capital. Yet Cockburn was ever insistent and with his greater experience of the Virginian and Maryland shores of the Chesapeake, and of every river and inlet between the Susquehanna and Cape Henry, who would deny him? The rear admiral had shown himself to be as at home leading his Royal Marines and sailors ashore as at sea: where other Britons had failed to take advantage of the undefended American seaboard in this internecine conflict, Cockburn had shone as an exponent of amphibious warfare whenever his small but dedicated force had landed. And 18 months experience had made him master of its topography.

13

Ross was disadvantaged in arguing his case against a man of Cockburn's persuasive power. As they had decided to move the army forward on August 23 and to bivouac for the night at Melwood on the road to Washington, Cockburn had agreed that he would send back his trusted aide-de-camp, Lieutenant James Scott, to Benedict on the Patuxent river to inform the commander-in-chief, Admiral Sir Alexander Cochrane, of their intention to attack. Scott had returned long before dawn with the commander-in-chief's explicit order to return to Benedict and re-embark, not at all what Cockburn had expected or wanted. But he was not to be deterred now. By sheer strength of personality and confidence in his own judgement he had convinced Ross that with Washington now a mere 16 miles away they could not turn back. He knew that in disobeying his superior's order, with no concessions for failure, he was gambling his professional career; and even success, while not damning him, would not necessarily endear him to Sir Alexander.

As a red-tinged morning sky gave hint of heat to come, the drums began to roll and a low murmur of enthusiasm from the men indicated well enough the popularity of the decision. There was no more time to lose. The oppressive heat soon drained the British. Dusty and thirsty, they had marched in their thick red jackets for hour after hour with but one short break, choosing the Bladensberg road to the north-east of Washington partly to deceive the Americans but mainly to be able to cross the eastern branch of the Potomac without relying on the bridges. The force had been formed into three brigades, with the 85th Regiment of King's Light Infantry in the van. Not only was this regiment well officered, but the men were lightly equipped and adept pacesetters, so it was no surprise that on arrival at Bladensburg, about noon, they were some way ahead of the second and third brigades. There in front of them on the heights above the town an American army was drawn up in prepared positions. The decision to attack without delay by the 1,400 or so men of the 85th, although crowned with success, was an extravagant move. Faced by some 10,000 men and artillery, well dug-in, the advance brought its inevitable cost in killed and wounded, but once the lines had been breached the untried American militia broke in headlong retreat.

The irrepressible Cockburn had been in the forefront. Mounted on a white charger and resplendent in his gold-laced hat and epaulettes, he was an obvious target for opposing marksmen. Corresponding in rank to General Ross his position on the battlefield was anachronistic; he could not lead the troops which, no doubt, he would have done readily given the opportunity, instead he busied himself with the marine artillery, directing their aim and firing their rockets. They were one of the few surprises which the British had up their sleeves in this sad quarrel with their American cousins. Recently invented by an army officer, Congreve by name, the rockets made up for their inaccuracy by creating fear in those opposing them for the first time. Smoke and flame added to the staccato noise of discharge sapped the morale of an untrained opposition.

Lieutenant Scott had attempted to persuade his admiral that he was over-exposed, commenting that however much they suffered the enemy would regard his death as ample compensation, but Cockburn quickly dismissed the suggestion; it was a point of honour to make himself conspicuous. As if to confirm Scott's warning, a musket shot promptly passed between Cockburn's leg and the flap of his saddle, cutting the stirrup leather in two. Miraculously neither he nor his horse was injured but, while he was temporarily dismounted, a marine by his side was killed by round-shot. Cockburn led a charmed life.

Not so fortunate was Joshua Barney, the American commodore, whose gunboats had recently been vanquished by Cockburn on the Patuxent. With his gallant seamen he had arrived late to reinforce the American lines. Now severely injured, Barney glanced up weakly as Cockburn was brought to his side. 'Well admiral, you have got hold of me at last', he sighed.[1] Cockburn, chivalrous as always, consoled and reassured him while an English surgeon bound his wounds. Barney was promptly freed on parole, as were some of his officers to see him to a place of safety. So deep an impression did this gesture make on the commodore's mind that he resolved, on recovery, to return his thanks to Cockburn in person under a flag of truce.

Barney's brave little force of 400 flotilla-men had held out to the last but to no avail. With the fighting over there was no question of a British pursuit – the men had sunk to the ground exhausted except for those detailed to remove the wounded and bury the dead. Some 254 had been killed or wounded but now, after brief refreshment, the survivors were needed for the prime objective – Washington.

Cockburn and Ross moved forward with the third brigade consisting of the seamen, Royal Marines, and the 21st Foot but before their arrival in the Washington suburbs it was dark. General Ross had repeatedly sounded a parley in the accepted manner by a loud roll on the drums, for he and Cockburn were anxious to spare the city if the right terms could be agreed, but no response was forthcoming. Washington had been abandoned. The president, statesmen, generals and soldiers had escaped as best they could. Secretary of State James Monroe and Secretary of War John Armstrong, along with General Winder, had thought to turn the Capitol into a citadel, but the idea was abandoned when the last semblance of discipline broke down. President Madison had arrived at the President's House around 4.30 pm only to find that Dolley, his wife, had left 30 minutes earlier whereupon the President made his own retreat into Virginia with similar despatch.

Hopes of a moratorium were fast fading and as Ross, Cockburn and their staffs, accompanied by a small guard, rode into the city and reached the open space where the Capitol stood, such dreams evaporated. A volley from the Capitol, supported by cross fire from the houses on either side, knocked Ross's horse from under him and killed one of the guard. It was time to fight.

At this point Cockburn took charge, for the present situation bore a striking similarity to many he had experienced in his Chesapeake landings. Then he had respected private property and only when arms had been found or there had been resistance had he lit the torch. The *National Intelligencer* under the guidance of its editor Joseph Gales Jr – 'Dear Josey' as Cockburn called him – had so misinformed his readers that the admiral was reviled by them all. But Cockburn was no Attila the Hun, nor were his seamen vandals even though strong measures were clearly now demanded. Moreover, he was fully aware of the feeling in the higher ranks of the British service that, in this wholly unnecessary war declared by President Madison, the Americans had burned and plundered Canadian settlements and townships inhumanely. Retaliation was ever an unfortunate consequence of war but the decision was taken at this moment not to spare Washington's public buildings.

Lieutenant Scott was immediately ordered by Cockburn to force an entry into the houses adjoining the Capitol. He was too late to deal with the snipers who had escaped by the rear; but as the buildings had been appropriated for war use, they were fair prey. Assisted by the Congreve rockets which quickly lit the rafters, they set the scene for a night of horror.

The Capitol was destined for the same treatment which might

have been avoided had it not been filled with armed men. But even before the fire-raisers could start their work, the sky gave warning of a huge conflagration to the south. Fearing that the moment was close at hand when the British would seize his beloved navy yard, Captain Tingey, its commandant, decided that he would fire it himself. Storehouses, sail and rigging lofts, paint shops and timber yard, were all consumed, the task being all too easy with the ready materials on hand – wood chips, pitch, tarred rope and gunpowder. One building, the Marine Corps commandant's house, was spared then and again when the British completed the devastation the following day. It may have been overlooked – no-one quite knew the reason why. Legend had it that the Royal Marines bore so much respect for the United States Marine Corps that they did not burn what is now the oldest government building in Washington, but the firing of two valuable warships by Tingey, the *Columbia*, a new frigate, and the *Argus*, a sloop, completed the destruction.

With the sky as bright as day, Cockburn's men turned their attention to the Capitol. Before entering, men of the third brigade were deployed in line facing the building. A smart volley was fired as a signal of intent and to deter any sharpshooters who remained. Then the doors were broken down and a party led by Lieutenant Evans, deputy quartermaster general, set to with a will. Lieutenant Pratt of the navy was an expert in the use of pyrotechnics but found the solid, classical building a challenge. Again those adaptable rockets were employed and the flames surged through doors, windows and roof into the night. It was a task which offered no great pleasure; even the troops were silent as they watched the destruction of so much that was fine.

The archives and a valuable library acquired to form the basis of the Library of Congress, went up in flames except for one small memento retained by Cockburn, *An Account of the Receipts and Expenditure of the United States for the Year 1810*. It contained information on subjects as pedestrian as the payment of bounties on pickled fish and salted provisions exported, the names of districts famous in fishing annals from Nantucket and Gloucester down to Passamaquaddy and southward to Mobile, and pensions payments to Monsieur L'Enfant as compensation for his services in planning the city of Washington. Cockburn removed it from the office set apart for the President for no better reason than to provide evidence of his presence there, later to be inscribed inside the cover, 'Taken in the President's room in the Capitol at the destruction of that building by the

British on the capture of Washington, August 24, 1814, by Admiral Cockburn, and by him presented to his eldest brother Sir James Cockburn of Langton, Bart, Governor of Bermuda.' (It is now in the Jefferson Library of Congress.)

The flames from the Capitol set light to four more buildings on North Capitol Street where the Congressional papers had been moved; by now the roar from flammable material and the glare struck a mixture of horror and fury in the hearts of Washington's unfortunate inhabitants.

At about 10.30 pm, Cockburn and Ross collected 150 men and made their way up Pennsylvania Avenue, admiring the spacious causeway with its side roads and paths for equestrians and pedestrians separated by rows of trees. But this was no time to dally: a momentary stop only was allowed to reassure a worried inhabitant that individuals and private property would be respected, for they were anxious to reach the president's house not far away. Cockburn was not sure whom he might find there, uncertain of the movements of President Madison and his lady. Always the gallant, he sent an advance message offering Dolley Madison an escort to a place of safety, unaware that already she had flown. After a short while the party reached the handsome stone building which, along with the Capitol, was the pride of Washington. Some were already calling it the White House, a name appropriate to its appearance.

In the deserted building's dining room they found the table set for the victory which the Americans had hoped to celebrate. The uninvited battle-weary guests could scarcely believe their luck: a supply of excellent madeira and other wines considerably packed in ice in their coolers, and food in plenty for the inner man awaited them. There was even fine china – and crystal goblets to help add to the sense of occasion as they slaked their thirst and toasted the Prince Regent. Lieutenant Scott mused on the irony of a situation where, in other circumstances, the toast would have been to the champions of republican freedom, and he blessed his absent hosts for their erring foresight.

The beautiful apartments were hastily visited. The president's dressing room provided evidence enough of the rapid departures with opened drawers and half-filled travelling cases. The snowy clean linen proved too tempting for Scott and his companions who gladly exchanged it for their own soiled apparel. As Scott himself said, the operation of thrusting his unworthy person into a shirt belonging to no less a person than the chief magistrate of the United

States equalled in luxury the feast of the banqueting room.

Apart from such understandable excesses there was no looting. Cockburn had with him, as guide, Roger Weightman, a Washington book dealer, whose wish to remove a valuable souvenir was not against *his* moral principles; but Cockburn forbade it. Sitting Weightman in a chair, Cockburn ordered him to drink to 'Jemmy' as he liked to call the president, and gave him a few odds and ends of no consequence. The ever ebullient admiral selected a cushion from Dolley's chair, to remind him of her seat as his schoolboy humour expressed it.[2]

A brief relaxation was followed by the firing of the house. Lieutenant Pratt took over and completed his task proficiently again. By now he was building up a useful score to which was added, shortly after, the adjacent brick treasury building; but the longed-for treasure from that source, legitimate plunder, had already been removed.

It was nearing midnight as Cockburn returned down Pennsylvania Avenue, his thoughts with 'dear Josey', the Irish renegade whose *National Intelligencer* had made Cockburn a special target of hate. The admiral was far from a vindictive character and indulged in no personal grudges, but here was a heaven-sent opportunity to interrupt the flow of vilification against him which rolled from the paper's presses if only he could find the office. A bystander duly obliged by pointing out the building which stood back from its neighbours. Hardly had he made the opening moves for its destruction when two ladies pleaded that it should be spared or theirs would burn too. Always courteous in his dealings with the fair sex, Cockburn decided that the offices could equally well be pulled down. A party of seamen was detailed for the task, work requiring the use of stout ropes and a 'long pull, and a strong pull, and a pull together' so familiar to the men in their shipboard duties. In two hours the offices were in ruin and a huge bonfire was fed with reams of paper, gazettes and much else. 'Be sure that all the c's are destroyed so the rascals can't abuse my name any more', quipped the admiral and the printer's type was consigned.

By now, a host of attractive ladies had gathered abandoned, it seemed, by their menfolk. They chatted gaily with Cockburn who was delighted with their friendliness. 'Now did you expect to see me such a clever fellow? Were you not prepared to see a savage, a ferocious creature, such as Josey represented me? But you see I am quite harmless; don't be afraid, I will take better care of you than Jemmy did!' he said to one of them.

When the destruction was complete, the admiral and Scott were entertained with refreshments. Scott was asked by the hostess the name of the delightful officer accompanying him. 'Why, that is the vile monster Cock--burn', was his reply[3], pronouncing it as two long distinct syllables in the American fashion. The effect was electrifying!

Having made his farewells the admiral returned to the headquarters on Capitol Hill. It was the end of what, by any standards, had been a remarkable day – 20 hours of never-to-be forgotten non-stop activity.

CHAPTER TWO

The Cockburns of Langton

IN THE SUMMER OF 1314, the English governor of Stirling, under siege by the Scottish forces of Robert Bruce, had sent word to England that if they were not relieved shortly he proposed to surrender castle and town. Stirling, the strategic key to Scotland, was not to be lightly lost so King Edward II, hastily assembling an army mainly recruited from the midland and northern counties of England, marched to the garrison's rescue. Bruce, saving his forces, made no attempt to defend the border country but took up his battle station south of Stirling near the stream known as Bannock Burn to await the enemy.

At this time a number of the great Scottish nobles and landowners had a difficult part to play holding, as many did, large estates both in England and in Scotland, lieges therefore of the English as well as of the Scottish kings. Among those who decided now to range themselves with Robert Bruce was Sir William de Veteri-Ponti – or Wepoynt as he was sometimes known – a member of an illustrious Norman family and owner not only of Langton Castle in the Border country, but of other estates both in Scotland and England.

Although heavily outnumbered at Bannockburn, Bruce achieved a sensational victory. On the English side one earl, 42 barons and 68 knights, 700 esquires and 10,000 foot soldiers were killed in battle or in the subsequent pursuit, while the Scottish army lost but two knights and 4,000 men. One of these knights was Sir William de Veteri-Ponti. In the words of an ancient ballad,

> And upon the Scottis mennys party
> There wes slayne worthi knichtis twa
> Welyame the Wepoynt was ane of tha
> And Schyr Waltre of Ross ane othyr

Sir William had no son so his estates were inherited by his daughter Mariota, the wife of Sir Alexander de Cokburn whose family owned land stretching from nearby Duns to Cockburnspath on the east coast of Berwickshire; Alexander's father Piers had been knighted by King Alexander III of Scotland.

The Border country where their families lived consists of territory on both sides of the boundary line between Scotland and England, a line which begins at Berwick and running south-west follows the River Tweed for 35 miles to continue west as far as the Solway Firth. South lie rugged glens and high bleak moorlands on which sheep and cattle graze, while to the north stretch beautiful and fertile valleys and dales. In the 14th century a chain of peel towers, now ruined, reached across the country from coast to coast, many the homes of early border families. Throughout the years there were innumerable fights arising out of feuds and raids giving the area a name for lawlessness and bloodshed.

The Cockburn family home was originally one of these peel towers, enlarged in ensuing years. Built on the slopes of a hill called Cockburn's Law, close to the River Whiteadder, no traces of the castle now remain, although the commanding site can still be seen with a neighbouring farm incorporating many of the castle's solid old stones in house and barns.

The Cockburns are thought to have crossed the border from Northumberland in the reign of King Malcolm of Scotland around the year 1057, and to have been given lands by him in return for their help in defeating his enemy, Macbeth. Another theory is that they were descended from a Danish invader called Colbrand who, circa 950 AD, landed on the coastline just north of Berwick at Colbrandspeth now known as Cockburnspath and, liking what he saw, returned later to settle there. Whichever legend is true, the Cokburns or Cockburns were well established and their shield, with its cock's crest, well known by the time Alexander's father-in-law was killed at Bannockburn.

In about 1335, Mariota de Cokburn with husband and family moved to her castle at Langton near Duns, and for the next four hundred years or so, with but a short break, it remained in the possession of the senior line of the family. Throughout the centuries between, the Cockburns were prominent in Border country history and in the friendship of the Scottish kings. In 1413 a Cockburn was

22

deputed as ambassador to the Court of England, and in 1513, Sir William Cockburn, who with his wife were close friends of James IV and Queen Margaret, was killed at Flodden Field as were many of his Border relations.

A grandson of William's who inherited the castle was a faithful follower of Mary, Queen of Scots, and lost his castle when it was seized as retribution by the English. Later, retrieving their lands at Langton, the Cockburns continued to be prominent in Scottish affairs, and in the early 1600's the then Sir William Cockburn was awarded an English baronetcy by James I, formerly James VI of Scotland, which also entitled him to a large tract of land in the colony of Nova Scotia.

The last Cockburn to live at Langton, Sir Archibald, has been regarded as a reckless waster of the estates whereas he was, more likely, an able and enterprising man in advance of his time. He attempted improvements in farming, probably carried out by agents wedded to old customs, the prospective value of which were quite beyond their comprehension or that of his contemporaries. He introduced the buying of Highland cattle for fattening and contracted with a John Campbell, later Lord Breadalbane, to supply him with 500 'highland cowes yeirly for the space of thrie years'. His enterprise was unsuccessful; his creditors, becoming importunate, had him placed in Edinburgh's Tolbooth prison from which he managed to escape in 1700. Five years later he died and was buried in Langton church.

By 1742, the estate had passed to Sir Alexander Cockburn, a promising army officer who, during the short time he held the title, managed to relieve greatly the pressure of Archibald's obligations. Sadly, in 1745, he was killed at the battle of Fontenoy during the war of the Austrian Succession. Unmarried, his lands and commitments fell on the shoulders of a 14-year-old cousin, Sir James Cockburn and his widowed mother. The creditors again moved in and the estates had to be sold so that, when the young man came of age, he had only a small property and lands near Peebles. The house and estate at Langton were bought for £60,000 by a Mr Gavin, described as having 'great welth in Middleburgh in Zealand (Holland) by head and marriage but of low birth and obscure'. Then obscure perhaps, but his name is commemorated today by the village of Gavinton close by the Langton ruin.[1]

Sir James, who in 1752 became member of parliament for Peebles, married twice. His second wife was Augusta Ann, daughter of the Very Reverend Francis Ayscough, Dean of Bristol, by whom he had five sons and a daughter. One history of the Cockburn family comments that 'there are few intervals in history of this country in which the name of at least one of the Cockburns is not found prominently mentioned either as soldier, sailor, diplomatist, statesman, or lawyer'; certainly Augusta Ann's sons were no exception. Her first and fifth sons became generals in the army, and respectively Governors of Bermuda and Curaçoa with Honduras. Her third son was Dean of York, the fourth achieved high rank in the consular service but George, born on April 22 1772 and the subject of this book, outshone all.

In London's National Gallery there is a portrait by Sir Joshua Reynolds of Augusta Ann and her three elder sons; a copy of it beautifully executed on enamel by Bone can be seen in the Wallace Collection, also in London. The boys are in their infancy – William, the future Dean, lies naked on his mother's lap, and James, heir to the baronetcy is draped in pink and kneeling beside her. George, similarly dressed and barefooted, looks over her shoulder. It is an outstanding painting of a beautiful woman and part of her family, the male members of which all achieved distinction. Their father, Sir James, died at Hillingdon, near London, in 1804, his title passing to James, later Governor of Bermuda.

George's early childhood is unremarked but his family at that time appears to have been living in or around Lisson Grove, then a fashionable area of west London, and it is recorded that George first went to school in nearby Marylebone. He also received additional instruction in the classics from a Reverend Mr Wells at Margate. Later, he was sent to a Mr Roy in Old Burlington Street to be completed in mathematics, navigation and other studies necessary for entry into the navy which career he, himself, had chosen. With such a large family less than well endowed, the parents in all probability welcomed his choice of so honourable a profession. They certainly had friends in high places with the influence to see him placed.

He began his career under the patronage of the Admirals Lord Hood and Sir Joshua Rowley when, as a 10-year-old, he was entered as a 'captain's servant' on the books of a frigate commanded by Sir Joshua's son. This meant that his service time started while he was

• The Reynolds portrait of Lady Augusta and her three eldest sons.
(National Gallery, London)

at school which was then customary for those fortunate enough to
have the right 'interest'. Subsequently, his name appears on the
books of the *William and Mary* , yacht, and in 1786, aged 14, he made
his debut as a fledgling naval officer on board the *Termagant*, a sloop
of war employed on the home station.

In January 1788, Lord Hood arranged his appointment to the
Ariel, under the command of Captain Moorsom, noted for his ability
in gunnery, who was to captain the *Revenge* at Trafalgar. In 1789,
young Cockburn sailed with him to the East Indies to survey har-

bours and shores then little known. Now 17, he proved keen and anxious to learn; his commander, realising his potential, gave him much personal attention and always employed him on the more important surveys. By the time he left the *Ariel* in 1790 he had become a thoroughly practical all-round seaman; his apprenticeship under Moorsom was to serve him well throughout his career[2].

His next ship was the frigate *Hebe*, Captain Alexander Hood; for seven boisterous winter months the vessel cruised in and around the Channel watching for the smugglers who were endemic along these coasts. Acting first as midshipman and later as master's mate, his professional abilities widened. Among his fellow midshipmen onboard was Thomas Hardy with whom Cockburn's career was to run almost in parallel for the two were to meet with uncanny frequency. At one stage Hardy served as Cockburn's first lieutenant when the latter commanded the *Minerve* frigate, and he also followed on as first sea lord from Cockburn at a later period. Although both officers became, arguably, Nelson's greatest favourites, it was Hardy whose association became better known as *Victory*'s captain at Trafalgar.

Another contemporary of Cockburn, Midshipman Thomas Dillon, was also in the *Hebe*; his autobiography, written when an admiral, records with pride that of the five midshipmen then serving in the gunroom, four rose to flag rank.

Having passed his examination for lieutenant, Cockburn was sent in 1792 to the flagship *Romney* bound for the Mediterranean where, shortly after arrival, he was appointed first to the frigate *Pearl*, and, a few months later, to the *Orestes* commanded by Lord Augustus Fitzroy. It was on returning to England in this ship that he learned that war had been declared against France.

In the collected papers of Admiral Sir Thomas Byam Martin, another of Cockburn's contemporaries, the admiral comments on the many who went to sea aged 12 or 13 and who, by zeal and application, rendered themselves ornaments of their profession. Among them Nelson, Collingwood, St Vincent and Cockburn are cited as examples worthy of comparison with the most distinguished statesmen and diplomatists of the age. Martin continues, 'it is very remarkable that there is scarcely an instance of a naval officer faltering in any position of perplexity and difficulty; they have always, on such occasions, acquitted themselves with honour to their country.'

Conflict with France was to launch young Cockburn on precisely such a path.

CHAPTER THREE

War initiation 1793-6

WITH 1793's ADVENT George Cockburn's career prospects took a favourable turn. First, he had achieved unusually early promotion to lieutenant, probably the most important step in any naval officer's career. The earlier the examination for lieutenant could be passed after the qualifying age of 20, the sooner an officer could expect promotion. True, Horatio Nelson was allowed to present himself before an examining board while still only 19, shortly after which he was appointed lieutenant of the *Lowestoft,* but he was an exception. Any officer who succeeded in being posted lieutenant under the age of 21 had done extremely well. Such was Cockburn.

Secondly, the Thursday night dinner toast celebrated in the wardroom of 'a bloody war and quick promotion', could not have been more apposite at that moment when Cockburn gained his majority. War's outbreak meant a rapid enlargement of the fleet thus providing continuing opportunities for quick advancement – if one stayed alive. Thirdly, interest made all the difference for those who were fortunate enough to receive it. Under the patronage and watchful eye of Lord Hood – now commander-in-chief, Mediterranean – Cockburn could not go far wrong provided he was keen, efficient, and hard-working. The best interest was usually bestowed on those who were the sons or relations of senior naval officers which Cockburn was not, but his father did have powerful naval friends. The influence which Lord Hood brought to bear in Cockburn's brief 18 months in the Mediterranean to 'place' him, is evidence enough of its importance.[1]

On the last day of January 1793, the French Convention annexed the Austrian Netherlands and next day declared war on Great

Britain and Holland. With world revolution as her objective, France believed that England could also fall to internal revolt. France now held the Scheldt estuary and surrounding coasts leaving Britain with no choice but to defend her trade.

At the start of this protracted war Britain's army and navy, appallingly run down, lacked leadership and equipment. War required a leading politician to stir the country to superhuman effort and in Henry Dundas, a principal secretary of state blessed with a business flair, found a man able to organise the services into a state of moderate readiness.

The navy's main fleet was despatched to the Mediterranean under the command of Admiral Lord Hood to support *inter alia* the numerous French royalists in Provence. Cockburn, now a fledgling lieutenant, was appointed to the *Britannia*, a first rate ship-of-the-line but a notoriously bad sailer. Many years later, at Trafalgar, her sailing qualities almost debarred her from any part in the battle. She wore the flag of the second-in-command, Vice Admiral Hotham, of whom Cockburn was to see much in the years to come. Hood intended that Cockburn should remain only temporarily under Hotham; consequently, after a bare two months' service, he was transferred on July 2 to the *Victory*, Hood's own flagship as tenth and most junior lieutenant. To be posted to a fine first-rate of more than 100 guns, where his performance would be seen by those who mattered, was both exhilarating and demanding.

Marseilles and Toulon were blockaded after the fleet had arrived off these ports on July 16. The French fleet, thoroughly disorganised as a result of the Revolution, posed no threat and remained steadfastly inside Toulon harbour. To subsist, the import of corn was essential to the inhabitants; by denying them, they might submit without the need of force. It was no easy task for the patrolling warships as the small republic of Genoa, to the east, owned most of the Riviera; although neutral, her merchants were prepared to run the blockade in their own interests.

When Toulon capitulated quite suddenly at the end of August, it was not the threat of starvation that was wholly responsible. Internal dissension between the royalists and the Paris government was a more fundamental cause. Toulon, in fact, had been outlawed by the National Convention. The city commissioners arrived on board the *Victory* without warning to parley with Hood. Terms were straightforward: in exchange for recognition of the restitution of monarchy in France, Toulon's great arsenal would be delivered to

Hood. By any standards this was a good start. Allied troops took possession of the powerful fortifications commanding the harbour while the dockyards and French warships were surrendered to the British fleet.

With a grandstand view of these remarkable events, Cockburn and his fellow officers must have been rubbing their hands. The addition of prizes to the fleet should create extra jobs, and so it turned out. His seniors, one by one, were appointed away until he, himself, had risen to the exalted position of first lieutenant of the *Victory*. Then it was his turn. On October 28, 1793, after barely eight months of war, Hood gave Cockburn his first command by appointing him to the 14-gun brig sloop *Speedy*. A mere 78 feet long, a beam of 26 feet, and of 158 tons, she was more suited to coastwork than in operating with an ocean-going fleet. Her 14 guns sound formidable enough for her size, but they were only four-pounders capable almost of being lifted and fired. She was lightly masted and rigged, the headroom below the maindeck a mere five feet. Yet later, under Lord Cochrane, the *Speedy* was to achieve fame before her eventual capture by the French battleship *Dessaix* in 1801. Under George Cockburn, the *Speedy*'s record was to become outstanding enough in the three-and-a-half months he was in command. It was the season of storms in the Gulf of Genoa and the year 1793 provided them in full. Rarely at anchor, the *Speedy* plied between Toulon and Genoa carrying passengers and despatches.

Genoese ships increasingly ignored their own neutrality landing large quantities of corn and other contraband in the Riviera harbours for the benefit of the French on the other side of the Maritime Alps. Stronger measures had to be taken. Under Captain Sutherland of the *Diadem* Hood, therefore, formed a small squadron with the *Speedy* as part, to blockade Genoa. Towards the end of the year the squadron experienced a succession of storms, and in great distress it was finally scattered, all ships, except the *Speedy*, forced to shelter where they could. *Speedy* meanwhile maintained station off Genoa while her consorts were repairing. It was inconceivable to Sutherland that she could have survived and when the *Diadem* sailed into Hyères Bay for repairs, he had to report the dispersal of his squadron to Hood and his fears for *Speedy*'s safety. When his ship was seaworthy, Sutherland returned to Genoa only to find the *Speedy* still cruising off the Mole Heads. Unsupported, Cockburn had maintained the blockade and had seized a number of small vessels attempting to run it. The *Diadem's* arrival was timely as the *Speedy* was down to a few gallons of water and could not long have remained on station.

Sutherland was impressed and on the instant wrote a flattering report to Lord Hood on the skill, perseverance and fine seamanship displayed by Cockburn in such adverse circumstances. The *Speedy* sailed immediately for Hyères Bay with Cockburn acting as the courier for Sutherland's glowing encomium delivered personally to Lord Hood in *Victory's* great cabin. Cockburn had shown himself able to shoulder the responsibilities of a man of more mature years and he was assured on the spot of his Lordship's continuing interest, evidence of which came with amazing speed. On the day following the interview, Captain Montgomerie of the 36-gun frigate *Inconstant* requested leave of absence, and Cockburn was given temporary command as a post captain.

Montgomerie returned after a month by when command of another frigate, the *Meleager*, had become vacant and Cockburn transferred to her, a fifth rate of 36 guns which had been in service for about eight years. Her length was 137 feet, almost double that of the *Speedy* and she was well appointed. Admiralty confirmed Cockburn's commission as post captain of the ship as from February 20, 1794. He was still only 21.

Only certain seagoing posts – those in command of frigates and larger ships – qualified for the appointment of a post captain, one

● **Toulon in 1789 (R N Museum, Portsmouth)**

who had qualified for his rank by virtue of his posting. In earlier days it was the 'post' which was important but now it was the 'rank', for the reason that further promotion to the admirals' list (flag rank), depended entirely on seniority as a post captain. It was of great consequence, therefore, to become a post captain as early as possible. The importance to Cockburn of his appointment to command the *Meleager* becomes doubly apparent.

Some three months before, while Cockburn was still off Genoa Mole in the *Speedy*, dramatic events were taking place both in Toulon and Corsica. The British had failed to occupy the former militarily and it was now threatened by a Jacobin besieging army. An able young captain of artillery – one Napoleon Bonaparte – organised an assault on a strategic fort at the harbour entrance realising, where others had failed, that its possession would compel the British fleet's withdrawal. The fort fell and the royalists' defences crumbled. The fleet had to sail on December 19, even while vengeance was being wreaked on those who had supported it. There was little to do except embark as many fugitives as possible and destroy French warships and the arsenal. Hood then retreated eastwards to Hyères Bay where his ships could lie safely.

In the same month Captain Nelson in the *Agamemnon* had been directed by Hood to cruise off the northern end of Corsica with a small squadron to enforce a minor blockade. Some 20 years earlier the island had been a dependency of the Genoese Republic subsequently ceded to France against the wishes of the inhabitants. Resistance to their new masters was such that the French now held only three or four of the principal seaports, so Nelson liaised with the Corsican rebel leader Paoli for the landing of troops, sending also a commission headed by Sir Gilbert Elliot as Britain's official representative. A satisfactory agreement concluded, Hood sailed from Hyères Bay with troopships to begin operations against San Fiorenzo which was to become a valuable fleet base. By February 19, the French had retreated to Bastia on the north-east of Corsica.

With Toulon lost, it was more than ever necessary to blockade that port and maintain a close watch on enemy shipping inside the harbour. Frigates were ideal for this and Cockburn's *Meleager* was allotted the monotonous and demanding task in company with the *Ariadne* of the same class.

With frigates ever in short supply, they were frequently detached for convoy work, for watching the movements of enemy warships, and for special inshore duties. Admiral Graves had commented aptly on them in the previous war, 'frigates are not inapplicably called the eyes of the squadron; they certainly are the scouts and the voice of it.'[2] In fleet actions they were to hold off at a discreet distance and provide assistance where and when most needed. Invaluable as 'repeater' ships, they stationed themselves between opposing fleets repeating signals for the benefit of their own side. Not the least of their duties was to tow disabled ships to safety for which they carried a variety of hawsers and stream cables. Nominally, they were known as fourth, fifth, and sixth rates depending on their size and the number of guns carried; most commonly used were the fifth rates of 36 guns, such as the *Meleager* whose task of controlling neutral shipping became progressively more difficult. The Italian republics were touchy and there were many complaints about unlawful seizure. The position of Genoa was the most difficult with her territory extending as far as Nice, and with a fine anchorage at Vado Bay which the British quickly recognised and used. To the east, Genoa owned Spezia then known as Porto Especia. Further along the Mediterranean littoral stood the Italian state of Tuscany with its main port of Leghorn, and also the Papal States who sought to maintain a difficult neutrality. South again, lay Naples, part of the

● **The Gulf of Genoa**

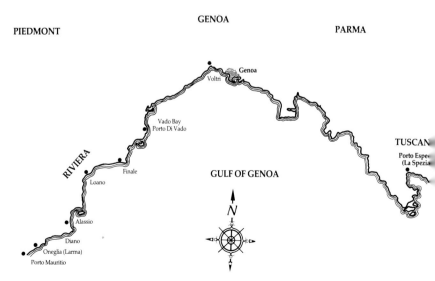

Kingdom of the Two Sicilies which, at this stage, sided somewhat ineffectively with Britain.

It was essential for the navy to prevent these republics allying with France. The problem of search was not confined to them but extended to neutrals from Baltic countries. For example, in March, 1794, Cockburn received warning from the Admiralty against ships from Denmark and Norway which were known to be conveying warlike stores to France under what were called 'Colourable Papers' – in laymen's language, a spurious manifest.

Vice-Admiral Hotham, Hood's second in command, had overall responsibility for the Toulon vigil. As well as his own *Britannia*, there was a division of seven ships-of-the-line, and frigates including the *Meleager*. On June 5, Hotham received warning that nine French ships-of-the-line were about to leave Toulon to reinforce Calvi – the last remaining French stronghold in Corsica. Hotham decided to quit Toulon and join Hood's force at San Fiorenzo in the belief that a combined fleet would register an overwhelming victory. He detached Cockburn in the *Meleager* and told him to continue to Toulon, to watch the motions of the French fleet, judge its strength, and ascertain from its course the most likely destination. The French fleet duly departed, and having remained in its vicinity for longer than was healthy, Cockburn crowded sail to find the *Victory* and tell Hood he had seen the French fleet the evening before to the north-west, some 40 miles off its own coast. Hood at once sailed in pursuit and sighted the French in the afternoon of June 10, but was foiled by light winds from engaging. The French, familiar with their coast, succeeded in towing their ships through the shoals and under the batteries of Golfe Jouan (Gourjean Bay).

The fickle winds thwarted Hood's attempts to follow into the Bay, favouring the French and giving them time to strengthen their defences. Hood prepared a detailed plan of attack in which Cockburn was given the responsibility for leading the fleet between the shoals into action. But a council held later onboard *Victory* decided that the continuing absence of wind and the now formida-able defences made the attempt foolhardy. One can only guess Cockburn's disappointment coupled perhaps with pride that his mentor and friend Lord Hood had shown confidence in his ability to lead in the fleet.

It was a sad end to an affair which reflected none too well on

Hotham. A Nelson or a Cockburn would have fought the battle off Toulon and not retreated to join Hood for tactical reasons. Hotham had parity in numbers as it turned out but lost an opportunity for combat which might have left the control of the Mediterranean beyond dispute. Some time after, Nelson judged Hotham in a letter to the Duke of Clarence, 'if he has a failing, and we are none of us without them, it is taking too much time to deliberate whereby opportunities are lost'.

Hood returned with the fleet to San Fiorenzo Bay on the north west tip of Corsica, now his best anchorage. His immediate task was the reduction of the last remaining French stronghold at Calvi to secure the island. The French fleet which had slipped him at Gourjean Bay would return, he guessed, to Toulon there to await reinforcement.

The threat of this fleet leaving Gourjean without warning limited Hood's options and caused great anxiety. That the conquest of Calvi should be achieved quickly was essential, particularly as many seamen and marines were ashore in support of the army. Cockburn in the *Meleager* was at Bastia at instant notice to re-embark these men should the situation require it. He was surprised to receive a letter from the newly appointed viceroy, Sir Gilbert Elliot, ordering him to provide transport for 500 Toulonese refugees from Porto Ferrajo in Elba to Corsica. Operational control of ships was the responsibility of the naval commander-in-chief and, at the very least, a request for this service should have been made to Hood; a diplomat, after all, should know his protocol better than most! Cockburn wisely passed the matter to Hood the same day avoiding comment except to say (probably tongue in cheek), that he proposed complying. Cockburn was told that other arrangements would be made, the *Meleager* being required for more important fleet duties. Sure enough, he was ordered to Gourjean Bay with despatches for Vice-Admiral Goodall and to follow his orders.

Before leaving the fleet, now at sea, there was a more pressing matter for Cockburn. Hood's flagship, the *Victory*, had exhausted her stock of wine, and as the *Meleager* from her recent provisioning had ample supplies, it was a straightforward matter to comply with Hood's request, 'August 12, 1794, at sea – I desire you will immediately deliver to the *Victory*'s launch, all the wine you have onboard except enough to carry you to San Fiorenzo, to which place you will proceed afterwards without a moment's loss of time, to store as expeditiously as possible with 30 or 40 pipes.' (A pipe was approximately 105 gallons!)

Wine was part of the seamen's ration. In the Mediterranean, a pint a day was the entitlement in lieu of the gallon of beer issued in home waters. To deprive a man of his liquid refreshment was unthinkable against the background of hardship he had to endure. Hood's order to Cockburn was not the triviality it may seem.

Following his previous orders, Cockburn now sailed for Gourjean Bay to place himself under Vice-Admiral Goodall's command. In the short period of British occupation of Toulon, Goodall had acted as governor so he, as much as anyone, understood the importance of preventing the French ships at Gourjean from returning to base. However, his squadron was too small to be effective as apart from his own flagship, the *Princess Royal*, he had only one or two minor vessels with him.

Having delivered Hood's despatches, Cockburn and his crew settled into the grind of watching and waiting. Some pleasure was derived by the circulation of a resolution, passed in the Houses of Parliament at home, congratulating the fleet on its success against the enemy in the expedition to Corsica. Otherwise, for the next seven weeks, little happened. With the approach of the autumnal equinox, the weather deteriorated. Each succeeding gale compelled Goodall in his cumbersome first-rate ship to keep well away from the lee shore. On one such occasion, a French ship made its getaway from Gourjean. Goodall, a rather overbearing man, laid the blame at Cockburn's door for failing to provide another frigate, the *Aimable*, with repeater flags without which she was unable to relay the movements of the enemy. Cockburn, hurt by the rebuke, hastened to reply, 'September 17, 1794 Sir – Having this instant received an order from you today wherein you say "you have been informed that I have neglected sending sundry flags and pendants to the *Aimable* which I ought to have sent, I have to acquaint you such information is incorrect, as a proof whereof, I have enclosed an account of the Colours the Boatswain was charged with, and the receipt from the Boatswain of the *Aimable* which you will find to be exactly the same, none having been expended to me . . ."[3]

The letter reveals much about Cockburn's strength of character. Conscientious to a degree, he was not prepared to lie down under an unwarranted charge; the language is quite strong, and certainly direct for a young man still only 22 in writing to a superior officer of twice that age.

Probably with a measure of relief, Cockburn informed Goodall on September 22, that *Meleager's* mainmast had sprung 12 feet below the cap, and that his carpenter had requested a survey on it. The mainmast being condemned, Cockburn was ordered to San Fiorenzo Bay where the storeship *Inflexible* lay. Failing supply from that source, he was to proceed to Leghorn – the main repair and victualling base used by the British – to buy a new one.

Cockburn arrived at San Fiorenzo Bay just as Lord Hood was preparing to leave for England in the *Victory*. The admiral, now 70 years old, still full of vitality and highly respected, needed a spell of inactivity. His intention was to reassume command in the spring of 1795 until when the fleet would be in Vice-Admiral Hotham's uninspiring charge. Cockburn took this opportunity to pay his respects to the man who had been a second father to him, unaware that this would be the last occasion he would serve under Hood. Never one to suffer fools gladly, Hood fell out with the Admiralty Board over several issues while at home, and was ordered to haul down his flag when on the point of returning to the Mediterranean.

His leadership and able administration was to be sadly missed. Hotham served longer in the post than anticipated and on many an occasion in the next year, opportunities were to arise which would have been turned to better account under Hood.

Equipped with new mainmast, the *Meleager* was now employed on arduous winter cruising. The capture of Corsica facilitated the control of those waters separating it from Leghorn, some 70 miles to the north-east. A close watch could now be maintained on much of the seaborne traffic sailing to and from Genoa. With these considerations in mind, Hotham ordered Cockburn on November 4 to cruise off Capraia for the protection of trade between Leghorn and Corsica. Capraia, a small island to the east of Corsica, reduces the distance to the Italian mainland to about 40 miles. It was not an inspiring task at the best of times; in the winter months of 1794 it was decidedly unpleasant and was relieved only by an occasional visit to Leghorn.

Matters were not helped in March of the new year by the signing of a treaty of neutrality between the French Convention and Tuscany, the threat to whose independence had increased with the growing power of France whom Tuscany had no wish to offend. Until now, Britain had been the most favoured country, her shipping allowed to enter and leave Leghorn at will. Now her warships would have to be more circumspect, particularly over the seizure of other vessels, if complaints were to be avoided; 'it becoming consequently necessary that due observance be paid to such neutrality by the powers in amity with the State of Tuscany' as the proclamation ran.

Conditions, both politically and militarily, had swung in France's favour. In northern Europe, the coalition against her had collapsed; she had virtually occupied Spain; and her growing army in Italy now threatened the opposing forces of Austria and Piedmont. Possession of the Riviera was of particular moment to her for it offered the only practical route into Italy. By the end of 1794 the French army had pushed as far as Vado Bay, not far from Genoa. *Faute de mieux*, that republic accepted this breach of her neutrality. It was, as it happened, of considerable pecuniary benefit since her ports along the Riviera thrived as depots in the trade of grain of which the French army was much in need; by the same token the Royal Navy's role was to deny that trade, causing dispute with the Genoese.

It was not a background calculated to encourage British optimism. The French fleet, too, had become stronger and was more inclined to make forays out of Toulon to threaten British convoys and to *reculer pour mieux sauter*. Against them, Corsica was of immense strategic importance, although the British, as with the French before, now faced problems from Corsicans who simply wanted independence.

Intelligence from French loyalists was an important factor in anticipating French moves. After intercepting a French coaster in January 1795, Cockburn received onboard a prisoner who previously had been a 'midshipman of the first class' in their navy. He relayed to Hotham the information given him by his prisoner, 'it is universally believed the French Fleet is coming out to convoy 60 transports (which have been got ready with the utmost despatch at Marseilles), to Tunis, Bone and Algiers to fetch corn . . . and believes they will sail very soon. They have instructions not to fight the English squadron, but to do it rather than lose the convoy, as there is a great want of corn about Marseilles.'[4]

The British fleet, after cruising in severe weather to the north of

● When *La Minerve* was captured by the British, Cockburn's next command was assured. (National Maritime Museum)

Corsica, arrived at Leghorn on February 24 where an express from Genoa brought the admiral news, on March 8, that the French fleet was at sea. Next day Hotham set off in chase. The rival fleets sighted each other in the neighbourhood of Genoa but light winds and heavy swell delayed close action. The resultant battle was inconclusive, partly owing to the baffling winds but also because Hotham failed to pursue the enemy after two French battleships, the *Ça Ira* and the *Censeur*, had struck. Nelson, who had played the leading role in their capture, boarded the *Britannia* to persuade Hotham to continue the chase, and to leave the *Meleager* behind to take charge of the captured vessels. 'But,' said Hotham, 'we must be contented, we have done very well.'

Throughout the *Meleager* had acted as repeater ship – a demanding and exhausting task. The British *Illustrious* was badly mauled and with the loss of her main and mizen masts was prey to the savage gales which terminated the action. The *Meleager* took her in tow but she ran ashore at Avenca on the Genoese coast whence the *Meleager* removed her crew. Valuable parts of the ship were saved subsequently; otherwise she was a total loss and was set on fire.

There was no respite for Cockburn and his crew. After a quick call at Porto Especia, the ship proceeded to Leghorn and left there on March 29 with an important convoy of vessels loaded with bullocks, lemons and onions bound for San Fiorenzo, by no means a trivial task as fresh meat and vegetables were essential for maintaining the health of seamen, keeping at bay the dreaded scurvy. Fortunately

38

such provisions were plentiful. On arrival at San Fiorenzo, Cockburn was immediately appointed a member of the court martial onboard the *Princess Royal* for 'the trial of Captain Frederick, the officers, and ship's company of His Majesty's late ship *Illustrious* for their conduct in the loss of that ship'. This was a formality, of course, as the ship was fought bravely and no-one was to blame, but in the loss or stranding of a ship a court martial was obligatory. Then away to sea again for the latter half of April, with a short break at Leghorn, before another seven weeks of patrolling, convoying and fleet work.

The fleet returned again to San Fiorenzo on June 29, the frigates *Dido* and *Lowestoft* being detached a few days earlier to look into Toulon. On June 24, they fell in with two French frigates and, after a fierce engagement, the smaller British frigates captured one, *La Minerve*, a handsome ship of 40 guns – all 18-pounders. The other frigate escaped after a severe mauling. The British frigate captains were not to know then that they had provided Cockburn with his next command!

At this time the Austrians and their allies, the Piedmontese, were preparing to recover the Genoese Riviera, ensuring Vado Bay as a safe anchorage for the British fleet. Hotham had received reinforcements from home and was now prepared to detach a small force under Nelson's command in the *Agamemnon* to support the Austrian General de Vins. On July 4, Nelson sailed from San Fiorenzo Bay with six smaller vessels which included the *Meleager*. A rude shock awaited them; confrontation with the French fleet believed to be in Toulon but now at sea! By dint of good seamanship they were able to gain San Fiorenzo before the 23 pursuing ships could catch up. Hotham was thus provided with a providential opportunity to turn the tables, and he in turn took up the chase. Although the opposing fleets sighted each other on July 13, constant shifts of light wind again prevented a decisive battle. The only casualty was the French *Alcide* of 74 guns which blew up.

The small squadron of which the *Meleager* formed part left San Fiorenzo Bay a second time for Genoa. Nelson's orders were to confer with Mr Francis Drake, the British minister in Genoa, and then to proceed to Vado Bay where he would liaise with the Austrians. His primary task was to prevent the flood of merchandise – particularly grain – which was being delivered in ever increasing quantity to the French along the Riviera. It could not be done without searching the many Genoese vessels engaged in this trade. At the same time the British squadron had to try to observe the instructions issued from England which said, *inter alia*, that warships were 'to avoid giving any just cause of offence to the foreign power (Genoa), in amity with His Majesty'.

The two objects were incompatible: if the job was to be done conscientiously, offence had to be caused. By their training, Nelson and Cockburn were single-minded – either the duty was done well or not at all. Over the next few weeks both played leading parts in the denouement.

They arrived off Genoa Mole on July 17. After receiving information from Francis Drake on the movements of Genoese vessels, Nelson ordered Cockburn two days later to 'cruise off Vado Bay till joined by me – which I expect will be tomorrow morning – taking under your direction, the *Resolution*, cutter, and the *Tarleton*, brig.'

A further order given Cockburn before sailing, was unequivocal.

'July 19, 1795, *Agamemnon*, Genoa Mole. You are hereby directed to stop and detail all ships and vessels to whatever power they may belong which may be bound to France, or any place occupied by the armies of France, and send them into a safe anchorage in Vado Bay, there to wait for my further direction concerning them.

'You will be as careful as possible in preventing any embezzlement of the cargoes, making the masters of such vessels remain onboard in charge of the cargo, and putting into such vessels, a sober, careful man or two, and taking out of them, such people, as may be deemed by you, improper to remain onboard.

'The sails of such vessels, I would recommend being unbent. Many vessels under Genoese colours being hourly expected from Marseilles with money, plate and jewels, you are directed to be particularly vigilant in searching for such vessels, and you are not to allow any vessels to pass along the coast without the strictest examination.'[5]

Cockburn was ideal for such a mission: he could be relied upon to carry out his instructions with moral courage and to the letter. Even if distasteful, it was necessary to help the Austrian troops' advance.

Word soon reached the Genoese secretary of state of Cockburn's activities. Towards the end of July, he wrote formally to Lord Grenville, the foreign secretary in England, complaining about recent violations of neutrality, and sending a copy to Francis Drake in Genoa. The second of these reported acts was 'the arrestation of the vessel commanded by Captain Bavastro which, while riding at anchor on the beach at Finale (near Vado Bay), under the asylum and protection of the Castle of Finale, which also hoisted Genoese colours, could not avoid being captured by an English frigate which, by armed force and musket shot, took possession of her, with a similar manifest violation of the territory, and the most glaring attempt against the Neutrality of the Republic . . .'

This had all the making of serious trouble which had to be nipped in the bud. The English frigate referred to of course was the *Meleager*. On August 3, Nelson sent Cockburn a copy of the complaint and asked for his comments. As instigator of the original orders Nelson ·was in a difficult position, and with pre-knowledge of the event he accordingly wrote to Hotham in explanation, 'July 22, 1795, Vado Bay. The *Meleager*, Captain Cockburn, brought in yesterday a valuable prize called *Nostra Signora di Belvedere*. I have no doubt her cargo is French property. The gold, silver and jewels which were found in the cabin, are onboard the *Agamemnon*; but things of much more consequence, I understand, are in the hold: indeed I cannot guess at the value of the cargo. She was deserted by the Master and all her crew . . .'[6] It must have been infuriating to Cockburn that, after carrying out his orders with such speed and efficiency, he should have now to vindicate his actions. On August 7, two weeks after the taking of the *Belvedere,* he wrote in a letter to Hotham a stinging indictment of the Genoese complaints, enclosing an affidavit together with remarks on 'some very glaring mistakes'. The burden of Cockburn's response was

1   The vessel was not boarded at anchor off Finale, but three-quarters of an hour after sailing therefrom.

2   The breach of neutrality was committed 'on their side' by threatening to fire at the *Meleager*'s boat when attempting to come alongside.

3   An incorrect accusation against Lieutenant Hardy who was in charge of the *Meleager*'s boat. Hardy had promised the liberty and security of the neutral after inspection.

4   The deposition of a passenger onboard the *Belvedere* which stated that some of the sailors onboard that vessel proposed 'to fight the *Meleager* or get under the batteries at Alassio, which conduct appears very unlike that of a fair trading neutral vessel'.

Cockburn ended his letter, 'I cannot help observing the quantity of mistakes in the above mentioned declaration which appear to be too many to be occasioned by want of memory or any other accident. The appearance of duplicity must be much heightened, in the eyes of every disinterested person, by a parcel of papers being thrown overboard in the evening, and the vessel bearing the name of *Il Furioso* on her stern, although called in all the papers I have been able to find *Nostra Signora di Belvedere*. Add to these, that when she was boarded her guns were all loaded with landgridge (sic), primed, and the matches lighted fore and aft – a situation rather extraordinary for a neutral merchant vessel.'[7] The reply must have been conclusive for that was the end of the affair.

July, August and September were months of intense activity. Nelson's small squadron was employed on a task which was rare in naval experience, affording an opportunity to take the war to the enemy, a welcome change from humdrum fleet work. 'What changes in my life of activity! Here I am having commenced co-operation with an old Austrian general, almost fancying myself charging at the head of a troop of horse,' wrote Nelson to his wife.[8] Co-operation was also essential with Francis Drake who fed the naval captains with valuable information on neutral ships, their cargoes and destinations. On one occasion, permission was given to Cockburn to arrange a safe passage in Genoese vessels for Frenchmen known to favour Britain's cause. The only condition was that the ships in which they were to embark should make their journey empty to prevent advantage being taken.

To police Genoese small craft hugging a familiar coastline demanded a high degree of seamanship from the British warships. Cockburn's frigate was too large to take the same risks, but he worked in shallow waters as far as his ship's draught and the shoreside batteries under French control would permit. The many harbours and anchorages along the Riviera were but a few miles apart from each other – Vado, Finale, Loano, Alassio and Oneglia, for example, were within easy sailing distance. Cockburn gained an intimate knowledge of them all.

Over the wider scene, the war was not going well for Britain. Spain, under some duress, decided to make peace with France. Her fleet had never been particularly effective as an ally, but the balance now hung in France's favour. Napoleon's reaction was immediate. 'Peace with Spain,' he said, 'makes offensive war in Piedmont certain; my plan is being discussed; Vado will soon be taken.' He was determined that no effort should be spared by land and sea to re-open communications with Genoa, the key to advance into Italy.

Hotham's failure to make the best of his opportunities against the French fleet was all too apparent. He could have made some amend by strengthening Nelson's squadron where positive results were being obtained but declined to reduce his own fleet strength.

In August, Nelson's force consisted of the *Agamemnon, Inconstant, Meleager, Tartar, Southampton, Ariadne* and *Speedy* which, although inadequate for the task, had notably supported the Austrian army by denying the French. On August 26 they did particularly well at Alassio in cutting out two French gun brigs, two five-gun corvettes, and five vessels laden with stores with no British loss of ships or men. Nelson's strategy on such occasions is illuminated by his signal to Cockburn the day before the action began, 'you will have the *Meleager* as near as possible to the French corvette, and be ready to engage her when I make the signal, but although the enemy are now in possession of the town, my particular desire is, to avoid as much as possible firing into the town, as I hope soon the Genoese will be allowed by the success of the Allies, to have quiet possession of the Riviere.'[9]

Alas, the wish expressed at the end of the signal was never realised. Nelson's optimism contrasted starkly with Hotham's own assessment of the war written four days later, 'whereas from the very peculiar circumstances of the war in Italy, it is absolutely neces-sary that a temporary suspension should take place of all navigation whatever, liable to just suspicion of carrying provisions, stores, cloa-thing, or other necessities to the Enemy . . .'

By the end of September, the *Meleager's* seams and decking had opened up and she badly needed recaulking, the only vessel in the British fleet which had not been refitted since leaving England. A dock and other facilities were available at Leghorn, whence she-proceeded. For two months the *Meleager* was 'out of routine' provid-ing her crew with a welcome rest until November 30 when she rejoined Nelson's *Agamemnon* off Vado Bay. There had been a violent turn in the fortunes of war in *Meleager's* absence, for Vado had been taken by the French and the Austrian army was full in retreat. Worse, Admiral Hyde Parker, who had temporarily succeeded Hotham as commander-in-chief, was even more uncooperative in providing

• **Action at Oneglia. (National Maritime Museum)**

Nelson with reinforcements. Inexplicably he reduced the squardron in early November to one frigate – the *Meleager,* and one brig – the *Speedy,* as Nelson's total support.

With winter's onset the campaign ended temporarily. Indeed with such a small force Nelson had little option. The *Agamemnon,* now desperately unseaworthy, retired to Leghorn for a six-week refit leaving Cockburn as the senior officer at Genoa, cooperating with Francis Drake ashore. He enquired by letter, 'in what manner the *Meleager* can be most beneficially employed' and was asked to keep a particularly watchful eye on Vado Bay. It was useful if not exciting work exemplified by an occasional report to Drake such as this of December 9, '...had the good fortune to fall in with theAustrian corvette which was going into Vado, she not having heard of the evacuation'.

The year 1796 began as the old had ended – with a lull at sea. Admiral Jervis arrived at San Fiorenzo to take command of the British fleet and quickly injected fresh confidence among officers and men. A boost to morale was needed for nothing could now prevent the forward march of the French army into Piedmont and the Genoese approaches. The blockade of the Riviera to the west thus became of less consequence, and sorties were restricted mainly to Toulon, Porto Especia, Leghorn and, of course, Genoa, all of which were of strategic importance in watching and containing the French.

In April both Nelson and Cockburn cruised with the fleet under Jervis. Then on the 23rd *Agamemnon* and *Meleager,* with *Diadem* and the brig *Petrel* in company, were again detached to blockade Genoa.

Evidence of the high esteem which Nelson now held for Cockburn is provided by the frequency their two ships were in company together. Nelson had long since discovered that Cockburn was a man after his own heart with an insatiable wish to hit the enemy hard. An opportunity came with surprising speed.

After a successful cutting out operation at Loana Bay in which squadron boats captured four valuable transports from under the enemy batteries, another seven French vessels laden with ordnance stores were discovered off Oneglia on May 31 attempting to run under the protective batteries of nearby Larma. Cockburn was ordered to lead into the anchorage 'which he did,' said Nelson, 'in a most officer-like manner'. He ran in as close to the batteries as the depth of water would allow, and started to engage the armed vessels and forts. Nelson, never happy if anyone was nearer to the enemy than himself, tried to sail between the *Meleager* and the shore. To achieve this his ship had to luff, but Cockburn had left no room for him, and the *Agamemnon* ran aground under the *Meleager's* stern. The attack continued without interruption: the forts were silenced, seven enemy vessels brought out, and the *Agamemnon* got off without damage. While she was aground, Cockburn had gone onboard to offer help but he found the commodore in his cabin writing letters – 'a singular trait in the character of that great man' as it has been reported. Few officers would have had either the nerve or the inclination to be so employed while their ship lay grounded under the enemy's battery, uncertain whether she could be refloated. Nelson later wrote to Jervis a glowing testimony of Cockburn's conduct. 'Much as I feel indebted to every officer in the squadron,' said he, 'yet I cannot omit to mention the great support and assistance I have ever received from Captain Cockburn, who has been nearly a year under my command on this station; and I should myself be guilty of a neglect of duty were I not to represent his zeal, ability and courage, which are conspicuous on every occasion that offers.'[10]

It was time for Cockburn to have a change of command and on June 3, three days after the Oneglia success, Nelson wrote to Admiral Jervis, '. . . I wish, Sir, that Captain Cockburn had the *Minerve*; he is worthy of her or a better ship.' The *Minerve* was the fine French frigate captured but a short while before. A few weeks later Jervis replied, 'I believe Captain Hotham will decline the *Minerve*, and Captain Cockburn shall in that case have her. She carries the new builder to Ajaccio who has promised me to fit her well.'[11]

Change was indeed on the way. In August 1796, an alliance was signed between France and Spain, which was to lead to Spain declaring war on Great Britain within two months. The balance of power in the Mediterranean maritime war had tipped dramatically – in favour of the French. Britain's tenuous hold on Corsica was threatened, and even Leghorn had been occupied by the French. Such was the backdrop when Cockburn left the *Meleager*, now released from Nelson's command. Nelson himself had joined the fleet in his new ship, the *Captain* of 74 guns.

A letter dated August 6, 1796, from Admiral Jervis shows the delicate nature of the *Meleager's* last mission now that Spain was hostile. 'You are hereby required and directed to proceed forthwith with the ship under your command off Barcelona, (but not to anchor there), and send your boat onshore with the utmost caution and circumspection, to deliver the accompanying letter to the Consul there, and to receive 35,000 lbs weight of onions and such other refreshments, as he may have to send to the fleet . . . having so done you are to rejoin me with all possible expedition.'[12]

The task performed, the *Meleager* was sent to repair. So Cockburn lost an old friend.

CHAPTER FOUR

The Minerve - Nelson's acolyte 1796-7

GEORGE COCKBURN TRANSFERRED from the *Meleager* to the *Minerve* on August 19, 1796 taking with him as ordered by Admiral Jervis 11 key men to facilitate the transition to his new command, which differed considerably from her British counterparts both internally and in her armament. With finer lines and built for speed, she had less hamper below the main deck. She carried 28 long 18-pounders and a dozen long eight-pounders, the latter distributed on quarterdeck and forecastle. Of French manufacture, they had minor differences demanding time and practice to overcome. Two British 36-pounder carronades were also embarked and since the 'smashers', as they were affectionately known, were by now almost standard in major British warships, they were at least familiar and helped infuse confidence.

With a ship's complement of 286, Cockburn was faced with the daunting task of getting to know a large crew quickly. (There were no volunteers as there would have been had he commissioned in home waters). No commanding officer ever surrendered his best hands when asked to contribute towards the manning of another ship, so the hasty commissioning of the *Minerve* with the British facing a crisis, doubtlessly forced Cockburn to accept a fair quota of lame ducks. Certainly the punishments recorded in the ship's log confirm that supposition.

It was a considerable compliment to a 24-year-old to be given such a command: George Cockburn's responsibility would have been more appropriate to a man ten years his senior. Whatever the limitations of his crew, there was consolation in being able to bring Lieutenant Thomas Masterman Hardy with him, to continue as first lieutenant. A magnificent seaman in Cockburn's mould, Hardy was the ideal selection for a job requiring selfless cooperation. Most important in commissioning *Minerve* was his ability to exert a firm but just discipline and – as with Cockburn – to lead from the front. The fact that he was three years older than his captain, and lacking the interest that had launched his senior so auspiciously, would not have bothered Hardy. He was not an easy man to overlook with his commanding height of six foot three inches, and it was not to be long before Nelson himself came to appreciate Hardy's worth, leading to a lasting association.

The first task was to shake down the ship and enable everyone to become familiar with his new surroundings. The carpenters were particularly busy replacing rotting timber; spare booms had to be secured, and the mizen-mast moved further aft to improve the ship's sailing qualities.

On August 28 Cockburn joined the fleet off San Fiorenzo, its sole anchorage in the Mediterranean now that Leghorn was in French hands. This Cockburn learned when he called on Admiral Jervis in the *Victory* next morning. The *Minerve*, Jervis said, was to operate under Commodore Nelson to assist in preventing ships from entering or leaving Leghorn without permission; to protect the remnants of British trade in the vicinity; and to secure safe withdrawal by providing convoy. As for Genoa, all ports of that Republic were now closed to British ships and the Riviera, which previously had been the centre of Cockburn's activities, was to be considered outside the operational theatre.

With British-held Corsica under threat from French partisans and other republicans, the sea lanes between Bastia on the north eastern coast of the island and Leghorn on the Italian mainland had to be strengthened. Between lay the small island of Capraia and the much larger Elba with its chief port of Porto Ferrajo taken by Nelson the previous July. Strategically, both islands were vital: to the enemy as staging posts in an attack on Corsica; to the British as defensive positions against such a challenge. Consequently, Capraia's seizure was Nelson's first objective.

Leaving the fleet on August 30 for Leghorn, *Minerve*'s log reveals a rash of punishments at this time: offenders' names recur sufficiently to suggest that there was a hard core – few in number – of constant trouble-makers. The ship carried a small detachment of the 11th Regiment (the Devonshires) – in place of marines who were in short supply – whose soldiers figured largely in the punishment book. Service in the cramped quarters of a frigate probably did not accord with their idea of military duty.

Off Leghorn, Cockburn had a brief rendezvous with Nelson in the *Captain*, a third rate ship of the line. Left with a small gunboat – the *Venom* it was not long before *Minerve's* close watch off the port bore fruit. On the ninth, an unidentified trading vessel quit harbour and was chased by the *Venom*. To escape she ran ashore but not before hoisting French colours. The crew of about 32 jumped into the sea, but by this time the *Minerve's* own boats were on the scene and by dint of good seamanship the stranded vessel was towed into deeper water as prize. Several of the French crew were picked up and taken onboard to place Cockburn in a predicament. The French merchant seamen were an embarrassment since, being non-combatant, they were not legally prisoners-of-war. Also they took up valuable ship space and ate a share of the provisions. On the other hand, by requesting permission to put the Frenchmen ashore he realised that the Tuscan authorities might prove awkward about the breach of their neutrality created by the ship's seizure.

Tongue in cheek Cockburn wrote to the Marquis Joseph de Silva,

● **The Western Mediterranean**

the Tuscan minister responsible, saying that he was prepared to release the men if the ship's cargo and crew on leaving the port were as on entering it. Put another way, he wanted assurance that the ship had left no supplies for the French occupying the port.

The British and the Tuscans still maintained a friendly relationship and Cockburn's bluff succeeded beyond expectation. Within a few days the Marquis replied, 'I am grateful for your good disposition to release the said individuals on condition that I occasion the vessel to be sent out again with a certificate under my hand that she is in the same state as to cargo and people, as when she entered the port. I will inform and communicate to the King, my master, this your generosity, as a new attestation of the many regards and loyal friendship, subsisting between our two Courts; but Sir, it is not in my power to profit by your offer, the execution not depending on me, and her condition being extremely changed at present both with regard to cargo and individuals that were onboard her; therefore I do not insist anymore for the deliverance of the said individuals, and you can dispose of them as you please.'[1]

Thus Cockburn's ploy allowed him to land the men and keep the prize, the best of both worlds: his flair for diplomacy, later to become one of his notable attributes, even now was burgeoning.

Nelson had already started to garrison the tiny Genoese-owned island of Capraia. Because that Republic had performed various hostile acts, including the firing by some shore batteries at Nelson's own ship, he had no compunction about its seizure. Cockburn joined the *Captain* off Capraia on September 15, after detaching his prize to Bastia. The next few days he spent assisting the landing of troops, stores and guns. On the 19th, the job complete, the British flag was hoisted. The island had fallen quickly because of the planning and efficiency of the assault in which Cockburn took a prominent part on shore. He was rewarded by a special mention in Admiral Jervis's subsequent report to the Admiralty, 'I enclose for the information of the Lords Commissioner, Commodore Nelson's report of the expedition against, and capture of the Island Capraia, the conduct of which reflects the highest honour on his skill, judgement and enterprise, and on the good training of those under his command, among whom Captain Cockburn of the *Minerve* stands eminently distinguished. He and Berry . . . have exposed their persons on all occasions with that cool, deliberate courage which forms so prominent a feature in the Commodore's character, and I beg leave to recommend them to Their Lordships' favour and protection.'[2]

There was still much to be done to make the garrison self-supporting, particularly in drinking water. The *Minerve* proceeded to Bastia to embark further provisions for the garrison. Water was not the only liquid refreshment to be provided, the log entry for September 28 reading, 'Received onboard 30 pipes of wine, 1 of brandy, 26 casks of provisions, 60 bags of bread, for the troops on Capraia'. Throughout this work of transporting from Bastia, Cockburn succeeded where other failed in maintaining good relationships with General de Burgh, the Army commander. Some found the general obstinate and reactionary, but replying to an invitation to use the *Vanneau*, a large prize converted for trooping, he replied to Cockburn, 'I have only just received your favor having been constantly employed throughout the day. I think the *Vanneau* can very well convoy the tartan (a lateen-sailed, single-masted Mediterranean type) and will arrange for their departure tomorrow. I wish you a pleasant cruise and success in *Minerve*. Whenever the service brings you to Bastia Roads, I hope you will make my house as convenient as possible to you.'

Cockburn was leaving for Montecristo, a small island to the south, to examine its potential as a watering place before landing provisions at Capraia. While there, he wrote to Nelson giving his findings but on broader matters saying that he felt he should renew the blockade of Leghorn as soon as possible in view of the menace to Corsica. Nelson's reply of October 2 reflects his high regard, 'I received your letter from off Monte Christo; we so exactly think alike on points of service that if your mind tells you it is right, there can hardly be a doubt that I must approve.

'I hope this will find you settling your affairs at Porto Ferrajo. As to convoy to Naples, you may tell Pollard, there can be none till the convoy comes up, which is not expected for a long time. I wish the ordnance brig was sold, if Mr Lamb will not give £700 he had better take her for six. If he really will not buy her, we must manage to heave her down and fit her for sea; she will sell well in many other places. My Dear Friend, endeavour to get clear accounts of the money lodged with us, but you know how to settle all better than I do, therefore I shall say no more.

'I am going over tomorrow to Felama Bay, from thence I shall call at Porto Ferrajo, on my way to Leghorn. The *Blanche* wants water, and I believe provisions. If only the former, she may come here; if both, desire Lord Garlies to send her to San Fiorenzo with strict orders for her quick return and say to his Lordship, I have received his letter of the 29th September, that in Corsica, they are not afraid were 2000 Corsicans to come there. I wish to see Lord Garlies as soon as I appear off Leghorn, as I want to send him on a particular service.

'PS You will dispose of the *Vanneau* as you please; if you think of anchoring or that she can cruise off Leghorn with you, take her there; if she is useless to us, let her stay at Ferrajo till I see her myself. I don't believe the Corses will quit Leghorn if they can help it. The Viceroy and Mr North have 10,000 Corses who are so kind at this moment to take pay from *us for good'*.[3]

The Mr Pollard mentioned was the British agent in Leghorn working with the Consulate and the British squadron. His function was to dispose of all goods and prizes for the best price or send them to Naples. Lord Garlies, captain of the frigate *Lively* attached to Nelson's squadron, presumably had informed Nelson of the darkening Corsican situation which had left Nelson unimpressed. The 2000 Corsicans referred to were partisans at Leghorn ready to help deliver the island from the British.

Two days after the first letter, Nelson wrote again to Cockburn. This second letter helps to amplify the first but also shows that Nelson's small force was stretched to the limits in a rapidly deteriorating situation, 'I have a letter from the Admiral saying that the *Lively* must immediately come here (Bastia) from Leghorn and yet Leghorn must be blockaded. The *Blanche* wants water and provisions, therefore my dear Sir, if you can manage to blockade Leghorn singlehanded with the *Bombard*, send *Blanche* to get some water at Fiorenzo and from thence to join the fleet.

- **Bastia at the turn of the eighteenth century (RN Museum, Portsmouth)**

'I have orders from the Admiral viz. you are to put the captain, officers and men to ⅔rds allowance of all species of provisions, except wine and spirits, and you are to direct them to take especial care that the officers of any distinction, are not allowed a greater proportion than the men. This reduction will be continued no longer than is absolutely necessary . . . Ever Yours, Horatio Nelson.'[4]

The position had become desperate. Live cattle and other fresh provisions were scarcely procurable after the closure of both Genoa and Leghorn to the British. Trading was at a standstill and Jervis knew that if the men of the fleet subsisted for too long on hard tack, scurvy must follow. Worse, Spain declared war on October 8 following the Franco-Spanish provisional treaty which had been ratified the month before. The Spanish Admiral Langara was now at large in the western Mediterranean with 26 ships of the line besides frigates. The French fleet, too, had been re-equipped in Toulon with 12 ships of the line ready to sail at short notice. The British lacked allies; even the Neapolitan fleet was unavailable now that Naples had decided to make peace with France, fearing her aggression. The entire Italian littoral was virtually denied to the British, thanks to Bonaparte's successes against the Austrians. Corsica was anything but secure and, on recent Admiralty orders, to be abandoned, although Nelson still thought he could defend it. Even the British hold on Elba itself was precarious.

The bitterest pill of all for Sir John Jervis was the non-arrival of Rear-Admiral Man with seven ships of the line sent from England to reinforce him.[5] Jervis was left with only 14 line ships in San Fiorenzo Bay to confront this huge Spanish-French armada should they happen to meet. The order which Jervis received on September 25, to retreat from the Mediterranean, seems to have been the only possible course in the circumstances.

This was the unhappy scenario when Cockburn sailed for his last single-handed blockade of Leghorn – leaving Nelson to begin Bastia's evacuation and Corsica's surrender. A successful blockade would lighten Nelson's task by preventing partisans from leaving Leghorn for Corsica. Who else, then, but Nelson's best frigate captain to undertake it?

As the *Minerve* might be on her Leghorn station for some time, Cockburn had to be provisioned. He arrived on October 4 at Porto Ferrajo where the small dockyard, but a day's sailing from Leghorn, supplied most of his immediate needs. Fresh beef and water were loaded; even the carpenter's and boatswain's requirements were largely met. The log for the sixth shows the following received: 3 barrels tar, 20 yards kersey, 4 log lines, 30 lbs twine, 6 lbs thread, 6 oars, 40 lbs tallow, deep sea leadline, 9 lbs yellow paint, and 40 block pins.

The *Minerve* was ready for sea on October 14 and, sailing to the north, tacked to and fro off the small island of Gorgona in the narrow channel between Cape Corse and Leghorn, a natural hunting ground for predators. This time, alas, there was no prey, those vessels boarded being able to give a good account of themselves. She arrived in Leghorn Roads on the 18th where a boat came alongside carrying a flag of truce. The bearer gave Cockburn a letter from M Belleville, the French Consul in Leghorn, 'le porteur de ma lettre est le Citoyen Sapey qui a longtemps traité de l'échange des prisonniers avec Mr Elliot; il vous justifiera de ce que j'ai l'honneur de vous avancer. Salut et considération respectueuse, Bellville,' so read the letter with an epistolary flourish. The content was interesting with a heading which ran, 'Consulat de Livourne – Egalité – Liberté' and then the date given in the French revolutionary calendar, 'le 26 Vendemaire l'an 5 de la Republique Francaise, Une et Indivisible'. M Belleville reported that Mr Elliot (Sir Gilbert Elliot, British Viceroy in Corsica) had returned, under flags of truce, approximately 700 Frenchmen who had been prisoners-of-war in Bastia. Accompanying them were deputies of the island to discuss the question of their onward passage to France. Belleville stressed that these prisoners – all French sailors – could not remain in Leghorn and would have to travel by sea. For that reason he was now asking Captain Cockburn to provide safe passage for their ships. He finished the letter gleefully with the comment, 'il est certain monsieur, que les troupes de sa Majesté Britannique evacuent la Corse'.

There was no doubting the authenticity of this request and, under the rules for the exchange of prisoners-of-war, Cockburn had no option but to approve it as in the course of time a corresponding number of British prisoners would be returned to England. Cockburn's reply was brief and to the point. He wrote, 'enclosed you will receive the passports requisite for the three cartels bound to Genoa and Nice, and to prevent their being chased or molested in their voyage, I would recommend them to carry an English Jack at their fore topgallant mastheads, whilst in sight of any ships of war.'[6]

M Belleville's titbit of news that he could confirm the British were evacuating Corsica was correct. Late on October 18 the French landed near Cape Corse and within 36 hours occupied the empty citadel of Bastia from which the British had already withdrawn. Nelson and General de Burgh had been the last to embark, retreating to Porto Ferrajo, Elba being now the only territory of any size left in British hands.

Cockburn, meantime, had completed his business ashore with Mr Pollard who took on charge all goods captured by Nelson's squadron. Together with the polacre *Fortuna* (a three-masted Mediterranean merchant vessel) they were sold for the best price and the net proceeds remitted to London.

The *Minerve* continued her monotonous task in unremitting equinoctal gales, work with which Cockburn was well acquainted. Only two years before in the little *Speedy* he had been applauded for the way he had carried on with the blockade of Genoa without support; now here he was again, in a larger ship but in equally bad weather. On October 25, a storm carried away the *Minerve's* fore topmast and she sprang a stay. Her topgallant masts were struck down only just in time to save further disaster, and her larboard bumkin (a short boom projecting from the bow), was lost. These were far from ideal conditions for chasing and boarding but on many occasions boats were lowered in heaving seas to inspect neutrals more closely.

About this time, the ship bore down on a polacre which answered the recognition signal. She was from San Fiorenzo bearing despatches, from Sir John Jervis, which related sightings of the Spanish fleet by the frigates *Inconstant* and *Blanche* and a Danish brig. These had been made at the northern end of Corsica but, from the course steered, it was difficult to assess the Spaniards' destination. There were two letters from Jervis written within a day of each other. In the first he suggested that Toulon and not Corsica was the Spaniards' destination as they were steering north-west in strong winds. In the second letter, with the benefit of further intelligence, he had obviously changed his mind, '. . . the wind chopping about suddenly in the evening from NW to NE, they hauled their wind on the starboard tack in great confusion, Cape Corse then bearing SSE by compass, 11 or 12 leagues. The probability is they were bound for Leghorn to conduct the expedition to Corsica; it is therefore necessary for you to be on the alert and have something to the westward to give notice of their approach; the small gunboat had best be sent immediately to Porto Ferrajo, and perhaps it will be wise to be all under sail when the wind comes to the westward. Give me notice if possible, of their approach to Leghorn.'[7]

When Jervis wrote these letters, he was still worried by the prospect of a full scale invasion on Corsica from Leghorn with the Spanish and French fleets in support. Nelson's efficient and rapid evacuation of Bastia had much reduced that likelihood, but with communications being what they were it was difficult to keep up with events.

Cockburn knew that the threat at Leghorn had probably diminished, but he hastened to reassure Jervis in his reply of the 24th, 'La Minerve being the *only* vessel left off Leghorn, I keep constantly under sail, not only more effectually to perform the blockade, but in consequence of information I had received similar to that you have now sent. As on the appearance of a Spanish fleet to the westward, I shall be obliged to make my retreat to the south, I cruise chiefly on the southern side of the town. Any vessels therefore, that you may send to me, had better approach on that side.'

For a number of days the *Minerve* continued her close blockade patrolling, in the main, the few miles which separated Leghorn from the offshore island of Gorgona. She continued to be buffeted by heavy weather, and one particularly large wave stove in the jolly boat. On that same day the sloop *Raven* hove in sight flying the private recognition signal and bearing the welcome news from Jervis that the blockade was to be abandoned, and that Cockburn was to rejoin him at Mortella Bay.

His departure was part of a general plan of withdrawal. Jervis, himself, was stretched to the limit with insufficient warships to escort the transports carrying the departing garrisons of Calvi and San Fiorenzo to Porto Ferrajo. After parting company with the *Minerve*, the *Raven* therefore sailed directly to Porto Ferrajo with orders for ships there to rejoin Jervis with all possible speed. Nelson, in the *Captain*, was already with his commander-in-chief, so that all preparations had now been made for the decision to quit the Mediterranean. The only element to be left intact was the military garrison under General de Burgh in Elba. The risk was great but there was little option, de Burgh preferring to take his orders from home and not from the naval command.

Had Admiral Man arrived with his squadron and extra provisions, Jervis might have wished to remain until an opportunity arose to challenge the Spanish fleet. Man's conduct was incomprehensible. He disobeyed Jervis's order to join him and instead cruised off Cape St Vincent in the Atlantic until such time as a council of war of his captains decided by a majority vote that they should return to England. Arriving at Spithead at the end of December, Man was ordered to strike his flag. He was never employed again.

By November 2, the British evacuation of Corsica was complete. Jervis, having learned that the Spanish fleet under Langara had arrived at Toulon, decided that this was the moment for his 15 sail of the line, his frigates, and a convoy of merchant vessels, to sail south. On the day following, while still close to Cape Corse, the *Minerve*'s log briefly records, 'saw several of the fleet firing at the shore', a *feu-de-joie* to celebrate their departure.

The first part of the voyage was passed in a relatively relaxed atmosphere with discussion taking place onboard the *Victory* between Jervis and his captains. Meanwhile the *Minerve*'s ship's company was employed drawing and knotting yarns, splicing, and painting. The sailmakers were making a trysail out of the ship's former mizen sail, 'it being much worn and eaten by the rats'.

On the 12th an unidentified frigate was met which made no response to signals. Decks were cleared for action but closer investigation revealed her as an Algerine. She claimed she was cruising, but smaller fry than the *Minerve* of any flag would no doubt have been victim to her predatory instincts.

The fleet passed Majorca in company when gales and heavy seas dispersed the ships; the *Minerve* sailed independently for a period. During this time another unidentified ship was met and chased. Brought to by gunfire she was found to be a Spanish polacre, laden with wool and bound for Port Mahon. This useful prize was taken in tow by *Minerve* but on the orders of Jervis was transferred to the *Diadem* two days later. Jervis had received news from a Swedish merchant vessel that she had been boarded by a Spanish frigate, and Cockburn was told to cruise off Cape de Gata until December 3, in the hope that she might meet the frigate. For more than a week the *Minerve* remained not far east of Gibraltar and although she met and chased many strange sail, the Spanish frigate was not among them. Six brigs were boarded – four Danes, a Swede and a Tuscan, bound for enemy-held ports. The right of search was enforced to which the Danes in particular objected; eventually Cockburn allowed them all to go on their way. It would have been an inconvenient time for diplomatic upsets.

Having received orders from Jervis to rejoin, Cockburn arrived on December 9 in Gibraltar Bay, where the fleet was already assembled.

The following day was to be eventful if not disastrous. A minor gale reached hurricane force – even ships of the line dragged their anchors and the *Minerve* kept them company. A dispassionate entry in the log for December 10 records an incident which, had it not been for outstanding seamanship, would have resulted in the ship's loss, 'strong gale from the south east. Dragging on the best bower anchor. Veered three cables finding the ship would not bring up, and being so far to leeward, obliged to cut at the bitts. Sheeted home the topsails and set foresail. At 2 came to with small bower in 50 fathoms of water. Veered 2 cables . . . Lost in the gale, 3 cables, one anchor, buoy rope 50 fathoms, 1 nun buoy and a boat.'

The *Minerve* escaped running ashore, but others were less fortunate. The 74-gun *Courageux* drove from her anchors and became a total wreck on the rocky African coast before the ship could be brought under control. More than 450 of her crew perished. Her commander, Captain Hallowell, with whom Cockburn was to be closely associated in the following year, was ashore at the time attending a court martial, and naturally enough was exonerated at his own court martial later. Two other ships of the line, the *Gibraltar* and the *Culloden*, also dragged and narrowly survived.

The same storm enabled a French squadron of five line ships and three frigates to escape downwind through the Gut of Gibraltar to Brest. Admiral Villeneuve had not even appreciated that the British fleet stood before him, to the chagrin of Jervis watching their escape from the Rock.

Minerve's crew deserved a rest: she had been at sea almost continuously for five months which included the arduous duties of garrisoning Capraia and the Leghorn blockade. A frigate's duties were so varied that they invariably spent far less time at anchor than ships of the line.

Jervis had just received orders from the Admiralty to evacuate Elba where two or three frigates still remained in support of the isolated garrison at Porto Ferrajo. Nelson was the obvious choice for this task but Jervis could not spare the *Captain*. The special relationship which had developed between Nelson and Cockburn made the *Minerve* a natural replacement. The day after that momentous storm, Nelson transferred his commodore's broad pendant to the *Minerve* with instructions to sail in company with the frigate *Blanche* (Captain Preston), to Porto Ferrajo, and evacuate the military garrison and their equipment and stores. On December 15 Cockburn weighed anchor with his distinguished friend onboard. While the *Minerve* and the *Blanche* made their way back into the Mediterranean, Jervis with the fleet sailed into the Atlantic to counter French and Spanish designs.

Three uneventful days passed for the *Minerve* and her consort, but on December 19 she met a Genoese Malaga-bound polacre whose cargo included a large quantity of Spanish silk which, being contraband, was removed. For the rest of the day the two British frigates remained in dangerous waters off Cartagena where after nightfall they fell in with two Spanish frigates, one of which might well have been the cause of Cockburn's fruitless search off Cape de Gata a fortnight before.

A fierce action began which was reported in the *Minerve*'s log, 'brought to on the starboard tack at 10. The *Blanche* made signal to speak to us, and bore down towards us. The captain informed us that he saw two Spanish frigates to leeward and we cleared for action and bore down on them. At 20 minutes before 11 passed under the stern of one of them, which proving to be Spanish we commenced action with her. At 11 saw *Blanche* engaging the other. At 14 past 11 our opponent's mizen-mast fell by the board. Wore ship occasionally to prevent her getting to leeward of us, which she endeavoured often to effect. At 20 minutes after 1 she hailed us to say she had surrendered. Sent our first lieutenant to take possession and the Spanish captain Don Jacobo Stuart returned in the boat. He acquainted us the frigate was *La Santa Sabina*, mounting 40 guns, 20 18-pounders on the main deck, and 20 below. Took her in tow and made sail to the SE. Sent another lieutenant and 24 men onboard to clear her decks. Our People employed repairing damages. At half past 3 saw another frigate standing towards us, supposed her to be the *Blanche*. At 10 past 4 she hailed our prize in Spanish and fired a broadside into her, in consequence of which we cast off the prize and ordered her to stand to the southward. At half past 4 commenced action with the second frigate. At 5 she wore ship and stood from us. Saw three other ships astern, which as daylight cleared away, proved to be two line of battleships and a frigate, which the ship we had last engaged with, joined, and they all made sail in chase of us. Light airs made all sail possible, our prize in sight bearing about ENE, *Blanche* bearing West. The People employed repairing damages and fitting the lower masts etc, being badly wounded. *Sabina* hoisted English colours over Spanish and stood to the NE, which induced the largest line of battleship to give up the pursuit of us and follow her. She brought *La Santa Sabina* to, when her fore and mainmast went over the side, and she was retaken. The other line of battleship and two frigates continued in chase of us. Saw the Spanish fleet bearing ENE. Made signal to the *Blanche* to join us, which she did not answer. In the first action had seven seamen and marines killed and 34 wounded. In the second action 10 wounded. At noon fresh breezes and hazy weather and the Spanish frigates and one line of battleship still in chase of us.'

At this point, the story is best taken up by Nelson. He wrote two reports from his cabin in the *Minerve*, one during the morning of the 20th, and the other at the end of the day. Both addressed to Jervis appeared subsequently in the *London Gazette*. The second read, 'I have to acquaint you that Lieutenants Culverhouse and Hardy, with a proper number of men, being put in charge of the *Sabina*, and she taken in tow at four AM, a frigate was seen coming up, which by her signals, was known to be Spanish. At half past four she came to action with the *Minerve*, who cast off the prize, and Lieutenant Culverhouse was directed to stand to the southward; after a trial of strength of more than half an hour, she wore and hauled off, and I am confident she would have shared the fate of her companion. At this time three other ships were seen standing for the *Minerve*; hope was alive that they were only frigates, and also that the *Blanche* was one of them; but when the day dawned it was mortifying to see they were two Spanish ships of the line and two frigates, and the *Blanche* far to windward. In this situation, the enemy frequently within shot, by bringing up the breeze, it required all the skill of Captain Cockburn, which he eminently displayed, to get off with a crippled ship: And here I must also do justice to Lieutenants Culverhouse and Hardy, and express my tribute of praise in their management of the prize; a frigate repeatedly fired into her without effect, and at last the Spanish Admiral quitted the pursuit of the *Minerve* for that of the *Sabina*, who was steering a different course, evidently with the intention of attracting the notice of the Admiral, as English colours were hoisted over the Spanish. The *Sabina*'s main and foremast fell overboard before she surrendered. This is, Sir, an unpleasant tale; but the merits of every officer and man in the *Minerve* and her prize were eminently conspicuous through the whole of this arduous day. The enemy quitted the pursuit of the *Minerve* at dark.'

First light on the 21st showed that the Spanish ships were still only three miles astern of the crippled *Minerve* which was not making much headway. She had lost two excellent officers and 40 of her best men in the transfer to the *Sabina*, and her crew were now desperately employed in clearing away wreckage and repairing damage. Perhaps Nelson was over-sanguine in thinking the pursuit abandoned, but certainly by five o'clock that evening the Spanish ships were hull down and had altered course to the north east.[8]

Superhuman efforts by the carpenters repairing shot holes in the boats, by the sailmakers restoring the shot-riddled mainsail, and by 'the People about the rigging', made the *Minerve* relatively seaworthy on the 24th. That day she chased and captured a privateer ketch – the *Maria* – carrying six nine-pounder guns and with a crew of 68. She was taken in tow, her crew removed and another officer and eight men from the *Minerve* placed in her. For all this to happen so soon after their struggle with the *Sabina* proved the resilience of Cockburn and his crew. Nelson was prompted to write immediately to Jervis, 'you will, I am sure, forgive me for interesting myself for our friend Cockburn; he is now near 90 short of complement, altho' I have some hopes that those taken in the prize may be returned to Gibraltar; they are all good men . . . my cox'n, an invaluable man is also a prisoner. If you can, pray Sir, procure some good men for Cockburn, he deserves every favour you are pleased to bestow on him.'[9] Christmas day, which followed, passed uneventfully.

The adventurous passage to Elba ended on December 27 when the frigate reached Porto Ferrajo to find lying there the *Inconstant* and three minor war vessels. Carpenters and caulkers arrived onboard immediately to assist further with repairs. Nelson, as solicitous as ever for his men, wrote to the Captain-General of Cartagena, 'Sir – The fortune of war put *La Sabina* into my possession, after she had been most gallantly defended: the fickle dame returned her to you, with some of my officers and men in her.

'I have endeavoured to make the captivity of Don Jacobo Stuart, her brave commander, as light as possible; and I trust to the generosity of your nation for its being reciprocal for the British officers and men. 'I consent, Sir, that Don Jacobo may be exchanged and at full liberty to serve his King when Lieutenants Culverhouse and Hardy are delivered into the garrison of Gibraltar.'

Captain Preston of the *Blanche* had done well by successfully engaging the Spanish frigate *Ceres* without being able to take possession of her, but the award of *victor ludorum* undoubtedly belonged to

● The sword Nelson personally
wanted to present to Cockburn.
In the event Earl St Vincent
performed the duty.
(National Maritime Museum)

George Cockburn on whom Nelson again reported to Jervis, 'you are, Sir, so thoroughly acquainted with the merits of Captain Cockburn, that it is needless for me to express them'. A measure of the stubbornness with which the Spanish seamen had fought was reflected in their loss of 164 killed and wounded.

Nelson thought so highly of Cockburn's virtues that he decided to present him with a special sword to commemorate *Sabina's* taking. By the time this handsome gift had been made by his London cutler, the two officers were no longer serving together. Nelson therefore asked Admiral the Earl St Vincent (as Jervis later became), to present it. Nelson wrote, 'after George Cockburn's gallant action with the *Sabina*, I directed a gold-hilted sword to be made for him, which I had hoped to present to him myself in the most public and handsome manner, but as Providence has decreed otherwise, I must beg you to present it for me.'[10]

The crew now had to work to a deadline for evacuating Elba, but the ship needed extensive repair before she could be considered fit for sea again. A new mainmast had to be stepped, much of the rigging replaced, and first aid applied to the defective coppering on the ship's bottom on which depended the hull's resistance to the depredations of the teredo worm (apart from affecting the ship's speed). A patched up job of nailing loose copper would have to suffice for the time being.

Cockburn's old acquaintance, General de Burgh, was onshore, adamant that having received no instructions to quit the island, he and the army garrison would remain. Nelson, having argued ineffectually confined his activities to the withdrawal of the naval element. Sir Gilbert Elliot, the late Viceroy, was in Naples and could not be left behind, so Captain Fremantle in the *Inconstant* was sent to fetch him. It was a mission to Fremantle's liking, for while in Naples he was able to arrange his marriage to Miss Betsey Wynne in the British Embassy. Elliot, his aide-de-camp Colonel Drinkwater, and Betsey, all made the return trip in the *Inconstant*.

With the benefit of Elliot's diplomacy, Nelson tried again with General de Burgh, who still insisted that he would not move without a direct order from England. Consequently, Nelson arranged for transports to be victualled and ready at short notice to remove the garrison, should the need arise. The brief stay in Porto Ferrajo provided much social activity. It was the new year, no enemy was immediately in sight, and many friends found themselves in company. The *Inconstant* with a ready-made hostess onboard in Betsey, provided a natural rendezvous. Here Nelson, Cockburn, and others were entertained to a 'noisy party'; Cockburn returned the hospitality in the *Minerve* in what turned out to be a bacchanalia to celebrate Fremantle's loss of bachelor status.

The fleet weighed and entered open water on January 29. In company with the *Minerve* were the *Romulus, Southampton, Dido, Dolphin, Dromedary, Sardine, L'Utile* and 12 transports. Next day, the *Minerve* and *Romulus* were detached to see how things were in San Fiorenzo Bay, while the main squadron sailed to the south and relative safety. The two ships also carried out a quick reconnaissance of Toulon Harbour before turning down the Spanish coast where there were the usual troublesome Danish brigs to be chased and released after inspection. As recompense, a number of feluccas were taken with their cargoes; too small to be taken in tow they were burned. Cartagena – as with Toulon – was empty of ships, confirming that the Spanish and French fleets had probably moved into the Atlantic.

Nelson and Cockburn pushed ahead, reaching Gibraltar on February 9, 1797. There they learned that 27 Spanish sail of the line and 12 frigates had passed through the Gut four days before. Two Spanish ships had been detached to supply the Spanish defences on the mainland opposing Gibraltar and there, in one of them, the *Terrible*, were Culverhouse and Hardy: Nelson's plea for their return had worked. The arrival of the two British lieutenants with the seamen who had taken the *Sabina* as prize was a cause for celebration in the *Minerve*. They were sorely needed for the tasks immediately ahead.

CHAPTER FIVE

The Minerve - in the Atlantic 1797-8

THE *MINERVE* WAS ABOUT TO ENTER the Atlantic for the first time under Cockburn's command, and the crew bore that air of expectancy which only imminent action can engender. Leaving Gibraltar on February 11, 1797, with Nelson's broad pendant still flying, Cockburn's immediate problem was to escape the Spanish ships of the line anchored under the batteries of Algeciras, watching the *Minerve's* movements and ready to intercept. Thus, the Spanish *Terrible*, which had played captor to Hardy and was to take up the pursuit, was able to follow a course sufficiently close to the shore for the crowds there to witness the chase.

In the early afternoon, William Barnes, one of the seamen working on *Minerve's* sails, fell overboard. Unhesitatingly, Cockburn ordered the helmsman to heave to, and the jolly boat to be lowered. Hardy joined the boat in an attempt to save the man but a strong current soon left them far astern of the *Minerve*. Poor Barnes could not be found and by now the *Terrible* was gaining fast. Seeing that the boat was falling even further behind, Nelson exclaimed, 'by God, I'll not lose Hardy'. The order was given for the mizen topsail to be backed, effectively stemming the *Minerve's* forward movement. Inexplicably, *Terrible's* captain failed to press home his advantage but decided instead to shorten sail and wait for her consort. *Minerve's* jolly boat was quickly alongside and hoisted in, and the British ship began to draw away. Eventually the Spaniards were lost to sight as *Minerve* cleared Cape Spartel and bore to the north. It had been a miraculous escape seemingly brought about by *Minerve's* unexpected manoeuvre which had unnerved her Spanish pursuers.[1]

Night brought worries – and fog. The sound of minute guns indicated the presence of a large hostile fleet close by but Cockburn managed to avoid detection and at noon on the following day, the 13th, joined Jervis and the British fleet cruising off Cape St Vincent. Nelson and Cockburn wasted no time in repairing onboard the *Victory* to warn Jervis of the approaching Spanish armada; a little later Nelson left Cockburn to rejoin the *Captain* from which he had been absent for nearly two months. At the same time the opportunity was also taken for the *Minerve*'s distinguished guest, Sir Gilbert Elliot, to be transferred to the frigate *Lively* for return to England.

The easterly wind which had taken the Spanish fleet into the Atlantic shifted to the west that evening, enabling their ships to head towards Cadiz. Jervis's fleet of 15 ships of the line cruised between them and Spain and by dawn the fleets were only a few miles apart in the persistently foggy weather. In company with the frigate *Niger* Cockburn spent the night watching the Spanish ships at close quarters; the ship's log for the day which followed, St Valentine's day, reads, 'At 6, 13 strange ships in the south west; at 7, Out all reefs; at 10, Fleet in chase of Spanish fleet, 5 or 6 miles; at 1120, Van of our fleet commenced action; at 12, In close action.'

The *Minerve* signalled enemy numbers and course which information was repeated by the *Culloden* leading the British line. Onboard the *Victory* Jervis counted them with Hallowell who, since the loss of the *Courageux*, had been serving as a supernumerary. Through the mist, the total gradually increased as Hallowell reported,

'There are eight sail of the line, Sir John.'
'Very well, Sir.'
'There are 20 sail of the line, Sir John.'
'Very well, Sir.'
'There are 25 sail of the line, Sir John.'
'Very well, Sir.'
'There are 27 sail of the line, Sir John.'
'Enough Sir, no more of that; the die is cast, and if there are 50 sail, I will go through them.'
'That's right, Sir John,' answered Hallowell with typical enthusiasm and a thump on the back. 'That's right! And, by God, we'll give them a damned good licking.'

Cockburn himself was soon to experience Hallowell's ebullient nature when he shared his company over a long period.

The battle of St Vincent provided a tactical lesson. *The Fighting Instructions* of the time still prescribed that, when enemy fleets were

● **The battle of St Vincent where Nelson broke the line.
(RN Museum, Portsmouth)**

met, the line of one's own fleet should be maintained at all costs thus making it possible for opposite numbers in the enemy's line to be engaged fleetingly, if rarely conclusively.

A combination of factors on February 14, including changes in the direction of the wind and the fact that the Spanish fleet was in two divisions, suggested an indecisive engagement. Nelson in the *Captain*, at the rear of the British line, noted this and committed the cardinal sin of breaking the line, thus enabling him to take the shortest cut to engage the enemy at close quarters. Having briefly exchanged broadsides with the huge *Santissima Trinidad*, a four-decker mounting 134 guns, he took on the *San Nicolas* which had run foul of one of her compatriots, the *San Josef*. By this time he was supported by his friend Collingwood in the *Excellent* who had followed Nelson in his transgression.

Although the *Captain* was battered by the overwhelming weight of gunfire against her, Nelson laid his 74-gun ship alongside the *San Nicolas* and gave the order for boarders away. Leading, as always, from the front, he entered the Spaniard through her stern windows, followed by his seamen. Overcoming resistance they made their way to the quarterdeck where her ensign was already being low-ered. Without delay Nelson turned his attention to the *San Josef*, the three-decker locked to *San Nicolas*'s other side. Then came what many believe was the most glorious incident in his career: calling for

67

more boarders, and shouting, 'Westminster Abbey or Victory', he and his party climbed into the ship by her main chains and overcame resistance a second time, and probably more quickly than it had taken to secure the *San Nicolas*.

The capture of these two fine ships virtually ended the battle. The only ship of this Spanish division to escape was the *Santissima Trinidad*. Although at one stage she had struck her colours, she rehoisted them before possession of her could be made. Her capture would have been a prize above all others, although her escape was by no means complete.

While Nelson was in action Cockburn had to be content with a more passive role, his frigate's function being to offer back-up assistance in the rescue of disabled ships and their survivors. When the *Colossus* lost her foreyard he immediately closed to take her in tow and continue in her station. Captain Murray declined the offer for the benefit of other ships in greater need. More pressing was the situation of the *Captain*, at that moment entangled with her two adversaries. She was eventually hauled off and Cockburn welcomed Nelson onboard the *Minerve* where he was offered the facilities of the captain's table before both proceeded to meet the commander-in-chief.

Within little more than four hours a remarkable victory had been gained, the importance of which went far beyond the value of the prizes taken. The morale-sapping effect of the events of the previous year, including Britain's withdrawal from the Mediterranean, had been more than compensated for by the achievements of one glorious day. When Jervis and Nelson met on *Victory*'s quarterdeck, far from reprimanding him for breaking the line, Jervis embraced him saying he could not thank him enough.

Nelson now shifted his broad pendant to the *Irresistible* (74), while Cockburn was ordered to take charge of the crippled prizes and organise the frigates which were to tow them to Lisbon. It soon became obvious that such orders were impossible to carry out in the light and baffling winds with a numerically superior Spanish fleet still in the offing. So Jervis told Cockburn to tow the *Captain* in the centre of the protecting fleet. The prime need was for the fleet to reform; fortunately nearby Lagos Bay, where the ships arrived on February 17, provided a reasonable anchorage.

The *Lively* was now available to provide passage to England for Sir Gilbert Elliot and take home Jervis's despatches. Two weeks later news of the battle reached London where it was received with acclaim. The thanks of the House of Commons in a long and flowing eulogy under the command, 'that Mr Speaker do transmit the said resolutions of this House to Sir John Jervis', was received in the *Victory* in short time and read to all ships' companies. Others were quick to follow the example with the King, the House of Lords, the City of London, and the loyal subjects of the Factory at Lisbon, (the latter perhaps, not entirely without self interest), all paying tribute. Each admiral and captain of line-of-battle ships, but not the commanding officers of frigates such as the *Minerve* and other minor vessels, received the King's Gold Medal. The seamen went unrewarded, although it was a nice thought of the City of London to authorise, 'a sum to be subscribed by this Court to the Fund at Lloyds for the relief of widows and orphans of the seamen, marines, and others who fell in the said contest'.

The *Santissima Trinidad* when last seen was detached from the enemy fleet in tow of a large frigate and Cockburn was signalled by Jervis to look for her. On the evening of the 17th, having had no respite since leaving Gibraltar, the *Minerve* was joined by the frigate *Emerald* whose captain, Berkeley, came with orders to seek out the *Santissima Trinidad*, and to place himself in command of a squadron comprising the frigate *Niger*, the sloop *Bonne Citoyenne* together with the *Minerve* and *Emerald*. After cruising for three days, the *Trinidad*'s unmistakable outline was discovered about 80 miles south-east of Cape St Vincent. She was still under tow but now assisted by jury sails on the stumps of her masts. Berkeley ordered a general chase and under a heavy press of sail in the easterly gale then blowing, the squadron closed rapidly on their adversary. The *Minerve* led the chase with her superior sailing qualities, and was some distance ahead. Cockburn wore round to bring her close alongside the *Santissima Trinidad*; at the same moment the Spanish frigate cast off her tow and sailed away to the southward. In theory, the *Santissima Trinidad* should have been well able to look after herself. Cockburn luffed up under the stern of the giant four-decker and was on the point of opening fire when Berkeley signalled for the *Minerve* to close with the *Emerald*. Cockburn had no option but to conform even though Berkeley was on opposite tack to the *Santissima Trinidad* and rapidly losing contact. With all ships of the squadron under full sail in the darkening gloom, it was not long before the *Santissima Trinidad* was lost to sight and could not be rediscovered.

The *Emerald* returned to Lagos Bay leaving the *Minerve* to continue her watch over the movements of the enemy fleet. To the casual observer it would seem that a magnificent opportunity to have conducted a trial of strength with the *Santissima Trinidad* had been lost – or had it?

On joining the British Fleet off Lisbon on February 28, Cockburn learned that an application had been made for Berkeley's court-martial. The complaint against him came from his own officers who believed that he was entirely wrong in calling off the *Minerve* at the moment she was about to engage. Cockburn who so easily could have joined the hue and cry waited to hear Berkeley's defence. Berkeley's reason for withdrawing the *Minerve* was that at that precise moment when she was most vulnerable, his lookouts saw a ship bearing down quickly from the direction of Cadiz. He had little doubt she was an enemy although in the event she proved to be the British frigate *Terpischore*. The favourable moment for attacking the *Santissima Trinidad* had been lost and could not be regained.

Cockburn's own observations on the case were a model of fair-mindedness in support of a fellow captain whose service career was at stake. He told Jervis that he was naturally sorry not to have been able to test the *Santissima Trinidad* having got so near to her, but he had no true knowledge of the state of this mighty ship with her 134 guns. As far as he could judge from her appearance she seemed capable, if managed with the least resolution, and in such weather, to overwhelm any number of frigates. She was quite steady and under perfect control; although the heavy sea would have prevented the opening of her lower gun ports, she still had three other decks from which she could have fired with ease. Moreover, the press of sail employed by the *Minerve* in her endeavour to close with the *Santissima Trinidad* had caused her maindeck to half fill with water in the weather prevailing. The *Emerald*, he understood, was in like condition and there was no hope of the *Niger* ever getting within range. There was the possibility, too, that the Spanish frigate would turn about and join any action, which must have weighed upon Berkeley's mind.[2]

Cockburn did not have to supplicate with Jervis; his reputation was far too high. A straightforward statement of the facts was sufficient to convince the commander-in-chief that Berkeley's court-martial should not proceed. Cockburn at least had the satisfaction of seeing justice done to an officer who was not well known to him but much his senior.

Not that 'Old Jarvie', as Jervis was known, could possibly have been a pushover. He had the reputation for maintaining an iron discipline not one whit less severe on his officers than on his men, never hesitating to punish wrongdoers and insisting on high standards in such matters as dress, fitness, and sobriety. He made it clear that each officer's duty was to lead and to have a proper concern for his men particularly in harbour or at anchor when they 'must not leave them to their own devices'. Officers who went ashore 'dressed like shopkeepers' were threatened with arrest.

These were the months when insurrection developed in the Channel and North Sea fleets culminating in the great mutinies at Spithead and the Nore. To prevent the canker spreading to his own fleet, Jervis realised that severity needed to be backed by judgement and foresight. One description of him relates how his hard-set, weatherbeaten face watched the expiring struggles of a mutineer dangling at the yard-arm. As the struggle ceased, St Vincent (as he had now become), turned to his companion, raised his hat in salute to the ceremony rather than to the man who had died, and said confidently, 'discipline is preserved, Sir'.

For all his apparent insensitivity St Vincent could display moments of humanity. While the fleet was lying in the Tagus, Cockburn and his fellow captains received an order from the commander-in-chief to be read to their ships' companies. It referred to a deserter in the *Niger* who was to be pardoned in recognition of the general good conduct of the whole fleet in the recent battle, and continued, 'trusting that an instance of mercy shown to a man, who has justly forfeited his life by frequent desertions from His Majesty's Service, may operate more powerfully upon the minds of those prone to this disgraceful practice; I do hereby pardon John Moloney, a prisoner under sentence of death, for desertion from HM Sloop *Speedy*, now in confinement in HM ship under your command.'[3]

After a few days in the Tagus, Cockburn's activity restarted. Nelson, now promoted rear-admiral, was to operate an inshore squadron keeping watch on the Spanish fleet's movements and maintaining a close blockade of the Cadiz approaches. Intelligence that a Spanish treasure fleet was on its way home from South America which, if captured, would be an outstanding prize, was also a potent factor. Foul winds prevented the squadron from getting to sea until March 5 when, on casting off her mooring, the frigate *Andromache* was swept on to the *Minerve*; fortunately no great damage was done. After that, the squadron comprising the *Irresistible, Leander, Minerve, Andromache, Romulus, Southampton, Bonne Citoyenne* and *Raven* sailed without further trouble. Five days later Cockburn was selected by Nelson to reconnoitre close inshore and assess activity in Cadiz harbour. His report revealed a formidable gathering of 25 sail of the line, 10 frigates and 50 merchantmen, all in varying stages of preparedness. The *Santissima Trinidad* was there looking in much better shape, with an admiral's flag at the fore topmast head, her mainmast shipped, and others being replaced with the aid of sheerlegs.

For the remainder of March the *Minerve* cruised between Cape Spartel, on the north western tip of Africa, and Cape St Vincent, keeping a good watch to westward for the treasure ships, but again looking into Cadiz on the 27th, where he found the Spanish fleet still refitting much as before. The tedium of the task, however, was beginning to show. Lack of opportunity to embark fresh provisions caused Jeremiah McCarty and Joseph Green to be buried at sea with suspected scurvy; a cask of salt beef when opened was found to be 54lbs short, and was duly surveyed in the hope that, in the course of time, the rascally contractor who had supplied it would reap his desserts. Cockburn allocated 20 gallons of wine to the sick, for that at least had an anti-scorbutic quality.

Early in April the inshore squadron joined Jervis' main fleet which had come south from the Tagus. The interception of the Spanish treasure fleet had become an obsession with Nelson who reasoned that probably they had taken refuge at Santa Cruz in the Canary Islands, a focal point on the trade route from South America. With the Spanish fleet blockaded in Cadiz, Nelson conceived the idea of leading an expedition against the island of Teneriffe, there hopefully to seize the treasure ships and raid the warehouses for which he would require troops. Since the evacuation of the British garrison in Elba was overdue, they could be made available from that source if St Vincent would agree to Nelson covering the withdrawal.

Nelson discussed his plans with his captains, including Cockburn who was due to leave immediately for the Tagus to reprovision his ship. The scheme as explained to him was that instead of accompanying Nelson with his small squadron to Elba, the *Minerve*, and probably one other frigate, would operate meanwhile in the Canary Islands waters, thereby paving the way for Nelson's own expedition which it was unlikely could be mounted before mid-1797.

Initially, St Vincent did not like the idea of reducing his force in the all important blockade of Cadiz but Nelson's persuasiveness won, and he duly sailed for Elba on April 12.

That day Cockburn arrived in the Tagus where no time was wasted in embarking stores, particularly lemons to prevent further spread of the scurvy. Portuguese neutrality and the strong British trading community made Lisbon and its river a pleasant break. Still at anchor there and under survey were the captured Spanish warships *Salvadore da Mondo*, *San Josef*, *San Nicolas* and the *San Ysidro*, reminders of the recent victory. April 16 saw the arrival of the frigate *Lively* from England to which ship Captain Hallowell had been appointed at St Vincent's request. Cockburn was placed under his orders for the forthcoming cruise.

Hallowell, a Canadian of gigantic frame and considerable strength, was popular with his contemporaries who admired his courage and generous spirit. Cockburn, his junior by 12 years, could not have had a better companion for the work ahead. Hallowell possessed a bizarre sense of humour – it was he who, after the Battle of the Nile in the following year, presented Nelson with a coffin made from the mainmast of the French ship *L'Orient*, accompanied by a note saying that he hoped when Nelson had finished his military career in this world, 'you may be buried in one of your trophies – but that that period may be far distant.'

After leaving the Tagus, both ships joined the fleet off Cadiz where the blockade was now complete and no ships were allowed to enter. They remained there until the 27th operating under Captain Sir James Saumarez of the *Orion*, to whom Nelson had handed over command of the inshore squadron.

By the end of April the two frigates were in the vicinity of Portuguese Madeira, and on May 2 arrived within sight of Santa Cruz but did not close the shore for fear of rousing suspicion. The Canary Islands form an archipelago extending some 300 miles from west to east, and 100 miles from north to south. Since a thorough search of all islands was required, the frigates had much to cover.

Throughout May the *Lively* and the *Minerve* worked their way along the shore of La Palma at the western extremity to a circumnavigation of Lanzarote at the other, with little reward.

The monotony imposed too great a strain on some members of the crew, and Richard Cambridge, soldier of the 11th Regiment, was flogged yet again with four dozen lashes for neglect of duty and disobedience. The Great Mutinies, naturally, had alerted all ships to signs of incipient mutiny. An occasional offender apart, the *Minerve* was remarkably free of trouble and remained a happy ship. At the same time, there were some encouraging signs that the lessons of the Spithead mutiny had been learned: the promulgation of *The outline of a Plan for the encouragement of the seamen and marines serving onboard His Majesty's Fleet* being one. The plan included improved wages and provisions; the entitlement of all wounded to receive pay until their wounds were healed or declared incurable; and that, if incurable, they would receive a pension from the Chest at Chatham, or be admitted into the Royal Hospital at Greenwich. Such redress was long overdue and had a beneficial effect.

It was time to look more closely at Santa Cruz without arousing suspicion of future intentions. The *Lively* and the *Minerve* arrived off the town in the early morning of May 27, 1797 when Hallowell sent in a boat under a flag of truce with a letter to the Governor. Suspecting, correctly, that the object was simply to examine the port, the Governor sent out a launch under an English-speaking emissary, Don Juan Creagh, who received the letter not far from the mole. While awaiting his reply, the English boat's crew memorised the anchorage and the defences. Secured under the safety of the guns of Santa Cruz lay a huge treasure ship, confirming previous intelligence of her arrival there. Also present was a war vessel which looked suspiciously like a French armed brig. Any uncertainty was dispelled by the stream of abuse when one of her boats approached. The Governor's reply duly arrived (the subject of the letters was the exchange of prisoners), and the *Lively's* boat withdrew. But the insulting rencontre with the Frenchmen was not forgotten and, after

● **Santa Cruz in Teneriffe. (RN Museum, Portsmouth)**

discussion with Cockburn, Hallowell decided they would return swiftly. As it was impracticable for the frigates to cut out the vessel in so strongly defended a harbour, the best chance of success lay in achieving surprise by boat action. The plan was formed: the operation would be entrusted to Thomas Hardy with the *Lively* providing four officers and the *Minerve* two to take charge of the boats.

On May 29 the frigates returned to the anchorage under cover of darkness. *Minerve*'s log records, 'moderate breezes with thick hazy weather … occasionally standing into Santa Cruz Bay. At 12 past 10 hove to, hoisted boats out. At 11 sent the boats in company with the *Lively*'s, manned and armed into the Bay to cut out a French man-of-war brig at an anchor there. At ½ past 3 they began to fire from the shore at our boats; our large cutter received so many shot that she sank and was lost. At 6 the boats returned with the brig in tow. She proved to be *La Mutine* from Brest bound to the Island of France (Mauritius), mounting 12 six-pounders and two 42-pound carronades and 140 men. At 8 filled and made sail with the *Lively* and brig in company. Received onboard 42 prisoners.'[4]

The matter of fact style of this entry masks the occasion's heroics. Although heavily outnumbered and outgunned, the attack was made with great resolution. The French colours in the *Mutine* were lowered and replaced while her commander – Captain Xavier Pommier – was ashore. A heavy fire was opened from the shore batteries, and the boarding was opposed by intense musketry fire from the brig's deck. Having boarded her, there was still the problem of taking the capture in tow and at the same time keeping the prisoners below deck. Finally, the boats' crews had to row for an hour before regaining the safety of their own ships.

It transpired that the *Mutine*, on her way east to foment trouble in India, had broken her voyage to embark supplies and water. Her two carronades, 100 gallons of brandy, much bread, six sheets of copper and a barrel of tar, were transferred to the British ships. Perhaps Richard Cambridge, that well known offender of the 11th Regiment, managed to lay his hands on the brandy, for again he suffered three dozen lashes for theft and drunkenness.[5]

With all prisoners removed, Hardy was given acting command of the *Mutine* and sailed for Lisbon on June 2 with a small prize crew. St Vincent was so delighted with this fine brig that he commissioned her into the navy, confirmed Hardy in command, and promoted him to Commander. From this moment on, Hardy's career went from strength to strength.

Two days later, while cruising off Gran Canaria, the *Minerve* was hit by a violent squall. Before she could shorten sail, the main and mizen topmasts and fore topgallant mast carried away and were lost overboard. In her disabled state it was important for Cockburn to rid himself of his French prisoners. On June 6, she was back at Santa Cruz and, under a flag of truce, the prisoners were transferred ashore with all speed. Both Hallowell and Cockburn were anxious to allay any suspicion that the port was receiving undue attention for fear they might increase its preparedness before Nelson's expedition. Teneriffe was avoided therefore, and the ships cruised around the other islands of the archipelago.

The *Minerve*, at sea for two and a half months since leaving Lisbon, and still not fully recovered from the recent storm, was short both of provisions and of water, with many of her crew sickly. It was a boon therefore, to have the island of Madeira, some 300 miles to the north, as a refuge. The ship sailed into the anchorage in Funchal Bay towards the end of June to be reassured by the sight of an allied convoy of 56 merchantmen lying off the town. Fresh beef and seven pipes of wine were immediately embarked but the receipt of 170 hanks of onions particularly gladdened the heart of the ship's surgeon. These, more than anything, would help to reduce the ever-growing sick list.

While at Funchal, Samuel Hoare, seaman, was found guilty of inciting others to mutiny and was punished with three dozen lashes. There were others who were guilty of mutinous language and breaking shore leave, but Hoare was adjudged the ringleader and was discharged from the ship. Cockburn's firmness nipped further indiscipline in the bud.

The two frigates left with the convoy on June 29, and escorted it as far as La Palma – the most western island. They then parted company and returned to the northern end of Teneriffe where they spent a profitable month chasing, intercepting and taking prizes. A Spanish schooner proved to be particularly useful with a cargo of live bullocks, nine of which were transferred with their fodder. Another prize, the Spanish *El Corse*, was manned by an officer and eight men from the *Minerve*, and proved her worth in short time by taking a prize herself. Such proliferation required a return to Funchal on August 4 to disperse the growing fleet, but *El Corse*, a useful satellite, continued to sail in company with the frigates for the remainder of the month.

During the night of September 1, a suspicious ship was chased, later to be identified as the 28-gun *Marseillais*, a French letter-of-marque. Early next morning she ran for shelter into a difficult harbour of Gran Canaria Island, defended by two batteries. The *Minerve* followed closely in her wake, the enemy's pilot serving for both ships until Cockburn succeeded in getting alongside her. A fierce contest ensued and, although the *Minerve* was subjected to heavy and continuous fire from the shore batteries, she overcame her opponent at five in the morning. It was one thing to chase the *Marseillais* in but quite another to take her out of the small harbour in light airs while on a lee shore. Only the account in the ship's log can provide the full drama: the seaman's argot in which it is written nevertheless reveals how narrowly the *Minerve* escaped disaster. 'Fresh breezes and cloudy weather. At 2 the chase hoisted French colours; fired several shots at her to bring her to. At 4 chase standing into Porto Confital Bay. Half past 4 chase anchored between the two batteries and opened a heavy fire on us, as did the two batteries. Anchored with a spring on the best bower in 10 fathoms; hove in on the spring and brought our broadside to bear on the batteries and ship, and then engaged them. At 5 the ship struck. Sent an officer onboard to take possession of her. She proved to be the *Marseillais*, a French Letter-of-Marque from Guadaloupe bound to the Mediterranean laden with sugar, coffee, cotton, etc., mounting 28 guns. At 10 minutes before 6, hove short but not being able to purchase the anchor, it having hooked a rock, and the forts keeping up a heavy fire on us, cut the cable by order of the Captain. Lost the anchor and 12 fathoms of cable, and the spring which was a six and a half inch hawser, and which was 96 fathom. Made all sail with the boats ahead at 7. Light airs with a heavy swell setting on the land. At 8 prize in company. At 2 pm finding the ship drifting fast inshore, let go the small bower in 30 fathoms about 2 cables length from the surf. Carried the stream anchor out with the stream cable, a 9 inch cablet and a 7½ inch hawser bent to it. At 3 carried the keg with 138 fathom of cablet bent to it. At 5 a breeze sprang up; set all sail, ran the ship ahead by the hawsers, and then cut the small bower cable and hawsers, and cleared the outer rock by about ½ cable's length.'

After this display of seamanship, a small prize crew was placed onboard the *Marseillais*, but the *Minerve* now carried an over-large number of prisoners onboard. Cockburn preferred to avoid nearby Santa Cruz, so recently the scene of British aggression, but chose, instead, a point at the western end of the island of Teneriffe where he landed 28 Spanish and 25 French prisoners under flag of truce.

He left a letter for the Governor informing him of his action and asking for the return of any British prisoners held. No reply came but Cockburn could not leave until he had received receipts for the returned prisoners. To make matters worse, when the prisoners were landed an armed mob had detained his officers bearing the flag of truce for a whole day without food. Notwithstanding, he sailed to Santa Cruz to obtain satisfaction. The peripatetic *El Corse* was sent into the harbour with a firm but polite letter demanding the receipts and British exchange prisoners. His tenacity was immediately rewarded.

Hallowell decided it was time for Cockburn to rejoin St Vincent for further orders. The *Minerve* badly required refit, and needed to be relieved of her prizes. Stopping at Funchal to reprovision, she continued her northerly course with the prizes in company. A sad entry in the log for October 6 reflects only too well that sickness and accident take more toll than enemy action; 'in hoisting up the jolly boat, the tackle fall gave way and John Slade, seaman, fell out of her and was drowned; although we lowered the cutter down immediately, yet was too late to save him.'

By hailing the *Hannibal* on October 13, Cockburn learned that the British fleet was at sea off Cadiz and, by making all sail, its heart-warming sight came next day. A friendly welcome awaited onboard the *Ville de Paris*, St Vincent's new flagship, where the admiral ordered him to Gibraltar with the prizes, and for repairs.

On his way Cockburn passed his old command, the *Meleager*, and spoke to her. Inside the new mole at Gibraltar, the process of reducing the ship for refit proceeded swiftly. The master attendant was first aboard to moor the ship alongside; powder was disembarked to render the ship safe while in dockyard hands; the sails were unbent and sent ashore for repair, and topmasts struck.

While she was non-operational a convoy of merchant ships, under the care of the frigate *Andromache*, was seen to be in trouble near the Spanish shore as it approached Gibraltar. The adverse tide and lack of wind had set the ships close to Algeciras, whence about 30 predatory Spanish gunboats were moving out. Immediate assistance was required to save the convoy and, as senior naval officer at Gibraltar, Cockburn took the responsibility. The three serviceable gunboats available were manned with a selection of his own officers and seamen and the boats were pulled within range of the *Andro-*

mache, commanded by Captain Mansfield. Although it was now dark, Cockburn told him he intended placing his meagre force between the helpless inshore part of the convoy and the enemy force now gaining rapidly on it. In the darkness positions could be judged only by the flash of guns but, supported by the *Andromache*'s fire, Cockburn succeeded in confusing the opposition which comprised not only the formidable gunboat flotilla and the shore batteries, but also a frigate lying at Algeciras. This fierce contest lasted for four hours, during which most of the convoy reached safety. The laggards posed the greatest problem. One brig – an army victualler – ran on shore and was taken, but only after a fierce struggle. The determination with which Cockburn tried to save her can be gained from his report of November 7, to St Vincent, '... the brig we lost having her master killed, and being abandoned by her crew. I put some hands onboard of her to endeavour to get her sails set again, but we found everything cut to pieces by the shot. I therefore took her in tow but the wind unfortunately springing up at south east, I could not keep her off; I kept her in tow however, a considerable time in the hopes of a change, till she drifted close to Algeciras, when seeing no possible chance of getting her off, and all the rest of the convoy having got clear, and being myself nearly surrounded by the enemy's gunboats, I thought proper after withdrawing my people from her, to make my way after the rest of the convoy, all of which safely anchored here by half past 4 o'clock.'[6]

One historical account of this remarkable episode finishes with the following valediction, 'Thus by Cockburn's timely exertions and spirited conduct, was this valuable convoy saved from capture, though his even making the attempt against such a superiority of force, favoured as the Spaniards were by wind and tide and a dark night, appeared to his own people as a kind of forlorn hope. Under these circumstances, it is not too much to say that it was his own personal genius and intrepidity, that it was his placing himself in one of the boats, and personally directing their movements, that the success which attended them was principally to be attributed.'[7]

There were many casualties and the *Andromache* was considerably damaged, but the three gunboats suffered little. Cockburn received a letter of thanks and appreciation from St Vincent, commending him for his conduct in the most flattering terms.

The Governor of Gibraltar, Lieutenant General O'Hara, 'Old Cock of the Rock' as he was more familiarly called, was approached by

Cockburn on a matter affecting the 11th Regiment, who for a considerable time had served in the *Minerve* as sea soldiers. 'Sir,' he said, 'a detachment of the 11th Regiment doing duty as marines onboard His Majesty's Ship *La Minerve* under my command, being very much in want of clothing, none of them having received any since July 5, 1794, and there being no officer of the regiment here to obtain any for them, I have thought it right to represent their situation to you and to request you will give such directions herein, as may appear to you proper.'

These 22 soldiers had served faithfully and well in an unfamiliar environment onboard ship and it was time for them to revert to their calling. Three weeks after writing this letter, Cockburn was instructed by the commander-in-chief to discharge the detachment and to receive marine replacements from the *Argo*. The much-flogged Richard Cambridge could have had few regrets!

As senior naval officer at Gibraltar, Cockburn had many problems. The Danish consul, for example, wrote complaining about the impressment of a Danish seaman into the British brig *L'Espoire*, always a sensitive issue when it affected neutrals. Any weakness on Cockburn's part in his reply could result in an avalanche of other requests for men to be released similarly. After careful investigation, he answered, 'I have made the necessary inquiries reference the Danish seaman you stated to have been impressed into HM Service, but I find that he came voluntarily and entered onboard *L'Espoire*. Nor was it till he was sent onboard the Danish ship some time afterwards for his things, that he found out he did not like it and then said he would not enter, he having been however, entered on the Roll as a volunteer for some days previous to this. I am sorry it is not in my power to give the order you request for his release, as it would be trifling with, as well as contrary to, the forms of our service.'[8]

Leaving Gibraltar on November 25, Cockburn was ordered temporarily to Lisbon and met the *Mutine* on passage. The ships hove to briefly for Cockburn and Hardy to exchange pleasantries.

On December 1, 1797, Cockburn received orders to rendezvous with Hallowell again between the Canaries and Madeira. 'You are to cruise in the best possible position for capturing the enemy's privateers which infest those seas, and interrupting the trade to and from Spain and her colonies until January 10, 1798, when you are to make the best of your way back to the Tagus.' He arrived off Funchal on December 11, but had to search for another eight days before meeting Hallowell who, since their last meeting, had been transferred from the *Lively* to the *Swiftsure*, a 74-gun ship of the line. With the *Theseus*, another 74, the squadron had been considerably strengthened to match the area's strategic importance.

For a month the *Minerve* was in constant pursuit of strange sail and the number of prizes mounted rapidly. A polacre under French colours, a tartan, and a Spanish polacre brig, all were seized on one day, January 18, 1798. After leaving his prizes in Gibraltar, he reached the Tagus in February.

The *Minerve*'s copper had degenerated. Commissioner Inglefield had refused to repair it during her refit at Gibraltar, perhaps because he had neither the men nor the materials, but St Vincent recognised that the ship could no longer remain on active service until the re-coppering was effected. He decided, therefore, it was time to send the *Minerve* home for a general refit.

Cockburn received orders on February 19 to go to Oporto to meet his old ship, the *Meleager*, and with her to escort a large convoy to the Scillies; there to detach the *Meleager* with those ships bound for eastern ports, and to continue himself with those bound for Ireland, Liverpool and Bristol. The *Minerve* would then sail for Plymouth.

It was a slow journey and he did not arrive off Oporto until March 10, where he was joined by the *Meleager* and convoy according to plan. On April 14, 1798, he wrote to Nepean, the Secretary of the Admiralty, asking him to inform Their Lordships of his arrival that morning in Plymouth Sound. Cockburn had been the bearer of a letter from St Vincent to Lord Spencer (the First Lord), requesting that the *Minerve* might be allowed to return to him after the ship had been re-coppered. This, too, was forwarded to Nepean.

George Cockburn, a week short of his 26th birthday, had been away from England for six years bearing a responsibility greater than most men experience in a lifetime.

● The Nelson portrait painted by Heinrich Füger in 18[...]
(RN Museum, Portsmouth and Mrs LM McCarthy)

CHAPTER SIX

The Minerve - maid of all work
1798-1802

A DMIRALTY RESPONDED with commendable speed to
Cockburn's arrival at Plymouth. If from the report of the officers
appointed to inspect the state of the ship, said the Secretary of
the Admiralty, a docking appeared necessary, Cockburn was to sail
the *Minerve* to Portsmouth for that purpose; so to Spithead she
indeed sailed.

By the standards of those days, Cockburn maintained a happy
ship but her arrival home provided its own anti-climax once the
novelty had worn off and strain began to show. Lieutenant Mayling
asked for a court martial to investigate the conduct of Mr Lamotte,
the Purser who, he claimed, had been guilty of ungentlemanly
behaviour towards him, attempting, 'to force me out of his cabin
while making ill founded reflections on myself as first lieutenant of
this ship'. Cockburn decided that court martial was hardly justified,
and smoothed ruffled feathers.

To his great disappointment Cockburn found that he had missed
meeting Nelson, recuperating from the loss of his right arm at
Teneriffe, by days. After hoisting his flag in the *Vanguard*, Nelson
had hurriedly sailed from Spithead on April 10, 1798 now that
Britain had decided to play a more positive role in the Mediterranean
to encourage her allies and combat French expansion. The navy
would send in a fleet under the command of an admiral of St Vincent's
own choosing. As Nelson's health was restored, he stood out head
and shoulders for the task. His selection was ensured by the First
Lord who wrote St Vincent, 'I think it almost unnecessary to suggest
to you that the propriety of putting it under the command of Sir
Horatio Nelson, whose acquaintance with that part of the world, as
well as his activities and disposition, seem to qualify him in a peculiar

manner for that service.'

Meanwhile Cockburn fretted at his inactivity in Portsmouth. Had not St Vincent asked for his return in the *Minerve*, he might have been given a ship of the line and joined Nelson as one of the 'band of brothers'. In refitting *Minerve*, Cockburn's knowledge of the ship's idiosyncrasies was invaluable: in July he argued with dockyard officers that she required more ballast than was standard for a 38-gun British frigate. They obstinately refused to accept the point so Cockburn wrote to the Admiralty for a ruling in his favour. This was refused but he was insistent. Writing a second time, he said, 'I have received your letter of the 6th inst and am sorry to find you disapprove of *La Minerve* being supplied with an additional quantity of iron ballast owing to the report made to you by the officers of Portsmouth Yard. Formerly in addition to her iron ballast, the ship had 225 tons of shingle onboard which she was able to stow as there was no deck between her keelson and 'tween decks; but now, having a fore and after cockpit six feet from deck to deck, and orlop for the cables, it will be impossible for us to stow above half that quantity, nor shall we be able to stow so much water or provisions as formerly.' The letter ended with his earnest hope that the ship would not have to return through 'proving leewardly and crank, which I am convinced will be the case if she is only supplied with 90 tons of iron ballast – the quantity allowed to 38-gun frigates, all of which are considerably less tonnage than *La Minerve*.'[1] No further argument was necessary. He had his way.

Cockburn naturally seized the opportunity to visit family and friends and was particularly solicitous to Lady Nelson, judging by her frequent reference to him in writing to her husband. At Nelson's request Cockburn had brought home a quantity of Madeira wine which had to be cleared by customs, the duty paid, and then sent to Lady Nelson whose movements were unpredictable. This involved considerable expense, for which Cockburn refused recompense. On May 6, Lady Nelson wrote, 'I received a letter yesterday from Captain Cockburn – it came from Bath. His ship is at Portsmouth and he writes me he has paid the duties and sent it by Clark's waggon, who has engaged to deliver it safe at Ipswich and begs not to trouble me with the expenses ...' And again on May 28, she wrote Nelson from Roundwood (their recently acquired home near Ipswich), 'I shall exactly follow your directions about the £175. Had I not been so exceedingly hurried down, I should have seen Captain Cockburn for he was in London. He will not allow me to pay the expenses of the wine.'

A two-way traffic developed concerning the delivery of a trunk to Nelson. On October 1 Lady Nelson informed her husband that, 'Captain Cockburn writes will take charge of anything for you. I have by this day's waggon sent a box containing nine small stone jars of cherries in brandy, five of currant jelly, and five of apricot ...'[2]

Minerve's long refit was nearing its end. On October 11, Cockburn informed Admiral Sir Peter Parker, Portsmouth's commander-in-chief, that the ship was ready and asked that the complement should be completed. Assembling the crew and sorting out personnel problems were the most tiresome aspects of a ship's commissioning. Cockburn had difficulty in persuading the Navy Office that a man he had recommended as *Minerve's* cook was qualified for the job. Cooks were appointed by virtue of disability and Cockburn's nominee, a pensioner to the Chest at Chatham who had lost a leg when *La Minerve* was captured by the *Dido* to which latter ship he then belonged, was finally accepted.

With six months provisions aboard, and a brand new launch – supplied normally only to larger ships, but suitable for attacking vessels at anchor – Cockburn took his much altered *Minerve* to Spithead 'in constant readiness for sea'. She sailed on November 20, 1798 with a Mediterranean-bound convoy and on December 27, met the fleet under Lord St Vincent, whence she escorted a convoy to Palermo, where Cockburn rejoined Nelson. Dramatic had been the changes since February of the previous year when they had made their hurried exit through the Straits of Gibraltar. Minorca with its valuable harbour of Port Mahon had capitulated to Commodore Duckworth; the remnants of the French fleet in Egyptian waters – following their defeat at the Nile – were locked in Alexandria harbour; French control of the tottering Italian kingdoms was insecure and their occupation of Malta under heavy siege.

Since the end of September Nelson had come increasingly under the influence of both Lady Hamilton – the British Ambassador's wife – and of the Neapolitan court. The Nelson Touch faltered. Attacks upon Leghorn and Rome by a Neapolitan army of 30,000, inadvisably prompted by Nelson, failed disastrously. Wisdom replaced valour in King Ferdinand's decision to transfer to the other half of his kingdom in Sicily. In mid-December treasure was loaded into Nelson's flagship, the *Vanguard*, under Captain Hardy's direction. Even Nelson himself was involved in the embarkation of the royal party which was undertaken clandestinely by use of a subterranean tunnel connected to the palace. On December 23 *Vanguard* sailed into storm, Nelson claiming that it blew harder than he ever remembered. The royals did little to help themselves and relied heavily on Lady Hamilton who behaved stoically; but for the young Prince Alberto it all proved too much. On Christmas Day, 1798, he died in Emma Hamilton's arms shortly before the ship anchored at Palermo. There Nelson remained for the next four months.

It was an unfortunate moment for Cockburn to renew acquaintance with his much revered friend. Allowance could be made for Nelson's poor health resulting from a head wound received at the Nile, but that was not the sum of things. Some time before, Cockburn had been questioned by a friend on his opinion of Nelson's character and he gave it thus, 'he is a curious compound of weakness, with power of high exertions, of intrepidity and talent; and blessed with a never failing kindness of heart'. His weakness now was evident to all. Passion and conscience, thanks to his developing relationship with Lady Hamilton, battled it out. Although Nelson's 'band of brothers' recorded their thoughts on this relationship, Cockburn remained silent. Throughout his life he maintained high moral values and, being much younger than Nelson, his intense loyalty would not have allowed him to voice an opinion, yet his recent contacts with Lady Nelson must have strengthened his sadness about the turn of events.

In April, Nelson employed Cockburn on a number of exceptional tasks. The first concerned Captain Troubridge who, with a squadron of four ships of the line, had been sent to seize the islands in the bay of Naples. The expedition was immediately successful but Troubridge was faced with the problem of how to deal effectively with the many traitors to King Ferdinand who were in his charge. Swift summary justice could be applied up to a point, and Troubridge made full use of it. However, among those sent aboard his ship to be tried was a party of priests over whom he had no jurisdiction, so he asked for a judge to be assigned. One, quickly rounded up in Palermo, took passage in the *Minerve* to Naples. He was not the man Troubridge had looked for. A week later he wrote to Nelson, 'the judge appeared to me to be the poorest creature I ever saw; frightened out of his senses, and talks of it being necessary to have a bishop degrade the priests before he can execute them'.

Cockburn also had a special mission to Leghorn, higher up the coast where, through an agent of the Austrian army, Colonel Baron d'Ospre, he communicated Nelson's views on military operations and Austrian support. While there, he wrote to the French commander on the exchange of prisoners. Under the convention between the two countries, prisoners were exchanged in equal numbers but, following the battle of the Nile, there was now an imbalance which greatly favoured the French. Cockburn's object, unsuccessful as it transpired, was to accept any British prisoners held at Leghorn, particularly seamen.

News reached Palermo on May 12 that a French fleet of 25 ships of the line under Admiral Bruix had escaped the Brest blockade, and was sailing for the Mediterranean where it hoped to retrieve France's lost sea power. To achieve success, Bruix had to run the gauntlet of the various British squadrons stationed at Cadiz, Gibraltar, Minorca and Palermo. The news galvanised Nelson into action and no time was wasted in recalling his scattered ships from Naples and Malta. *Minerve* rejoined the squadron which then took up its battle station off the island of Maritimo, at the western end of Sicily, but after remaining inactive there for a few days Nelson turned back to Palermo.

Admiral Bruix's fleet had passed Gibraltar on May 5 and remained in the Mediterranean for just over two months. It had been followed by an allied Spanish fleet of 17 line ships, but the two forces failed to

- **Track of the *Minerve* November 20, 1798 – September 5, 1799 in pursuit of Admiral Bruix**

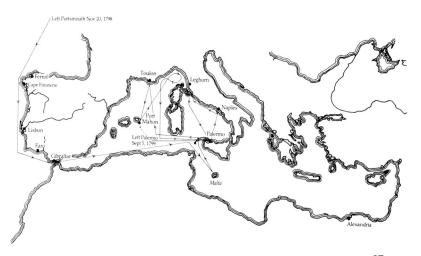

unite effectively. Their movements, and those of their British pursuers, provided an intricate pattern, and only rarely were they within striking distance of each other. None of the British admirals involved enhanced his reputation. Lord St Vincent in the *Ville de Paris* should have provided the co-ordinating drive between his subordinates, but his health was failing. Keith, lacking flair, was unable to detect it in others. With such contrasting personalities as Keith and Nelson, a clash between them was almost inevitable. Discord reached its apogee with Nelson's refusal to join Keith's fleet of 31 sail of the line off Minorca when there was a distinct possibility of meeting the enemy fleet of 40. Nelson's infatuation with the Kingdom of Naples was the cause of this dereliction, an incident wholly out of character and sufficiently grave to earn him a severe reprimand.

Eventually Keith pursued Bruix out of the Mediterranean but his chase was abortive. Bruix reached the safety of Brest again after a round cruise of three and a half months. The Bruix interlude, as it affected Cockburn, had been frustrating. He had not enjoyed his relative inactivity at Palermo where Nelson provided such a sorry contrast to the man under whom he had matured. The feeling of belonging, inspired by Nelson's leadership, was dissipated by Nelson's stay ashore in an alien society.

Hence it came as no disappointment when *Minerve*, in company with the frigate *Emerald*, was detached to look into Toulon harbour and then report to the commander-in-chief at Mahon. Toulon was empty but the capture of a French privateer, the *Caroline* of 16 guns, provided a useful prize before he rejoined Keith at sea. Keith had now assumed overall command and proceeded vainly to scour the Riviera and the coast as far as Leghorn, in search of Bruix. At the end of June Keith withdrew.

The Genoese, on the pretext of neutrality, had customarily supplied the French with essentials for prosecuting the war; Keith discovered on his short cruise that nothing had improved. Indeed he had been fired upon whenever his ships came within range of the shore defences. 'The Genoese forts at Porto Mauritio (near San Remo) having this day fired at the squadron under my command,' he ordered Cockburn, 'it is my positive direction that all Genoese vessels be hereafter taken, burnt, sunk, or destroyed, and in every respect treated as enemies of the British nation, instead of being only as hitherto, provisionally detained.'[3]

This was a bold step for any commander-in-chief to take without ministerial backing. To give effect to it, he issued instructions to Cockburn on July 7 to take the frigate *Santa Theresa*, and the sloops *Petrel* and *Vinceyo* under his command, 'to cruise off Genoa City and Cape Delle Melle to prevent vessels entering Genoese ports with provisions (wine, hay, oats, rice, sugar, cocoa, beans, etc) and to cruise one month on this service'.

With his special and detailed knowledge of the coast, Cockburn was the ideal choice and he set about it with his usual thoroughness. In quick time he made his presence felt by capturing a Spanish polacre with a cargo of wine, silencing the batteries in the town of Diano, and taking two Genoese tartans at Porto Mauritio.

Towards the end of July, he made Porto Mauritio, which place had so upset Keith, his special target. Having destroyed the forts by sailing the *Minerve* almost dangerously close inshore before engaging them, he completed his task by taking a French polacre and Genoese tartan off San Remo.

By now Keith had left the Mediterranean still in pursuit of Bruix, and as Cockburn's month of service on the Genoese coast had expired, he rejoined Nelson at Palermo. Nothing had improved. Nelson was still obsessed with Italian affairs; while he remained onshore, his ships were dispersed at Naples, Civita Vecchia and Malta, his captains gradually being appointed elsewhere.

After only two days, Cockburn left Palermo with orders to join the Lisbon station where there was a stronger likelihood of taking prizes. It was the best frigate appointment at Nelson's disposal but neither he nor Cockburn would have realised its significance: it was to be the last time their paths crossed. Before Cockburn returned to the Mediterranean, Nelson had left for England, travelling overland, and it is unlikely that they ever met again. Their relationship had been one of true friendship. Cockburn, virtually a tyro when he first came under the influence of the great man, had gained immeasurably both in stature and sheer professionalism from the association.

Cockburn left on September 5, 1799, with despatches for Mahon and Gibraltar en route. After a week's stay at Gibraltar for provisioning, he sailed to Faro where he rendezvoused with Rear-Admiral Duckworth, promoted after the painless capture of Minorca. But Duckworth was universally disliked and had the uneasy reputation both of brute and sycophant. Cockburn received his orders from 'Old Tommy', as the seamen called him, to watch the movements of the Spanish squadron at Ferrol and to reconnoitre both Ferrol and

Corunna and pass on any information to Lisbon. In the event of actually meeting a squadron at sea, he was to pursue it until its destination could be established, after which he would rejoin Duckworth with all haste.

It was the start of a lonely vigil off Cape Finisterre which continued on and off for the next 16 months, with only the occasional break at Lisbon. Of immediate concern was an outbreak of sickness in the ship which spread with alarming speed and forced Cockburn to seek the shelter of the River Tagus only four days after leaving Duckworth. He reported on October 22, 1799, 'since my parting with you on the 17 inst, 20 of the crew have been taken ill with scorbutic eruptions attended with a contagious fever, of which one man died this morning, and two are now given over by the surgeon. I therefore determined to anchor at this place (which owing to northerly winds and a very heavy sea I have only just been able to fetch), to procure some lemons and fresh provisions, which my surgeon represents as absolutely necessary to check this disorder in its infancy. Having obtained these, I shall proceed without a moment's loss of time to execute your orders and trust the above circumstances will appear to you sufficient to authorise my conduct herein ...'

He was away again four days later, hauled round the lighthouse of Corunna on November 13, stood into the Bay to reconnoitre, passed close to the entrance to Ferrol, and was able to report to Duckworth in remarkably quick time that only a small number of warships of no great consequence lay in these ports.

Entering the enemy's stronghold in this manner was dangerous; when repeated a few weeks later, Cockburn varied his approach by employing a *ruse-de-guerre*. He transferred his first lieutenant into a small schooner sailing in company with the *Minerve*. At daylight, American colours were hoisted in the schooner and she embarked a Spanish pilot. She was thus able to run close inshore and obtain a detailed survey without arousing suspicion.

It was a monotonous and demanding task involving long periods at sea frequently in tempestuous Atlantic weather. Clothing became clammy and many men reported to the surgeon with rheumatism. One particular hazard early in January 1800, was graphically reported to Duckworth, 'after parting with you on December 23, to see the Spanish brig *Volcano* into the Tagus, I met with nothing but strong SW winds against which it was with the utmost difficulty after carrying away three hawsers, and a stream cable towing her, that I got far enough to the southward to fetch in; on the evening of January 5, *Minerve* having sprung her foretopmast the night before, and split most of her sails, I thought it prudent, it then blowing a gale of wind from the west, to anchor also for the night, during which we shifted our foretopmast and repaired our sails, and were ready for sea again in the morning. But the gale continuing from the SW it was impossible to get out and excepting for a few hours on the

● **Track of the *Minerve*. Legend** --- **September 6, 1799 - January 31, 1801 (Cockburn as Senior Naval Officer, Lisbon)** —— **February 1, 1801 – February 4, 1802 (in the Mediterranean theatre and in chase of Ganteaume's squadron)**

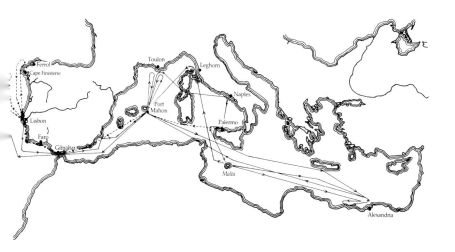

10th, which were moderate, (and during which we got very nearly to the Bar, tho' forced by the sea and gale to go back again), we have had an incessant gale from SW to W till today. There have been several vessels lost attempting to run in during the gale and I fear several are English Newfoundland ships …'[4]

When the *Minerve* repaired to the Tagus, it was usual for her to remain for about a fortnight to provision, carry out minor repairs, and for Cockburn to exercise his duties as Senior Naval Officer, Lisbon. A contemporary account of Lisbon runs as follows, 'it is a long straggling town including I believe Buenos Ayres and Belem, nearly five miles in extent, and without exception, the most dirty, filthy, stinking town I ever was in. Indeed the dirt of Lisbon is beyond description, and the fronts of the houses look wretched. It stands on rising ground above the river, and from some terraces, and many of the houses, there is fine view of the Tagus and shipping.'

Cockburn's main problem there was to secure the British Consul's co-operation in rounding up deserters, and pressing badly needed seamen into service, a need highlighted by Keith, who had now returned as commander-in-chief, Mediterranean. 'As men are much wanting to compleat the establishments of several of His Majesty's ships and vessels on this station, you are hereby required and directed to request that the Consul General at Lisbon will pay the usual allowances to the police there for picking up deserters and stragglers in the streets of that city which I have no doubt he will comply with as I have already written both to him and Rear-Admiral Duckworth on the occasion.'

- **Lisbon as it was in 1800 or thereabouts. (RN Museum, Portsmouth)**

The wretched inns of Lisbon harboured many of these men but Mr Arbuthnot, the consul, did not apply himself to his task with notable zeal. Masters of merchant ships, too, were content to conceal deserters from HM ships if it helped to relieve their own manning problems. Cockburn's unenviable duty caused him to write to Arbuthnot from time to time in irritable vein. One letter read, 'on my arrival here, I wrote to you requesting that you would give the necessary directions for the seamen about Lisbon to be apprehended as formerly and sent onboard *Minerve*; since when I have only received one man, tho' several have deserted and the captains of the other ships acquaint me that they continually lose men by desertion. I have, therefore, thought it right to acquaint you with these circumstances that you may make arrangements for this service being more effectually performed. If you will order a general press of English seamen for tonight, one of my men shall attend the gang, to assist them and look for deserters.'

The *Minerve* was also losing hands in other ways. All too frequently throughout 1800 the entry 'departed this life' appeared in the ship's log. One severe loss was Lieutenant Newall, the second lieutenant, whose body was committed to the deep with three volleys of small arms. The strain on the ship's complement rose in proportion to the number of prizes taken. The much frequented shipping lanes converging on Cape Finisterre were *Minerve*'s hunting ground where she was constantly in chase with captures to match. On each occasion a prize crew was necessary and, although the depletion in the *Minerve* lasted only until she next returned to the Tagus, the men were overstretched.

The catalogue of prizes was impressive – *La Mouche*, *Le Furet*, *El Legero*, *L'Active*, *Victorieux*, *El Rey Carlos*, *Bordeaux*, *La Vengeance*, *Notra Signora del Carmine*, *Mexicano*, and others, some of which were privateers or letters of marque of not inconsiderable size. The *Bordeaux*, for example, had a crew of 145 men and 20 guns, and *La Vengeance*, 130 men and 15 guns. In many instances Cockburn received the congratulations of Lord Keith and the Admiralty who invariably were 'much pleased with the *Minerve*'s success'.

Strategem played an important part in the war at sea. Spanish ships laden with valuable cargoes from America were not averse to the protection afforded by Portuguese convoys and using Portuguese colours to enter the Tagus. Cockburn was directed to examine such convoys without offending Britain's faithful ally – Portugal which, of all friendly countries at this time, was vital for Britain's prosecution of the war at sea. Trouble enough had been brewing with the neutral Baltic states over the rights of warring nations to inspect ship cargoes for contraband. Cockburn, himself, had undertaken the delicate task of searching the numerous Danish vessels about.

Bonaparte, now first consul of France, realising his own inability to defeat the British navy, sought other means of forcing Britain to her knees. He informed Denmark and Sweden that he proposed waiving his right of search, the ploy working exactly as planned. By December 1800, Sweden, Denmark and Prussia, had joined him in an armed neutrality of the north with the declared intention of resisting by force any attempts to search their shipping. The following month, Cockburn received Admiralty instructions to bring into the nearest port all Danish and Swedish shipping.

For Britain the time was critical. Timber and hemp supplies from the Baltic on which she relied for the building and repair of her ships, were no longer available. Her allies, including Austria, had temporarily withdrawn from the fray; the French had re-occupied northern Italy and Leghorn, and King Ferdinand of the Two Sicilies – now under pressure – forbade the entry of British warships to his ports.

Both Britain and France decided for their own strategic reasons that it was time to revive the Mediterranean as a theatre of war. Keith sailed from Gibraltar for Egypt towards the end of 1800 with a large fleet and 80 transports carrying 18,000 men under General Abercromby. Rear-Admiral Sir John Borlase Warren had also arrived off Cadiz with a squadron of ships; the concentration of forces had begun. Fortunately Malta, doggedly defended by the French General Vaubois, had surrendered in September and was serving as a fleet base.

For Cockburn and his stalwart crew off Cape Finisterre the moment had arrived for a change of scene. After a three-month storm-wracked vigil at sea, he arrived in the Tagus on January 7, 1801, to find orders there to join Warren. He wrote hurriedly to explain the delay in complying with these instructions which had been issued many weeks before, 'Tagus, January 14, 1801. Sir – I arrived at this place on the 7th inst. after a long and bad cruise off Cape Finisterre making about 16 inches of water an hour, with rigging, sails, etc, in a very shattered condition . . . and will join you off Cadiz as soon as possible'.

To make the *Minerve* seaworthy, caulkers were essential. Fortunately, Lisbon had good facilities including a dry dock, anchor wharf, gun wharf and rope walk, with supporting skilled labour. Cockburn's diplomatically worded request to the local governor for a party to be sent onboard to caulk the *Minerve*'s bends and sides, she 'having become extremely leaky', met a ready response. No less than 27 caulkers worked continuously for a fortnight with carpenters in support.

While *Minerve* lay unoperational, a French squadron of seven ships of the line and two frigates under Admiral Ganteaume, left Brest on January 23, 1801, to reinforce the French army in Egypt. The privilege of sighting this fleet off Finisterre fell to the British frigate *Concorde* which had relieved the *Minerve* on station. She had a sharp engagement with the frigate *Bravoure*, and then hastened to Lisbon with her intelligence. It was ironical that having spent so many months patiently watching for a Spanish or French squadron, the sighting off Finisterre should have taken place so soon after the *Minerve*'s withdrawal. By February 1 she was ready for sea again and sailed in company with the *Phoenix* (Captain Halsted) to forewarn Warren at Cadiz of Ganteaume's squadron.

Ganteaume passed through the Straits without hindrance on February 9 but was shadowed by the frigate *Success* for the next four days. Then, with a sudden change of wind, the *Success*, unable to keep her distance, was captured. She was a valuable prize for Ganteaume but one which Cockburn later was to recapture in brilliant fashion. Learning from the *Success* that Keith had gone to Egypt, Ganteaume altered course for Toulon.

At this stage Cockburn, who had been ordered by Warren to follow, was probably only 48 hours behind, handicapped by not knowing Ganteaume's destination. On February 11, *Minerve* made her first Danish capture – a fine Danish brig of war of 20 guns and a crew of 100. Cockburn looked swiftly into Carthagena for Ganteaume but found only merchant ships. Then, near Minorca, he decided to send his prize into Port Mahon to free him to pursue the French. More importantly, though, he wanted to inform that port's Senior Naval Officer of intelligence he had gained from the captured Danish officers. Dated February 15, at sea, his letter read, 'understanding from some Danish now onboard *Minerve* that there is a Danish frigate at anchor in Port Mahon, I have thought it right (passing the island), to send you the enclosed copy of a general order against that nation, in pursuance of which I have captured the Brig of War (the *Glommen*) which brings you this, and onboard of which I must request you will have the goodness to order some sailors from the transports in Port Mahon till the Admiral's orders concerning her shall be known. I am under the necessity of withdrawing *Minerve*'s people from her, now being in pursuit of a French squadron that has entered the Mediterranean and I believe gone to Toulon. If you have any information at Port Mahon respecting the French squadron, I shall thank you to send it to me. You may expect Sir John Warren with his squadron any day, to whom please deliver the enclosed letter. The Danish officers and sailors you will, of course, act with as most consistent, be it either to send them onboard the prison ship, allow them to land on their parole, or to stay onboard their own ship. I think the captains of the men of war should certainly be left onboard their ships, at least till further orders regarding them.'

Here is evidence of the 28-year-old Cockburn's highly developed maturity. The information is comprehensive, well reasoned and humane. It suggests his preference for liberality in the treatment of the Danes, born of the knowledge that the war with them was of a limited nature.

Shortly after leaving Mahon the frigates *Pearl* and *Santa Teresa* joined the *Minerve*, bringing Warren's confirmation to sail to Toulon and watch Ganteaume's movements. Such progress was made that, on February 17, the enemy squadron of 11 sail was sighted and a cat and mouse game ensued. The British ships were chased but succeeded in keeping their distance without losing touch and every tack by the French squadron was repeated by Cockburn until Toulon was reached. Leaving her two consorts on watch, the *Minerve* made a quick passage to Mahon to report to Warren the seven sail of the line and four frigates in Toulon harbour.

Warren's resources were small, and some of his ships were being refitted at Mahon, but surely a more resolute commander would have enforced the blockade. Instead Warren was content for *Minerve*, *Pearl* and *Teresa* to continue this demanding and wearing task for a month without Warren once appearing on the scene. Not a day passed throughout the first half of March but that the *Minerve* closed Toulon roads to confirm Ganteaume's presence. On March 19, with a heavy gale blowing, *Teresa* lost her topmasts and had to bear away in distress. Ganteaume decided this was his opportunity to slip out from Toulon unobserved, a move which almost succeeded.

But Cockburn had been particularly vigilant as he had noticed unusual activity within the port the previous day. Soon after daylight on the 19th, a straggler of Ganteaume's convoy was sighted from *Minerve*'s masthead. She and the *Pearl* gave chase and by noon the frigates were able to cut off and take the neglected charge from which Cockburn was able to learn the squadron's strength, number of troops and destination. As the ships were bound for Alexandria, the first need was to inform Keith for which purpose the *Pearl* was promptly detached. She carried Cockburn's despatch, 'I do not lose a moment in sending the *Pearl* to acquaint Your Lordship that last night during a very strong gale from the NW, M. Ganteaume sailed from Toulon with seven sail of the line, three frigates, one xebec and six merchantmen, one of which I have just captured. The merchant ships are certainly bound for Egypt and the squadron is supposed to have the same destination but it does not appear to be certain. I send all the letters etc, taken. I have examined them and the only information I obtain by them is that several merchant ships are now fitting with all possible despatch at Marseilles, destined for Egypt ... I am going immediately to join Sir John Warren according to an order I have received from him.'[5]

Cockburn was to join him at Naples in the event of Ganteaume being at sea. Taking the shortest possible route by night through the narrow pass of Bonifacio (between Corsica and Sardinia), he reached his rendezvous on March 27, only to find that Warren had sailed leaving no word of where he would be found. Sending a number of his French prisoners ashore, Cockburn made all sail down the Italian coast to Palermo where, he reasoned, he would find Warren who was neither there, nor at Malta. Cockburn's options were now limited; from Malta he correctly chose to stand to the east where his persistence was rewarded: he found Warren's squadron on April 10, off the African coast roughly half way between Malta and Alexandria.

Although a patient man, Cockburn's cup must have overflowed on learning that Warren had actually sighted the French squadron to the south of Sardinia, but had lost contact through not having a fast sailing ship to keep up with them. Had Warren left word at Naples of his movements, *Minerve* could have joined him and carried out this vital function. Three years before, Nelson in his vain search of the French fleet prior to the Nile, had written 'no frigates' as the cause of his failure, stressing the need for lookout ships.

Warren's resources were also slender but he made no use of those he had. Twenty years older than Cockburn, he lacked aggressiveness and, on this occasion, showed himself a poor strategist. 'Memory of him has grown dim except perhaps in his native county where a public house in Nottingham still bears his name', history records.

Minerve received 20 tons of much needed water from the *Alexander* and carried out a quick but unsuccessful reconnaissance in search of Ganteaume before pressing on to Alexandria where Cockburn came under Keith's orders.

Bonaparte ordered Ganteaume to make a second attempt to reach Egypt and he left Toulon again on April 27 with instructions to land troops in Elba and take possession of the island in support of operations on the mainland.

Without positive news of Ganteaume's activities, Keith's anxiety for his troopships and transports lying in Aboukir Bay was understandable. He wrote to Cockburn on April 20, 1801. 'The French have an idea to land men to the westward, which I hardly think practicable, therefore be so good as to look out as close inshore as is safe about 20 leagues to the westward for five days and then return here if you do not see the enemy sooner. Take care, I fear they have got our signals.' Cockburn found nothing.

Reassured, Keith sent the *Minerve* to Minorca for more active employment. A huge convoy, which Cockburn was now detailed to escort, had been forming at Port Mahon to transport army reinforcements to Aboukir Bay. Leaving Mahon on June 23, in company with the frigate *Phoenix* and 31 other sail, the convoy arrived intact in Aboukir Bay on July 17, where Cockburn received the pleasurable news that the general embargo on Danish ships had been lifted, and that all such were 'to pass free and unmolested'.

Cockburn rejoined the hunt for Ganteaume who, it was now known, was in Tuscan waters. He was then ordered by Keith to Malta with despatches and thereafter to join Warren off Taranto but, if he had left there, Cockburn was to pass by Elba, Tuscany, Genoa and the Riviera to gain information about the enemy.

Minerve suffered adverse winds and sail damage, hence it was three weeks before she reached Valetta harbour on August 11. By the time she sailed again ten days later, Cockburn knew that Warren would no longer be at Taranto. Proceeding towards Leghorn, *Minerve* met and spoke to the frigates *Phoenix* and *Pomone* on September 1. Then, before losing sight of the British ships, two French frigates were spotted. Cockburn stood towards them with a heavy press of sail while the enemy turned about hoping to reach Leghorn. *Minerve*'s log reads, 'Shortened sail and hove to off the northern end of Elba SW 4 or 5 miles. At 4.30 made sail. Two strange sail to the NE standing towards us. At 5.30 made the private signal which was not answered. Hauled our wind on the starboard tack, the island of Capraia 4 or 5 leagues. Made the signal to HM Ships *Phoenix* and *Pomone*, the enemy in sight. Fired several guns before the signal was answered. At ½ past 7 bore up in chase; made all sail. At ½ past 9 came up with the *Success* French frigate which had struck on the shoal off Vada. Fired one shot when she struck her colours. Made the signal to the *Pomone* the ship on shore had struck but we had not taken possession of her. Still in chase of the other frigate beating up towards Leghorn; fired at the French frigate as we passed on opposite tacks. The enemy ran ashore under the batteries of Lonlivera when her fore and mainmast went by the board. At ½ past 5 after much firing she struck her colours. Out all boats and sent them with the 1st and 3rd lieutenants to set her on fire, but finding a number of prisoners onboard that could not get away owing to the surf on the beach, the boats were obliged to return with the captain, first lieutenant, and as many more of the prisoners as they could bring. Sent the boats for more prisoners but the night coming on and the heavy fire from the batteries, and soldiers on the beach, was forced to quit the prize and return onboard. Boats hoisted. At 9, filled and stood off.' Thus Cockburn captured one, and destroyed another, of the enemy's frigates from under the protection of some formidable batteries; for though the *Phoenix* and *Pomone* took possession of the ship captured earlier they were barely within sight when *Minerve* forced the second to surrender.

In fact, it was the crew of the *Minerve* who saved the *Success*, the ship which had grounded. The following day, with a party of 20 men and a petty officer, the ship's launch got her off, the very launch which Cockburn acquired for such purpose before leaving Portsmouth. Then the second lieutenant, master's mate, two midshipmen and 30 men were transferred to help sail the *Success* to Mahon.

The account of the action forwarded by Keith to the Secretary of the Admiralty was duly gazetted. Warren's own letter written from his flagship, the *Renown* on October 26, nearly eight weeks after the event, failed to convey the degree of gratitude which was due. 'Having received the commander-in-chief's direction to communicate to you his thanks and approbation for the activity and exertion manifested by you in the recapture of His Majesty's ship *Success* and destruction of *La Bravoure* French frigate, I am happy in conveying the same to you, and request you will accept my thanks also upon the above important service.'[6] So outstanding a success deserved better praise.

A few days later *Minerve*, although severely overcrowded with 158 French prisoners, chased and took a Genoese vessel before arriving at Mahon on September 11. Here the prisoners were discharged to the prison ship *Courageux*, and the *Success* seen safely into port.

Watch off Toulon was renewed in mid September. The equinoctal gales made sure that Cockburn and his men retained a lasting memory of this irksome and final duty. It was particularly unfortunate that with relief close at hand Robert Taylor, caulker, fell overboard and was drowned. Murmurings of peace were confirmed when on October 24 a French brig under flag of truce brought news of peace and an invitation to enjoy Toulon's hospitality. The news was welcomed but the invitation was politely declined.

Cockburn wasted no time in repairing to Mahon to inform Warren who, anxious to get home quickly, hoisted his flag in the *Minerve* and returned in her to England. The log records the pleasures of homecoming – 'December 2, running up towards Cowes. Anchored Motherbank; December 3, Spithead; December 13, received 15 puncheons of beer;' and perhaps best of all, 'December 26, agent onboard to award and pay prize money.' How pleasant to receive some well earned remuneration even if a day out!

In February 1802, *Minerve* sailed for Deptford where stores were landed. The last log entry reads, 'Saturday, February 20, 1802. At Sunset, sent the people away in the gunboats to go to the Nore. The men being all gone, hauled the pendant down.'

Except for *Minerve's* refit in 1798, George Cockburn had been active throughout the war. His deserved rest, however, was to be short.

CHAPTER SEVEN

Mission to New York 1803-6

THE AMIENS PEACE declared on October 22, 1801, was fragile; continuing belligerency between Britain and France renewed the conflict 19 months later on May 16, 1803. The problem was Bonaparte's European dominance. Ever resentful of Britain's resistance he addressed his legislature in early 1803, claiming that 'this Government says with just pride, England alone cannot today contend against France'.

After the signing of the Treaty of Amiens naval strength had inevitably declined, this time by more than a half to approximately 50,000 men. Funds were slashed and ships rapidly deteriorated.

The time available for the navy to re-equip itself for war was restricted to a few months. As ships were paid off when peace was signed so, too, did an ever-swelling cadre of officers revert to half pay. Unlike the seamen the resumption of war presented few problems as the officers were immediately available for active duty. Indeed for them renewed war could only enhance prospects of a steady advance up the promotion ladder and possible prize money. For George Cockburn and Lord Nelson the short peace provided rest, recuperation and a rare taste of domesticity. Cockburn's service abroad had been almost continuous since 1786; how pleasant then to surrender command and enjoy the society of relations and friends. Now 31, his naval career had been unblemished. From 1794 he had served continuously for nine years as a frigate post captain, his professional experience outstanding for an officer of his age and seniority.

The *Victory* of 100 guns, named for Nelson's flag, was about to commission. No doubt, Cockburn would have prized her command above any other. Chance, however, had gone Thomas Hardy's way;

the guiding star of Cockburn's former first lieutenant had shone brightly since that day he had been given the captured *Mutine*, whereafter he had served almost continuously with Nelson. Moreover, that association had been cemented at the Nile and Copenhagen; his selection for the *Victory* followed naturally.

Within a few days of the declaration of war, Nelson sailed from Portsmouth to take up his post as commander-in-chief, Mediterranean, there to enforce the Toulon blockade. Cockburn had longer: 'Friend George' as Nelson familiarly styled him was appointed on July 12 to command the frigate *Phaeton*, a fifth rate of 38 guns, reputedly a fine, fast sailer. She was destined for special service abroad, thus denying Cockburn the opportunity to return to the Mediterranean or to see Nelson again.

When the *Phaeton* commissioned a fortnight later at Deptford where she had refitted, there was no shortage of seamen volunteers. It was largely the captain's responsibility to recruit the numbers required to bring his ship up to complement, his success dependent upon his own popularity and reputation according to the local grapevine. Any shortfall could be made good only by recourse to the press-gang's activities, or by men convicted and recommended for naval service by the magistrate – the King's Hard Bargains. Frigates were usually popular as their wide-ranging duties brought in a large share of prize money and, much as today, routine was easier in small ships than in large as officers tended to be less taut in their discipline. There were, of course, exceptions.

It was not all plain sailing for Cockburn. He had to write to the Admiralty on July 25, pointing out that many of his volunteers were men already serving in the London Militia, and requesting permission for their discharge from that regiment. Approval was given, but the fact that men were prepared to leave one service to join another where life was notoriously tough, is evidence of Cockburn's acceptability as a commander. On the other hand, the quota of King's Hard Bargains which Cockburn was obliged to accept were shortly to stir up trouble.

On August 17, 1803, Cockburn wrote to Sir Evan Nepean, the Secretary of the Admiralty, reporting that with two other frigates forming the squadron under his command, he was waiting to proceed from Long Reach (near Sheerness), and 'would have sailed this evening for the Nore but for the pilot's refusal to take charge'. Bad weather was the reason, and no doubt the pilot's judgement was sound, but the letter reflects Cockburn's understandable impatience to shake down his ships at sea after so long in dockyard hands.

The squadron's immediate task was to investigate a report that the French were collecting a force at Havre de Grace (now Le Havre) to invade England. Before the recent treaty had even been signed, the likelihood of a French invasion had so exercised the country and Admiralty that a special squadron had been placed under Nelson's command. Operations had taken place mainly off Boulogne, then regarded as the most likely place for an invasion fleet to be massed, although Calais, Dunkirk, Ostend, Flushing and, to a lesser degree, Le Havre, were also probable despatch points. Having thoroughly investigated the position at the entrance to the River Seine and off Le Havre, Cockburn was able to reassure authority at home that no such threat existed at that port.

Cockburn's next assignment represents a watershed in his career. So far there had been nothing exceptional in his appointments but in addition to his outstanding proficiency as a frigate captain, Their Lordships had also detected in him a flair for diplomacy which would be appropriate to the nature of a job on hand. *Phaeton* was to carry a new British Minister Plenipotentiary to the United States to negotiate and receive on arrival in New York the first cash recompense for the loyalists' losses following American independence.

On receipt of the specie Cockburn was to proceed to India and transfer it to the East India Company. An East Indiaman (the *Sir Edward Hughes*), would join Cockburn in America to transport part of the treasure. The decision in favour of India rather than Britain was taken for a variety of reasons. For one thing, the East India Company, founded simply as a trading venture, had grown into a vast territorial empire whose sea lanes to America were safer than the western approaches to Europe. Once the dollar coins arrived in India, Britain could make her own arrangements through the East India Company for a later exchange.

The American debts stemmed from the treaty of 1783, after the War of Independence, which was badly negotiated – largely because of mutual hostility. Besides refusing to establish diplomatic relations with the United States, the British showed remarkable ineptitude at the peace conference. Apparently ignorant of American geography, they had surrendered the all-important forts from Oswego to Niagara on the Great Lakes which secured the fur harvest.[1] Worse, they had ceded the forests south of the Great Lakes and north of the Ohio, totally disregarding the Canadian fur trade, the most profitable industry in North America.

In turn, the Americans had dishonoured their undertaking to repay the pre-revolutionary debts owing to British merchants, the states in which debtors lived having refused to enact laws that would enforce compliance. As the federal government lacked the power to bring the delinquent states to order, the British used this breach of the treaty as an excuse for not surrendering the forts. They also armed the Indians and incited them to resist in the ceded areas on the theory that the Indians still held title to the lands.

This unhappy and unstable relationship between the two countries continued until 1794 when John Jay, Chief Justice of the US Supreme Court, was appointed Envoy Extraordinary to London to revise the 1783 treaty. The Jay Treaty, as it became known, was signed in 1795 with many provisions considered unsatisfactory by the United States. The British contracted to evacuate the north-western forts on June 1, 1796, and the Americans, for their part, abandoned thoughts of sequestrating the funds owing to the British. By 1803, a proportion of the oustanding dues were ready for collection but by no means was Cockburn's task to be straightforward.

After celebrating the anniversary of George III's coronation on September 23 with a salute of 21 guns, reading the articles of war, and punishing Seaman Jeremiah Kelly with 30 lashes for repeated drunkenness, Cockburn and the *Phaeton* sailed from Spithead on September 25, 1803, immediately after embarking Mr Anthony Merry, the Minister Plenipotentiary.

Following a slow and stormy passage she anchored in Hampton Roads in Chesapeake Bay (later to become so familiar to Cockburn), where Mr Merry landed.[2] After a short stay, the *Phaeton* continued to New York, where she was moored snugly off the lazaretto at Staten Island on November 3. The ship having suffered considerable storm damage, Cockburn's priority was to refit and repair her so that she would be ready to sail again at short notice. When he tried to buy naval stores to undertake the work, difficulties were placed in his way. After much procrastination he was obliged to write to Thomas Barclay, the British Consul in New York. His letter is written off Staten Island on November 11.

'Whatever Nations are in a state of amity with His Majesty, must afford shelter in their Harbours, Rivers, etc, to his ships, and it is the

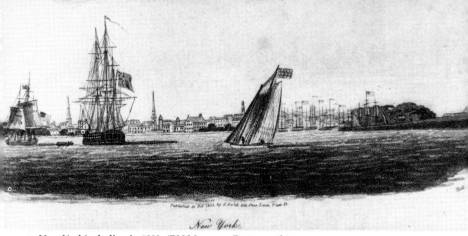

● New York's skyline in 1803. (RN Museum, Portsmouth)

indispensable right of Captains and Commanders of vessels of every description, to employ their crews about the hull, masts or rigging of their ships as to them, may seem necessary. Therefore, with respect to refitting the ship as far as depends upon ourselves, there can be no difficulty. Whether we have a right to procure from the shore what may be called Naval Stores, may perhaps bear an argument, but in the present instance where we have obtained permission from the Chief Magistrate of this place, it surely cannot be our business to investigate by what authority he acts …

'In the particular instance of the *Phaeton*, we have a much stronger claim, not being a cruiser forced into port, but being appointed *directly and purposely* to bring to this country, an Ambassador to render more intimate the mutual intercourse of the two Nations. On this voyage she sustained from the elements, such damage as to render some repairs necessary before she can, with safety, proceed to sea again, to refuse which, would therefore, most certainly be against every principle of justice and common sense.'

The American attitude was caused by the increasingly severe restrictions imposed by Britain on neutral trade, an understandable grievance. Relations worsened with the passing of Britain's orders in council in 1806 until three years later the United States enforced its non-intercourse act which made it illegal for British or French ships to enter their harbours, or to be afforded supplies. In view of the diplomatic nature of his visit Cockburn was within his rights and no further trouble arose during the remainder of the ship's stay in New York. Naval stores were made available – on a cash basis!

Then a more serious problem erupted. However efficient and happy a ship might be, the temptation to desert – almost overwhelming in North American waters where the dividing line between genuine and assumed United States citizenship was very thin – was ever present among pressed men. A British seaman found no difficulty in obtaining employment aboard an American ship at any of the bustling seaports of Baltimore, New York and Boston and this, to many, was preferable to servitude as a pressed man in the Royal Navy. The true citizenship of such men had become a highly contentious subject between Britain and the United States.

The *Phaeton* had been at her mooring off Staten Island for only a few days when the problem arose, as this letter dated November 14 to De Witt Clinton, Mayor of the City of New York, makes plain, 'I am extremely sorry at being obliged to trouble you herewith, in complaint of a man calling himself a subject of the United States, who came onboard His Majesty's ship under my command yesterday evening, in consequence of being hired to assist in calking her ... no sooner, however, was the work of the day over, and the People gone below, that he went down amongst them to induce them to desert and tell them how they might effect their escape from the ship. The Master-at-Arms (who I send herewith to prove to you the fact), and to whom he addressed himself by mistake, identified the same to me, but I am sorry to say not till after eight men had but too well succeeded, by the plan I suppose he had laid down. This was for one man to jump overboard and pretend he was drowning, and when a boat was consequently sent to pick him up, those men in the secret took care to jump into her, as if from the anxiety to save him but as soon as they had got hold of him, instead of coming back to the ship, they pulled on shore and landed.

'Now Sir, I trust you will be induced by the villainy of his transaction, added to the man's extreme personal insolence to myself, which the Officer I send herewith will relate to you, to give me such satisfaction as a Captain of an American frigate would under similar circumstances most undoubtedly receive in England – and so far punish the man as to prove that no country will sanction such conduct in its subjects; and I have likewise to request you will give such directions as may to you seem best, for having those men apprehended and returned to me, who have been so seduced from their duty.

'I feel the more confident in making these requests when I consider the Ship I command came hither *expressly and purposely* to bring to this country, an Ambassador to render more intimate, the intercourse of the two Nations.'

Cockburn must have felt like a husband cuckolded! The crimp in question, who had induced the seamen to desert, had hidden them in the town hoping that they would avoid detection before the *Phaeton* sailed.[3] But Cockburn, straining every nerve to deny them, secretly gained knowledge of their hideaway. He obtained permission from the Mayor to flush out the deserters, (all King's Hard Bargains) but not to return them onboard until his claim to their bodies had been agreed with the local authorities. The following night a few armed Royal Marines and trusty sailors under their officers apprehended the downcast deserters who were thereupon lodged in the local prison as agreed.

Then the authorities refused to release the men from New York's Bridewell prison. Cockburn, needing all the support he could get, wrote to Mr Merry, the Minister Plenipotentiary, asking for diplomatic intervention which was readily given.

Cockburn sought to prevent the men's release from prison *after* the ship had sailed, bad all round and hardly conducive to good discipline in his ship. His firmness won the day, the authorities gave way and finally delivered the deserters onboard. It was a remarkable victory against the odds, and its reward was that no man again attempted to desert from the *Phaeton* during Cockburn's command.

Recovery of seamen on the basis of citizenship was a game that two could play and the United States, young in nationhood, was equally determined to maintain her rights. What better opportunity while a British frigate remained anchored in American territory to pursue the claims of a number of men serving in the *Phaeton* who professed to be American when they were pressed into service? So thought De Witt Clinton, New York's Mayor, who wrote on December 9, 1803 to Cockburn on the subject even while the return of the British deserters was under debate. 'I have been informed that John Felton, a citizen of the United States, was impressed in London, and is now detained against his consent onboard of the frigate under your command, within the jurisdiction of this State. I will thank you to cause an enquiry to be made into the truth of this representation, and if correct, I feel persuaded you will order him to be released.'

This was extremely worrying for Cockburn as he could not possibly press men into service as replacements for those released. The undermanned state of his ship caused him – almost in desperation one suspects – to write to Sir Evan Nepean, the Secretary of the Admiralty, suggesting the offer of bounty money to secure recruits in these special circumstances, even though the regulations did not allow it in foreign waters, for which reason, as Cockburn guardedly observed, 'not to charge the sum against my private wages'. Time permitted no reply.

The two to three months Cockburn was in America provides a microcosm of his character. Of unflagging energy and determined in the pursuit of principle – almost pigheadedly sometimes – he was never one to court cheap popularity, yet was admired by his seamen for his sense of fair play. A tendency to aloofness perhaps reflected his Scottish background; he lacked the warmth – only marginally one suspects – which was one of Nelson's outstanding attributes. Not one to wear his rank on his sleeve he was nevertheless accorded great respect, the perfect choice in fact for this special duty. If other naval visitors to America had acted as fairly and firmly with deserters and citizenship problems, the later unfortunate war of 1812 with the United States might have been averted.[4]

Meanwhile, the Indiaman, the *Sir Edward Hughes* with Captain Barrow in command, had arrived at the end of December. Half the specie was to be embarked in the *Phaeton* at New York, and the other half in the *Sir Edward Hughes* at Hampton Roads, off Norfolk, Virginia. When the *Phaeton's* consignment came onboard, it was found to be in unsealed boxes. Understandably, Cockburn refused to sign the certificates of receipt. In reporting the fact to Mr Merry – who seems to have kept himself at a convenient distance from the transaction – Cockburn wrote reassuringly, 'I, however, on these being stowed away in the Spirit Room of this Ship, had the hatches thereof sealed

● **The high land of Never-Sink and Sandy Hook lighthouse as seen by the *Phaeton*. (RN Museum, Portsmouth)**

down in the presence of the First Lieutenant, Master and Master's Mate'. The wrangle continued for, from the American point of view, nothing short of signed certificates would do; eventually after the wording on the certificates had been suitably amended, the necessary signatures were given.

In the January gales of 1804, the two ships had a rough passage from New York to Hampton Roads, and although the *Sir Edward Hughes'* half of the treasure was there embarked without problem, departure was delayed until the Indiaman's storm damage had been repaired. Finally, on January 28, 1804, Cockburn was able to report from Cape Henry to Sir Evan Nepean in England that 'the ships are now underway to proceed according to Their Lordships' ultimate orders'.

The four-month voyage to Madras was uneventful. Before leaving Hampton Roads, Cockburn had received valuable intelligence from the British Minister,[5] advising that a French squadron of an 84-gun ship and three frigates under Admiral Linois had been in the area of the Ile de France (Mauritius) recently. In fact Linois with his well-trained raiding force had been based on the Ile de France and Batavia (now Jakarta) since 1802, and had savaged British shipping thereabouts. With treasure and a relatively defenceless Indiaman in his charge, clearly it was Cockburn's duty to keep out of the way. Unknown to him at that very time, February 15, 1804, when he was but a short way on his journey, Linois in the *Marengo*, and with the *Belle Poule*, *Semillante* and *Berceau* in company, was engaging the Honourable East India Company's China Fleet in the Indian Ocean. Fortunately for Cockburn, Linois returned to Batavia after the engagement.

Cockburn's immediate worries included the inability of the Indiaman to achieve the seamanlike standards of a warship. *Phaeton's* signals were either answered slowly or ignored; the East Indiaman's station-keeping was abysmal, from time to time she was out of sight over the horizon and even gun signals had little effect. On February 8, Cockburn sent a letter by boat listing his main complaints and asking for an officer, (other than the officer of the watch), to be detailed as a lookout – particularly for signals. Barrow was requested to follow in *Phaeton's* wake employing as much sail as the weather permitted. The medicine worked.

The ships arrived in Madras Roads on May 25, 1804 to discharge their valuable cargos. The *Phaeton* was soon required to serve in a small local squadron under the command of Captain John Osborn of the *Tremendous* – a ship of the line. The predatory Linois was capturing valuable prizes with his well trained force and the Ile de France centred in the area where he was most likely to be discovered. Although Linois was not found a successful blockade of the island was carried out by the British force. Several French vessels were captured and Cockburn carried out a programme of engaging shore batteries around the coast. Off Pointe Cannonière, where a French ship had run under the shore guns for protection, the *Phaeton* engaged the fort while her ship's boats captured and set fire to the vessel.[6] During this contest a furnace, used by the French for heating their shot, suffered a direct hit by which the fort, barracks and other buildings were engulfed in the blaze.

The length of service abroad, most of which in recent months had been spent at sea and in a hot and debilitating climate, began to have its effect on the ship's company. Scurvy, which could decimate a crew in double quick time, had erupted. From Bombay on January 27, 1805 Cockburn wrote to his senior officer in the *Tremendous*, 'the Surgeon of HMS *Phaeton* under my command having represented to me that one hundred of the said crew are affected with the scurvy and that an allowance of vegetables is necessary for the re-establishment of their health; I beg leave to state the same to you and to request you will order their being supplied with a proportion of vegetables accordingly'.

Fresh meat was a welcome replacement for the salted variety and there are interesting entries in the ship's log such as, 'January 22, 1805 – killed two bullocks 202 lbs; January 23 – killed 3 bullocks – 282lbs; January 24 – killed 3 bullocks;' and so on. Among the fresh vegetables and standard provisions embarked on one day, is an entry for 15 casks of arrack. Beer was still the normal daily drink as part of standard provisions in home waters, but when the beer was exhausted substitutes were allowed on foreign stations.[7] Thus in America, the *Phaeton's* crew received a daily ration of rum, but in Asian waters, arrack – a strong spirit distilled from rice and other materials – all that was available.

Admiral Sir Edward Pellew (later Lord Exmouth), was the station commander-in-chief and, in April 1805, he gave Cockburn command of a squadron in the upper part of the Bay of Bengal to protect the East Indian settlements. The real object, in fact, was for Cockburn to convey Marquis Wellesley, then Governor General of India, to

England. After calling at Colombo, Trincomalee, and elsewhere he arrived at the Hoogli River which flows from Calcutta to the sea where he transferred from the *Phaeton* to the *Howe* at Diamond Harbour on June 5, 1805. This ship, an Indiaman, had recently been purchased and equipped with 20 guns for service in the navy.

Cockburn was quick to find a discrepancy in the *Howe*. Next day he reported to Admiral Pellew, 'as it may be the same in other ships, I feel it right to inform you, Sir, that the measures supplied at Bombay by Mr Halliday are short in the proportion of ½ pint to the gallon'.

What was known as the 'purser's pound' of 14 instead of 16 ounces, was an abuse openly allowed by authority; the underpaid purser could make a good thing out of his job only by indulging in what to others seemed to be downright peculation. To give short commons through faulty *drinking* measures, was criminal.

Wellesley embarked on August 23, 1805, and the *Howe* left the Hoogli two days later for passage round the Cape of Good Hope back to England. An enduring friendship was struck between Cockburn and Wellesley who at St Helena, a regular port of call in sailing ship days, disembarked for a few days rest. Little did Cockburn know that he was to become far better acquainted with the place later in life. It was here in St Helena that 32 officers and men from the East Indiaman *Brunswick* captured by the French and now aboard the American brig *Eliza* gladly joined the *Howe* for passage home.

The *Howe* arrived at Spithead on January 7, 1806 five months after setting out during which period the Battle of Trafalgar had been won and Cockburn's friend, Nelson, lost.

CHAPTER EIGHT

Commando in the making 1806-9

COCKBURN'S NEW COMMAND in early July, 1806 was the *Captain* which, under Nelson at Cape St Vincent in 1797, had defeated the Spanish *San Josef* of 112 guns and *San Nicolas*, 84. She was completing with stores at St Helen's at the eastern end of the Isle of Wight – the Spithead arrival and departure anchorage.

On commissioning the ship, as usual, was short of men. To remedy this Cockburn applied to the Marine Society, an organisation founded by Jonas Hanway (the inventor of the umbrella), supplying orphans to serve as seamen. If not exactly volunteers they were preferable to pressed men for these were disciplined, trained boys and most welcome.

Every available source was tapped to make up numbers. Two smugglers, whose punishment was impressment, joined; such men were usually fine seamen but these two, however, petitioned – unsuccessfully – for their release, offering substitutes.

Young officers had usually been found by ships' captains from the sons of their friends. The system, whatever its failings, provided many outstanding officers, but for some time Admiralty had disliked such autocratic powers and had set up a Naval Academy at Portsmouth where theory ashore replaced the initial practical education at sea. Naturally it was disliked by the old school who objected to their privileges being whittled away, but Their Lordships insisted on providing their quota. The First Lord, Marsden, wrote Cockburn saying, 'whereas Mr John W Montagu has been educated in the Royal Academy at Portsmouth and is well qualified to serve His Majesty at sea, he is to be entered as one of the complement.'[1] Marsden enlarged on the duties and the privileges to be afforded him; although performing as an able seaman he was allowed to walk

113

the quarterdeck; was obliged to keep a journal and to draw the 'appearance of headlands, coasts, bays, sand, rocks and such like,' and so instructed that after two years he could be rated midshipman if deserving and given a certificate of sobriety and good behaviour. Prejudice, however, in such a conservative organisation as the navy was not easily overcome and success stories of officers who had started their training at the Naval Academy were relatively few.

The *Captain* sailed from St Helen's in convoy for Plymouth where she joined Rear-Admiral Sir Thomas Louis under orders to intercept a French squadron in which Jerome Bonaparte held a command. The attempt was unsuccessful and the French succeeded in making port; but the sortie was not entirely without reward as, on September 28, the French frigate *President* of 40 guns was captured and 58 members of the crew taken onboard the *Captain*. On October 11 Cockburn was sent back to Plymouth: after seven weeks seatime the veteran *Captain* was badly in need of repairs to masts and rigging.

Early in February, 1807 the *Captain* returned to Spithead in company with the *Ganges* and *Defence* to take a large East India Company convoy to Madeira and the Cape Verde Islands. Although the Company had transferred some of its powers to the government, it still had a virtual monopoly of the Indian and China trade. Its wealth, built up from the early 17th century, was prodigious and its fleet of ships – well built and admirably administered – was run as a paramilitary force.

Before sailing, the Company's secretary at East India House wrote to Cockburn enclosing a code of signals and instructing him on their use in language which can only be described as peremptory. 'The Court of the Company request you will be particularly careful to return them all to me upon the conclusion of your voyage,' the letter ended with some additional orders about maintaining secrecy and destroying the signals if captured. Cockburn ran true to form. 'I acknowledge receipt of your letter of February 21 with the code of signals for use by the East India Company stating, "where the Court of Directors request I should keep them" and likewise that "you are commanded to desire me to take the earliest opportunity of informing you should any accident happen to the Plate of Flags." In answer I have to inform you that I have already given sufficient instructions to the Indiamen and other ships going under my convoy and am returning yours. I beg further to inform you that the only mode of sending *instructions and orders* to captains of His Majesty's Ships is through the Board of Admiralty.'[2]

The Company could not have hit upon anyone less likely than Captain George Cockburn to comply with their directions; however it caused them to cease issuing such abrasive edicts.

The convoy reached Madeira without hindrance. Of all the duties devolving upon warship captains the charge of a convoy under sail was perhaps the most onerous and frustrating and making masters observe and comply with signals was ever a problem. One stray sheep would be followed by another; one would make too much sail, his companion too little. Unless well regulated from the outset, the voyage could become a nightmare.

But the East India ships, commanded by a superior class of officer, presented few problems to Cockburn who always assumed the role of ringmaster with outstanding success. His plan was to place the slowest ship at the head of the convoy, making her carry all possible sail with safety and permitting no other ship to pass her beam. Offenders received a salutory shot across their bows, the expense of which was paid for by the erring masters!

When the convoy reached Madeira this well-disciplined procedure had its rewards as reflected in the words of J Kirkpatrick, master of an Indiaman, 'whatever merit you may have conceived me entitled to from having used my endeavours to obey your signals and in keeping the *Henry Addington* on her assigned station, I cannot but feel particular gratitude for the handsome terms in which you have expressed it and shall ever make it my study to prove my conduct what it has been under your command.'[3]

Cockburn was replaced on June 30, 1807 and was rewarded with a few months respite from active service before joining the *Aboukir*, 74, at Chatham. Within a few days, on March 20, Their Lordships decided a more suitable command would be the *Pompée*, 80 guns, also lying at Chatham and reputedly one of the navy's finest line-of-battleships.[4] Lieutenant Bigland and Midshipman Scott, for whom Cockburn had developed a particular regard, came with him. The first few months were spent in the Channel Fleet blockading Rochefort on the Biscay coast. There were no major engagements but numerous opportunities were presented to pursue chasse-marées with the ship's boats, splendid training for younger officers and men, Midshipman Scott among them. So well did Scott perform that during the latter part of the cruise he was elevated to mate of the first watch and then to acting lieutenant. That rank carried with it the responsibility for occasional charge of the ship, an honour which was speedily threatened as Scott himself explained. 'It was the middle watch, and we were sailing in line with the *Impetueux* and *Theseus*, when the Commodore made the signal to tack in succession. We followed in his wake, but the *Theseus*, who previously to our going about, was to windward of her station three or four points on our weather quarter, instead of going astern of us according to the signal, and then tacking, endeavoured to pass between us and the Commodore, though our jib-boom was nearly over the taffrail of the *Impetueux*. Not supposing that the *Theseus* would persist in this mad course, and knowing I was in my proper station, I stood on. Too late she perceived her error, and altered her course to pass astern. Finding that she must inevitably come in contact with us, I put the helm down to lessen the shock, and slap she took us on the quarter; her jib-boom passing abaft the mizen rigging, knocking away the quarter-boat, and dealing out sundry other damage and detriment to His Majesty's Ship *Pompée*. The captain was on deck in a trice. Believing, at the first glance of affairs that I was to blame, he was on the point of opening out his lower-deckers upon me, when I requested him to take notice of the Commodore's position. The storm that was ready to fall heavily upon my shoulders, was shifted to those of the unfortunate lieutenant of the offending ship. Next day an enquiry took place, when I was perfectly acquitted by the evidence of the officer of the watch onboard the *Impetueux*. The culprit lieutenant got off with a few days' arrest, and the payment of the value of the jib-boom.'

By the end of August the *Pompée* was back at Plymouth completing with six months provisions for foreign service. She was instructed to proceed 50 leagues south-west of the Scillies where she was to open Admiralty sealed orders. Their allotted station was the West Indies for operations against the French island of Martinique. *Pompée* immediately set course for Madeira to gain the trades whence she could run westward to her destination, Carlisle Bay in Barbados.

It was a pleasant, incident-free passage until a few days from Barbados when a distant sail appeared on the starboard quarter. Quickly identified as a French man-of-war brig, an exciting chase ensued which tested the seamanship of both ships. Strong squalls demanded constant sail handling – at one moment crowding on canvas, at the next shortening and reefing. Prey proved equal to pursuer; throughout the afternoon and evening advantage passed from one to the other. By nightfall the wind had dropped favouring the brig which distanced herself from the *Pompée*. Most of the latter's officers considered further pursuit hopeless as the night was moonless; they expected the hammocks to be piped down from their upperdeck stowage for the hands to turn in and the ship then to renew her normal course. Cockburn, however, thought differently. With the judgement that can be acquired only by an experienced seaman, he reckoned that the brig's captain, having made good his escape, would regain his position near enough to where the chase had begun, and resume *his* normal course. From the wind's strength and relative ship positions, he calculated when, on this assumption, to alter course to intercept. A sharp lookout was maintained particularly at dawn and sure enough, within two hours, a sail appeared to weather which was quickly confirmed as the French brig's. With the element of surprise favouring the *Pompée* she quickly had the Frenchman under her guns, so close that any attempt to escape would have resulted in the brig's certain destruction whereupon the French captain hauled down his colours. She was a splendid capture carrying sixteen 32-pound carronades and a crew of 109. The Frenchmen had been congratulating themselves on their success up to the moment of capture. In an officer's journal appeared the interesting entry, *'Dieu merci, nous ne serons pas pris aujour d'hui. Adieu! Jean Boull, adieu ros bif!'*[5] How was he to know that their adversary was the redoubtable Cockburn!

The capture of *Le Pylade* had an unfortunate sequel. In the hurried confusion of sending the prisoners onboard the *Pompée*, the French surgeon was removed with the rest. It was not until later that several of the French crew were discovered on the lower deck of *Le Pylade* – with yellow fever! Contagion spread quickly to the British prize crew. In one night 25 Frenchmen died and six of the prize crew had to be transferred back to the *Pompée*. By the time the ships reached Carlisle Bay, the fever was endemic in both ships. The entire prize crew of 33 men was transferred to the island's hospital where nearly all succumbed.

Drastic measures had to be taken. At the end of October Cockburn received orders, 'you are hereby required and directed to return immediately outside Carlisle Bay Bar, and send the bad cases to the hospital and such others as Doctor MacArthur, the surgeon of the hospital, shall recommend. You will then, as the most probable means of putting a stop to the sickness, continue to cruise off that Bay, and the moment a man is taken ill, land him. You are at liberty to direct the purser or surgeon to purchase such extra vegetables, fruit, etc, as you may deem necessary. You will remain off that island until you think the sickness is completely put a stop to – and then apply to General Beckwith and receive onboard as many soldiers of the detachments expected from Madeira as will make up the numbers victualled onboard to about 100 above complement. Having so done, you will rejoin off Point Salines.'[6]

The ship's company recovered and, operational again, the *Pompée* took up her cruising ground in Fort Royal Bay, Martinique. British interest in this valuable French colony was stimulated in the summer of 1808 by learning of a shortage of French troops to defend it. Preparations for an attack began at Barbados in November of which intention the French soon became aware. Until the troops arrived, Rear-Admiral Sir Alexander Cochrane, who commanded the naval squadron, had first to enforce a blockade (particularly of Port Royal and St Pierre). Cockburn was allocated ships for this purpose but if, as Cochrane warned, a French fleet of 19 sail of the line arrived to relieved Martinique, Cockburn was to attack it with his inadequate force. Fortunately the intelligence proved false, but why did Cochrane choose that moment to depart for Barbados in his flagship *Neptune* with two valuable ships of the line – the *Belleisle* and *York*?

Throughout January 1809, troops were embarked in Carlisle Bay, and on the 30th the expedition arrived off Martinique to join Cockburn. The British brought 10,000 troops under Lieutenant General Sir George Beckwith. The French had only a quarter of that number in effective regulars although they were supported by a considerable militia. Strong defences largely countered the disparity. Martinique's governor-general was a distinguished aristocrat, Vice Admiral Villaret-Joyeuse, Admiral Lord Howe's opponent at the battle of the 'Glorious First of June', some 15 years earlier.

If Cockburn had been given the main naval responsibility for blockading before hostilities started, he assumed no less an aggressive role ashore. It was not his nature to remain passive if, by showing initiative, opportunities to hit the enemy were presented. While waiting for the main force to arrive he had taken soundings as close inshore as possible to the heavily defended Pigeon Island – commanding a strategically important position near the main island. He had already decided that the neutralisation of Pigeon Island was worth a try even if the military thought otherwise. When the action

118

● A sailor entertains with the story of a chase and a capture. (RN Museum, Portsmouth)

against Martinique started at the end of January he landed, with Sir Charles Shipley, the brigadier commanding the Royal Engineers, to reconnoitre.

Although the near perpendicular cliffs of the land facing Pigeon Island were daunting, the two leaders decided that as a preliminary to further action a mortar could at least be set up on a projecting rock at their base to annoy the fort. The *Pompée's* boats moved in by night and landed the 13-inch mortar and the materials for making a gun platform. The crews succeeded in setting it up without drawing the attention of the French garrison who, at daylight, were dismayed to be saluted by a shell in their midst. As the mortar was protected by rocks forming a natural parapet, their retaliation was ineffectual.

The capitulation of the Pigeon Island fort was necessary for British command of the all-important Port Royal Bay. Morne Vanier, a precipitous mountain overlooking the fortifications, was climbed by Cockburn and Shipley next day; the French, considering it inaccessible, had left it unprotected. Shipley declared that while there was no better spot for a battery, he could see no practicable way by which guns could be brought up. 'If you fix upon this spot, I will be answerable that in two days the guns shall be placed here,'[7] was Cockburn's con-

119

fident reply. A disbelieving Shipley could not refuse such an inviting offer; the work was set in hand.

The task was undertaken with copybook precision and skill despite being constantly under fire. Carpenters cut away the trees from the bottom to top, the valley alive with the busy hum of 200 seamen and marines under Cockburn's direction. It was dangerous, exhausting work causing many casualties, but by nightfall a way had been cleared to the summit. A stream cable was then secured and led downhill as straight as the irregularities of ground allowed. After breakfast next morning the first of the howitzers arrived on its hastily-made platform. With the aid of blocks, luff tackles, hawsers and toggles, whose usage was familiar to the seamen, the gun was slowly hoisted from one projecting ledge to the next until it safely reached the top.

Throughout the day the operation was repeated until five guns had been manhandled to the crest of this commanding height. Before sunset the battery was operable without a single accident except from enemy gunfire. Cockburn had accomplished the seemingly impossible within 12 hours of his promise, sharing his men's fatigue throughout. Lieutenant Scott of the *Pompée* who had also participated, remarked of his captain, 'he always imposed upon himself extra effort when the welfare or benefit of the service was concerned: his unbounded zeal in face of an enemy never allowed him to feel weary, or want of rest to oppress him; and he could not suppose others to be differently affected. Impossible was a word on these occasions erased from his vocabulary.'

When the hill battery began firing on February 3, the fort on Pigeon Island was literally pounded into submission. Within three hours a white flag was hoisted by the French. Cockburn's success was rewarded instantly by Cochrane with a commodore's broad pendant – and Captain Brenton to succeed him in command of the *Pompée*. He was also honoured by being at the table which decided capitulation terms.

Meanwhile General Beckwith's troops made good progress, overcoming all resistance from the French forces in the open and compelling them to retreat into Forts Royal and Bourbon. Fort Royal's occupation was shortlived as the garrison, in danger of being cut off, concentrated at Fort Bourbon – the island's last and most formidable stronghold.

The *Pompée* having moved to the other side of the bay, Cockburn landed the naval brigade to support the army. As a considerable distance had to be covered before the force with its guns reached its appointed station near Fort Bourbon, it came under intensive daily fire and suffered many casualties. But the resolution and cheerfulness displayed was as great as on the previous occasion and by February 17 the three batteries, now manned by sailors, were ready. The opening salute was fired in the afternoon on the 19th and, with Cockburn's swallow-tailed commodore's pendant fluttering proudly overhead, a full broadside of naval 24-pounders hit the fort. After three days of unceasing and accurate bombardment, much admired by their army companions, the white flag was hoisted over Fort Bourbon. Its surrender led to Martinique's swift submission.

For a second time, Commodore Cockburn was appointed one of the commissioners to negotiate surrender terms under which the Fort Bourbon garrison was allowed to march out with the honours of war.[8] Treaty terms were generous and fair; the sick and wounded would be cared for, the fortifications demolished, and the property of the inhabitants of Martinique respected. Most importantly, it was agreed that the French prisoners would be conveyed home to Quiberon Bay in British transports under the guard of a few warships. An exchange of prisoners would take place there on a rank for rank basis; because of the high respect held for Governor-General Admiral Villaret-Joyeuse, he would be taken to France free of all restriction.

Under Cockburn's signature Martinique became a British colony. In his co-operation with the army in their land operations he had shown all the qualities of a present-day commando and had been granted the temporary rank of brigadier-general while ashore. Cochrane graciously acknowledged Cockburn's conduct, his official letter commenting, 'I entrusted the whole of the naval arrangements on shore to Commodore Cockburn; his exertions have been unremitting and his merit beyond praise'.[9]

In due course Cockburn was thanked by both Houses of Parliament, and given the honorary appointment of Captain of the port of St Pierre in Martinique.

Directed to shift his pendant from the *Pompée* to the *Belleisle*, he returned to Europe with the surrendered governor and garrison under his charge. Admiral Villaret-Joyeuse, an honoured guest in the *Belleisle*, was treated courteously. From the beginning of the assault Cockburn had had a friendly relationship with him. On an earlier occasion Cockburn had returned some of Villaret's personal property which had been seized from a captured French cutter, Cockburn himself paying the prize agent the estimated value of the items. He had received Villaret's sincere thanks and a present of rich liqueurs and noyau. The friendship ended sadly; shortly after landing in France Villaret was tried and disgraced for surrendering Fort Bourbon. It was too much for him; he died of a broken heart on his Normandy estate.

The *Belleisle* had left Martinique on March 14, arriving at Quiberon Bay on April 27. Talks began immediately with the French authorities but, finding that their object was to persuade Cockburn to free his prisoners without an equivalent exchange, he broke off negotiations and landed only Admiral Villaret-Joyeuse and his suite. Cockburn reached Spithead on May 15, 1809, struck his pendant and boarded the London coach.

CHAPTER NINE

Cloak and dagger
1809-10

APART FROM ONE SHORT BREAK Britain had been at war for 16 years, and Cockburn's opportunities for relaxation and social pleasures had been both brief and intermittent. Those who knew him well say that he enjoyed female company and treated the ladies with an old-world courtesy and gaiety. Scarcely in one place long enough to develop a serious alliance he was a classic example of one 'wedded to the service'. There were many like him in the navy.

One regular companion during his short leaves was his cousin Mary Cockburn, a native of Jamaica, who returned to England after her father, a planter, had died in 1801. The relationship was one of mutual affection rather than of deep love but George, now 37, decided to ask for her hand, and was accepted. Before a wedding day could be arranged he was told by Lord Mulgrave, the First Lord, of a forthcoming expedition to the River Scheldt in which he was invited to take part. As every available ship would be required for this mammoth undertaking, he readily agreed to remain in the *Belleisle* temporarily, postpone his marriage plans and surrender his commodore's pendant for the time being.

The Scheldt expedition had its origins in the belief of King George III's ministers that with Bonaparte's armies fully extended, a continental diversion in a sensitive area might be decisive. The French were already actively employed on the banks of the Danube against the Archduke Charles; in Portugal in combat with Sir Arthur Wellesley; and in Spain against Spanish guerillas. An invasion of Holland would provide the Netherlanders with an opportunity to declare themselves against France which, if successful, might deny that country's commerce through Antwerp.

Massive military and naval preparations had been mounted in Britain for some time with this in view; a force of 37,000 soldiers under the command of the Earl of Chatham was to spearhead the attack and virtually every warship in commission in home waters was to transport and support the army.

At Portsmouth the *Belleisle's* lower deck was cleared of guns to maximise room for troops, the hold made ready to accommodate horses in makeshift stables, and extra boats embarked for landing purposes.

By mid-July all was ready. The crack 71st regiment of Highlanders, commanded by Colonel Sir Denis Pack, embarked in the *Belleisle* from Southsea beach,[1] and the strong Portsmouth division of ships left Spithead to join the force waiting at the Downs off the Kent coast. Here the operation's magnitude was clear, the sea alive with stately 74s, dashing frigates, and countless sloops, brigs, cutters, gunboats and transports.

Prior to sailing the duties of each division were assigned, George Cockburn being chosen by Admiral Sir Richard Strachan, the naval commander-in-chief, to command the flotilla of bombs, brigs and gunboats responsible for seeing the army ashore and acting in its support.

Belleisle sailed with her consorts on July 29, and a stiff breeze brought them speedily to the island of Walcheren at the entrance to the perilous Scheldt, the initial target for capture. The river enters the North Sea in two branches known as the East and West Scheldt separated from each other by a mass of low-lying islands and moving sandbanks where swift-flowing currents hazard navigation. The anchorage selected for the *Belleisle* went by the strange name of the Roompot – which belied its true nature. Although well sheltered in the East Scheldt and ideal for attacking Walcheren, the North Sea pilot embarked in the ship considered any attempt to reach it would inevitably run her aground and promptly relinquished responsibility. Equally promptly Cockburn took over and by dint of constant soundings brought the ship to her allotted anchorage. Three or four following ships were temporarily grounded but otherwise the squadron met with no mishap.

The flat-bottomed craft and ships' boats were hoisted out, the gunboats brought alongside for their guns, and the launches armed. The troops were soon in the boats and under Cockburn's direction were assembled for the intended landing on the sands of Walcheren between Domberg and East Capel (see diagram). The dykes provided excellent cover for the enemy but the bombs and small craft proved more than a match for them during disembarkation.

Success swiftly followed. Colonel Pack and his Highlanders pursued the retreating French and within three days Terveer and the larger town of Middelburg were taken; only Flushing, Walcheren's important and heavily defended arsenal into which the French had been driven, frustrated the occupation of the island. Flushing could be attacked effectively only from the West Scheldt; Cockburn was given command of all sloops, gunboats and lesser craft to negotiate the difficult passage of the Sloe, connecting the river's two arms, for a frontal attack. The channel's narrowness, a fast flowing tide and good shore defences caused vessels to ground in every direction but, with his usual perseverance, Cockburn succeeded in this exacting task. Command of these small craft may appear to be of small significance but the role of the little ships throughout the Scheldt campaign was the most important of all the participating warships – including battleships and frigates. Because of their size and mobility they were able to operate inshore and take risks denied to larger ships; although individually they carried few guns their total armament in company provided an effective bombardment. Those serving in them led exacting and uncomfortable lives, but the

- **Walcheren and the River Scheldt**

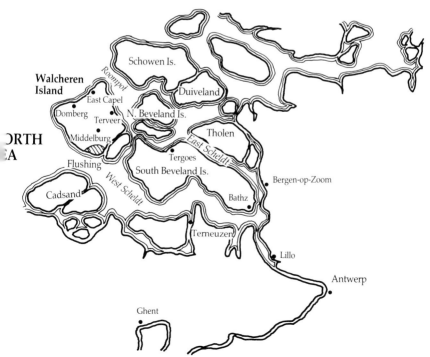

consolation of being away from big-ship routine more than compensated for the hardships. George Cockburn, an obvious choice to command such a hybrid force, was instantly rewarded by Admiral Strachan with a commodore's broad pendant flown in the sloop *Plover* while he was detached from the *Belleisle*. Because so many men were transferred to gunboat duty, the *Belleisle* became unoperational: only 63 seamen remained onboard.

Although Flushing was beleaguered it was still possible for French reinforcements to cross over the West Scheldt from Cadsand on the opposite shore. Upwards of 3,000 men had made the crossing before Cockburn's small craft prevented further transfers. The *Plover* and her 'chickens' now routinely engaged the Flushing defences by day while patrolling off Cadsand by night: sleepless and exhausting work, but effective.

All was ready for a final assault on Flushing by mid-August. Batteries set up by Cockburn on the town's coastal surrounds then opened a devastating cannonade supported by the flotilla's fire. Even the 74s had found a passage through the sandbanks and lent their support with stunning broadsides. Two – the *St Domingo*, Admiral Strachan's flagship, and the *Blake* – grounded abreast the enemy's principal battery; again it was Cockburn with his small craft who helped refloat them on the flood tide.

Flushing capitulated on August 15 and Cockburn was given the honour – as at Martinique – of landing to arrange terms. Blindfolded he was escorted into the fortress on the 16th, and countersigned the surrender under which the 5000-strong French garrison became prisoners of war. His flair for diplomacy and fair dealing at the conference table was recognised by his superiors as matching his leadership in action.[2]

Historians claim that the surrender of Flushing, instead of producing that advantage which might have been expected, seemed to be the commencement of disaster. Although the army had captured many of the surrounding islands, notably Schonen, Duiveland, North and South Beveland, these had no bearing on the final outcome. The winding River Scheldt with its low-lying polders was manned as far as Antwerp by some 30 – 40,000 enemy troops; a co-ordinated plan for a British advance became increasingly elusive. Within a fortnight shortage of provisions and swamp fever caused hundreds to die and rendered 8,000 unfit for duty.[3] On August 27 the Earl of Chatham and a council of seven generals decided that nothing more could be done and a general retreat was ordered.

After Flushing's fall Cockburn had renewed the fight with vigour. Continuing up the West Scheldt in the *Plover,* accompanied by a flotilla of assorted small craft, he played a leading part in compelling the French forces to evacuate the Bathz fort. Further up river, he was preparing to bombard Lillo, not far distant from Antwerp itself, when he received news of the withdrawal, a sad ending to an enterprise which, although disastrous for British forces overall, had been singularly successful for Cockburn and his party. In recognition, Cockburn was ordered by Strachan to take the post of honour and form the rearguard of the retreat. Hotly engaged by pursuing enemy craft as far as Flushing the *Plover* succeeded in covering the main force from attack. While the fleet reformed at Flushing and the troops re-embarked, Cockburn received Strachan's plaudits, 'I am always pleased with your zealous conduct but never more so than yesterday,' was his opening remark in a long letter of congratulation.[4] The Earl of Chatham gave him a special mention too, 'the constant and cordial co-operation of the navy on all occasions, and my warmest congratulations and acknowledgements are most particularly due to Captain Cockburn of the *Belleisle'*.

With Cockburn back on board the *Belleisle* on September 7, the fleet returned to the Downs where the troops were landed. At Spithead *Belleisle* was de-stored and taken out of commission. His pendant was hauled down on October 7; now he could look forward to Christmas at home. But before that there were the arrangements for his marriage to Mary Cockburn on November 28 to attend to, a quiet affair witnessed probably by only those relatives and friends immediately available. Certainly it went unreported in the leading journals of the time.

In the latter half of 1809 the same Marquis Wellesley who had sailed from India in Cockburn's ship, the *Howe,* some four years earlier, became Foreign Secretary. The Grand Mogul as he was known in appreciation of his achievements as Governor-General of India, had more recently returned from Spain where, as British ambassador, he had unsuccesfully tried to bring the Spanish government into effective co-operation with his younger brother Arthur

Wellesley – later Duke of Wellington – then fighting the Peninsular War.

The marquis believed that the Spanish people's efforts and guerilla activity against French domination of their country, would be invigorated if King Ferdinand VII could return to Spain as the rallying point of national resistance.

Ferdinand's character justified no such assessment. Captured by the French in degrading circumstances he had acted supinely and was now under strict military guard at Talleyrand's chateau of Valençay in central France. Wellesley's contacts thought they knew how to effect his escape: the plan involved the landing of two agents at a suitable point on the French coast from a warship which would then wait for the agents' return with Ferdinand.

Wellesley's thoughts flew immediately to Cockburn who, enjoying his new domestic circumstance, was fortuitously available. A request for his services was made. How could Cockburn refuse? On February 2 he joined the *Implacable,* another third rate of 74 guns. Later he was allocated the frigate *Imperieuse* and two schooners, the *Nonpareil* and *Pickle,* to act under his command for the duration of the operation. The *Implacable* – ex *Duguay Trouin* of the French navy – had been captured in the aftermath of Trafalgar and was a fine ship.

Shortly before sailing from the Plymouth anchorage of Cawsand Bay the two foreign agents who were to rescue Ferdinand came onboard. One was the Baron de Kolli, of French and Polish extraction, who had given proof of his ability for the undertaking and of his sympathies with the object.

By special courier at the same time came two boxes of jewels valued at £6,334 and £1,093 respectively, to assist the baron in bribing where necessary – the jewels to be sewn into clothing before setting off. A further £800 in foreign coin was supplied to cover other necessary expenses.

Cockburn's destination was Quiberon Bay on the Brittany coast where he arrived on the night of March 7 during a heavy gale. He reported to Wellesley, 'having the next day reconnoitred the adjacent shores and taken all necessary precautions, I safely landed the Baron de Kolli and his friend about 11 o'clock on the night of the 9th without the least disturbance or molestation, nearly on the spot which I pointed out to your Lordship in London as that on which I judged it most advisable to make our first attempt. They were in high spirits at the facility with which they thus gained their first point, and seemed very confident of further success'. Cockburn arranged with de Kolli a cypher for communicating to each other and understood by only the two of them; he also happened to find, on the nearby island of Houat, a certain Baron de Ferriet, a general of the Vendéean insurgents who, as Cockburn reported to Wellesley, 'was in England a little while ago imploring the assistance of our government for his party, and has since been employed here smuggling British manufactures and colonial produce into France. This traffic has afforded him a facility of intercourse with the adjacent coasts which I judged might be turned to the advantage of our present undertaking'. Cockburn assured Wellesley that both he and de Kolli had established de Ferriet's bona fides before agreeing that he should assist them, and they had not divulged the nature of their enterprise except to say that it would redound greatly to the advantage of the Vendéean cause so close to de Ferriet's heart. The latter's role was to act as an agent for receiving and sending news to de Kolli, using Nantes as his base, and communicating with Cockburn by means of a chasse marée from a nearby point on the coast in the heart of the royalist Vendée country.

For days Cockburn received no news of de Kolli's progress while the *Implacable* swung off Quiberon Bay. He was beginning to fear for de Kolli when on April 20 he received a letter through the Nantes link. Cockburn replied next day using the same messenger – a certain Monsieur de St Ange whose credentials had been previously vetted. The letter for de Kolli was couched in cryptic language and is given here as it is open to varying interpretations. 'I was made very happy yesterday by the receipt of your note of April 6, as it was the first intimation I had had of the safety of yourself and *sister*. I much wish, however, you had been a little more explicit concerning *her*, that is to say whether you have seen *her at all* since you landed on the continent or had communication with her and if so, *when* and *where*. I am very anxious to know this and have therefore sent M de St Ange in the schooner to procure for me an answer hereto, if he can find you, or to bring you to me if you like to come yourself. M de St Ange is not in our secret respecting *your sister*. You need not impart therefore, more than advisable. Let me know *everything* that has occurred to you.'[5]

The most reasonable interpretation of this strange letter is that de Kolli's 'sister' was King Ferdinand VII. Cockburn had to anticipate the communication falling into enemy hands. Even de Kolli's name is not mentioned.

Cockburn must have been full of doubts. To receive a note which gave so little factual information – and none at all on Ferdinand – suggested it was spurious. However, he had no option but to remain at Quiberon Bay until positive news came about de Kolli. This duly arrived on May 14; de Kolli and his companion had been caught by the gendarmerie soon after their landing. They had already made contact with Ferdinand who, in consultation with his minister in captivity, cravenly gave the game away.

The *Implacable* returned to Spithead on May 21 when Cockburn wrote to Wellesley. 'Prior to the receipt of Your Lordship's letter on the subject, I had learnt from the continent the disastrous news of Baron de Kolli's apprehension and was consequently about to return to England in the *Implacable* when the *Britannia,* cutter, arrived with Your Lordship's commands thereon. It is now my intention to proceed to London with the least possible delay for the purpose of waiting on Your Lordship to give every explanation and detail respecting the service which you were pleased to confide to me. Although I feel most sensibly grieved at its failure, yet have I a confident hope of being able to convince Your Lordship that no exertion has been wanting on my part nor on the part of those employed under me to afford it a happier issue, and that had it not been for the unexpected and disgraceful conduct of Ferdinand and his minister Amezaga, we had every reason to hope for a successful termination to our endeavour in his favour.'

From this distance of time, Cockburn's assignment appears of doubtful value from its inception. Ferdinand's reputation justified no assumption that his return to Spain would rally his countrymen. The plan to land Baron de Kolli seemed foolhardy, lacking the required preparation to ensure success; and, most importantly, de Kolli himself was a poor selection for a key role. It transpired that, contrary to Cockburn's direction, he went to Paris which gave rise to his subsequent detection. Only Cockburn carried out his instructions with ability and to the letter but even he, one suspects, must have viewed the undertaking sceptically.

Clearly, Wellesley was pleased with Cockburn's conduct. Two months later the Foreign Secretary wrote, 'His Majesty has commanded me to signify to you his gracious approbation of your conduct, and of the zeal, ability and prudence manifested by you in the execution of the important duties entrusted to your direction. It is with great satisfaction that I have the honour to notify to you his Majesty's commands on this occasion'.

CHAPTER TEN

Special envoy
1810-12

A FORTNIGHT'S RESPITE WAS ALL that Cockburn was given before leaving home shores again. A French fleet, confident that the Scheldt was now safe, had dropped down the river to Flushing inviting attack. The *Implacable* sailed to investigate this report leaving Spithead on June 5, 1810, and arriving off Walcheren six days later, but saw nothing. As the ship was urgently required at Cadiz in support of the Peninsular War now at a critical stage, Cockburn wasted no time in returning to England to embark Rear Admiral Sir R G Keats whose flag the *Implacable* would fly on passage.

She was ready on July 17 and beat down Channel from St Helen's to reach Cadiz ten days later, when the flatboats embarked for the journey were hoisted out to assist in the town's defence.

At this time, the French general – Soult – was besieging Cadiz. Wellington, on the defensive behind the lines of Torres Vedras in Portugal, was able to spare a few troops who, together with the navy offshore, put up a stern resistance. Three factors favoured the British – Cadiz was virtually impregnable; the French army had to live off the land of a hostile country; and the sea was denied them: nevertheless a successful defence depended entirely upon the British forces. A flotilla of gunboats, flatboats and bomb ships was the navy's main contribution, while the army manned the advance batteries on the Isla with the troops stationed around. Constant fire was maintained by the French upon the town and shipping without material effect and, generally, the situation when Cockburn arrived was stalemate. British policy required that even if Portugal had to be evacuated, they would remain to defend Cadiz – little problem, thanks to its proximity to Gibraltar.

In August it was decided to create a diversion north of Cadiz at

Moguer where there was a substantial French force. The expedition was to consist mainly of Spanish troops who were to be embarked in two brigs and armed boats of the fleet led by Cockburn. The party left Cadiz on the night of August 22, landing 24 hours later to the south of a river which intersected their approach to Moguer. This the French considered relatively immune from attack without reasonable warning since the river extended for a considerable distance into the country and provided a natural protection. The Anglo-Spanish force marched along the bank of the river with eleven flatboats in attendance until they reached a convenient crossing point. From here the troops were able to take the most direct route to Moguer and achieve that element of surprise which was the undoing of the defending garrison of 1,100 men. Cockburn wrote his official account from the sloop *Jasper* in the Huelba River, 'the cheerfulness with which the Spanish troops bore the fatigue of marching 22 miles, after being without rest for three successive nights, and the steadiness and valour they displayed in the action that ensued, has excited my highest admiration, and made me more sanguine than ever in the hope that such people in such a cause, must be ultimately successful'. To which Admiral Keats replied, 'the attack ... reflects the highest honour on the troops and does infinite credit to the officers and men under your command and particularly to Lieutenant Westphal of the *Implacable* whose zeal and exertions have been so conspicuous on the occasion. In transmitting to the commander-in-chief the relation you have made, I cannot with justice omit an opportunity of expressing how much I feel obliged by your voluntary services.'[1] The Spanish Secretary of State also wrote adding his glowing approbation of the event and the way in which it was conducted.

When the Spaniards decided to send two of their huge 120-gun ships lying in Cadiz to Havannah for their better safety, the Council of Regency asked Admiral Keats for Cockburn in the *Implacable* to conduct them there '... on account of the confidence which Captain Cockburn deserves, as well as for the good services he has already rendered to Spain, and also on account of his acknowledged zeal, enthusiasm and peculiar attachment to our just cause which he has constantly manifested on all occasions', read their supplicatory letter. After reaching Havannah, the *Implacable* was to proceed to Vera Cruz, Mexico to load with such treasure as the viceroy of New

Spain might have ready for the use of the Spanish government and to return to Cadiz.

The *Santa Ana* and the *Principe de Asturias* – dwarfing the *Implacable* – sailed with her in company on September 6. A lieutenant and 20 seamen were transferred to the *Santa Ana* to ensure good communication and navigation. Weeks of boredom in the horse latitudes and the lack of fresh provisions brought their inevitable consequence; in early November scurvy broke out, the ship's log recording many deaths. One of the earliest to go was the ship's chaplain at the moment his services were most required.

The two Spanish ships were detached close to Cuba and made their way to Havannah while *Implacable* sailed on into the Gulf of Mexico until she reached her destination on November 21. The Governor of Vera Cruz came onboard and Cockburn explained his predicament. Everything possible was done – the sick were landed on Sacreficias Island and placed in a temporary hospital of tents under the charge of the ship's surgeon; ship's decks were scrubbed and sprinkled with vinegar, but scurvy continued unabated.

Appreciating the Spanish love of protocol, Cockburn wasted no time in stating formally the object of his visit so that, hopefully, there would be no delay in completing his task. He wrote to the viceroy of New Spain, 'I have had the honour to transmit to Your Excellency three letters confided to me by the Regency of Spain which will I believe point out to your Excellency the object for which they requested that HM Ship under my command might be sent to this place. I have now therefore, only to state to your Excellency that the *Implacable* is ready to return immediately to Cadiz with such treasure as you may think proper to confide to my care for the Spanish government, but I must beg your Excellency will have the goodness to inform me with as little delay as possible what quantity that is likely to be; and how soon it can be sent onboard that I may make my arrangements accordingly. Permit me now to offer your Excellency my most heartfelt congratulations on your Excellency's late brilliant successes against the enemies of Spain in this country, and I trust for the cause of justice and virtue that the glorious efforts of the Spanish nation may be crowned with equal success in every other part of the world. Should it lay in my power to render any assistance during my stay in the port I request your Excellency will not hesitate to command me.'

The expectation was for at least two million dollars of public money, increased by private funds in the hands of merchants, to be transferred in the patriotic cause, but the response was not quite as hoped. His Excellency proposed to send only one and a half million dollars and no private monies although Cockburn continued to stress that he was permitted to accept the latter provided it could be carried conveniently. He pursued the point by asking for licences to permit merchants to embark 'such money as they have ready', and to allow them also to send onboard their stocks of cochineal and indigo – both valued local commodities.

The viceroy continued to show unwarranted obstinacy, intended probably as a gesture of his authority, which Cockburn found irksome, particularly as he had now been at Vera Cruz for nearly a month and was anxious to sail. He wrote on December 12, 'I am honoured with your Excellency's letter informing me that your Excellency does not think proper to accede to the request I made for the *Implacable* to be permitted to carry to Cadiz such money as the merchants of Vera Cruz might have here in readiness to ship for that destination. I cannot Sir, but lament this determination of your Excellency, as in the present state of Europe, money going there though an act of private individuals, must be of the greatest public importance and I am not aware that it would take more time to embark such treasure as is here ready for shipping than to receive the precious produce of this Country, the embarkation of which you have been pleased to authorise. In compliance with your Excellency's letter I will not lose a moment in proceeding to Cadiz immediately after the precious produce and members destined for the Cortes are embarked'. As a sweetener he ended his letter, 'permit me now to congratulate your Excellency on the good news which is just arrived, of the victory gained by the allied army under Lord Wellington over the French army commanded by Massena – if the account prove correct which there seems no reason to doubt. I think I may venture to hope that by this time there is not a Frenchman remaining in Spain'. The battle was Busaco but it was by no means the final victory.

Cockburn won on all points but there was continuing irritation over charges for the return to Vera Cruz of the officers and men lent to navigate the Spanish ships into Havannah. A hired schooner had been employed for the purpose as no armed vessel could be spared, and Cockburn , quite rightly, expected His Excellency to defray the expenses for work done 'wholly and solely in the service of Spain'. Once this contentious issue was settled, the *Implacable*'s sick were re-embarked and the long return journey began on December 27.

It was some while before the sickness subsided; the assistant surgeon and two midshipmen died but otherwise a general recovery took place under the recuperative effects of good weather and a pleasant voyage. Cadiz was reached on February 18, 1811, and Cockburn's unusual assignment was successfully completed with the landing of the treasure and cargo.

The siege of Cadiz was still in progress although events in the Peninsular War were now more favourable. At that moment combined Spanish and British troops were attacking the rear of the French beseiging army, and Cockburn proceeded with the armed boats in support. The battle of Barossa had been won before he could play a useful part but his sailors and marines arrived in time to help secure the French prisoners.

Britain's envoy at Cadiz was Sir Henry Wellesley, brother of the Marquis and the Duke of Wellington. Cockburn's experience in Mexico led Sir Henry and Admiral Keats to believe that an attempt should be made to reconcile Spain's differences with her American colonies. There was a strong move towards independence as Cockburn had seen at first hand while at Vera Cruz causing a reluctance by the colonies to part with valuable resources for prosecuting the war against France. Henry Wellesley felt that mediation might arrest the progress of revolt, and decided that Cockburn should go to England to inform the government of their similar views. So Cockburn left on May 5 in the frigate *Druid*; in London he waited on his old acquaintance Richard Wellesley – still the Foreign Secretary – to lay before him his brother's despatches.

Government discussion took time but by the autumn it was decided to appoint commissioners who would offer to mediate in the name of the Prince Regent and attempt to bring Spain and the colonies to agreed terms. Two civilians were selected to fill the role – a Mr T Sydenham and Mr J P Morier – but perhaps the most surprising nomination was Cockburn himself, an unusual appointment for a naval officer but one which reflected the trust placed in his flair for negotiation and diplomacy. All three were named as envoys extraordinary and ministers plenipotentiary.[2]

While these deliberations were proceeding, Cockburn had a rare opportunity to relax and enjoy a summer at home. His daughter Augusta was born at this time; then, on August 1, he was granted the rank of colonel of the Royal Marines in addition to his naval rank. This was an unusual honour dating back to 1760 when the strength of the Royal Marine corps rose to more than one quarter of the total of the navy. The Admiralty, considering that there should be more senior RM officers, created three paid posts for naval captains as colonels – one for each division of Royal Marines. The system became increasingly unpopular and was referred to as 'that pernicious system of naval sinecures called Blue Colonelcies',[3] blue naturally enough, after the colour of the naval officer's uniform. It was an iniquitous arrangement since it inhibited the promotion of Royal Marine officers thus restricting incentive; yet in Cockburn's case it would have been difficult to have found a more deserving officer for the award. He had always shown an affection for the royal corps and had distinguished himself already in amphibious operations, the marines' forte. In the remaining war years ahead he would demonstrate that, far from the appointment being a sinecure, he would lead these men so successfully in person.

The *Grampus*, 50 guns, had fitted out at Portsmouth as the commissioners' accommodation ship. In recognition of his appointment as senior commissioner Cockburn was again ordered to hoist a commodore's broad pendant. The ship's departure for Cadiz, however, was delayed by political uncertainty in England; Wellesley's position as Foreign Secretary became increasingly tenuous at the beginning of 1812, and it was not until he resigned in February of that year and government became more settled, that the go-ahead could be given for the party to depart. The ship left St Helen's on April 9 and arrived back in Cadiz a little under a fortnight later with the intention of continuing to South America once agreement had been reached with the Cortes on the mediation policy. The commissioners started discussions but soon discovered so many prejudices among members of the Cortes that they realised their's would be a long drawn out task.

Although Cadiz was still besieged by Soult its fall was now quite remote enabling Cockburn and the officers of the *Grampus* to enjoy the town's extensive social life. Cleaner than Lisbon in 1812, Cadiz appeared beautiful from the bay but was crowded – many families, several of high rank, having come from the interior in consequence of the country's disturbed state. The ramparts, ideal for promenading, afforded good views to seaward. The streets were narrow – for shade – and lined with white-stuccoed houses many of whose windows were not even glazed, protected instead by iron railings. The better houses had balconies or verandahs rather similar to the modern London houses of the period. Cadiz was still the emporium of Spanish trade and strongly fortified as the French had discovered. As an officer from the *Grampus* so aptly put it, 'here were to be found concentrated all the excitements of war which love and glory can produce; one hour sighing at the feet of a mistress, the next engaged with the foe'.[4]

The talks with the Spanish government went badly and it soon became evident that the cramped and illiberal powers proposed for the commissioners in their dealings with the colonies precluded success. Sir Henry Wellesley, now promoted from envoy to ambassador, authorised the commissioners to return to England with their mission unfulfilled. The *Grampus* reached Spithead on August 4. For all the disappointment he must have felt Cockburn received consolation eight days later. Promoted Rear-Admiral of the Blue he was to fly his flag in the *Marlborough* and return to Cadiz and assume overall naval command. 'It was an event which was hailed by the officers who were to follow him into the *Marlborough* as the *ne plus ultra* of good fortune' were the words with which Lieutenant Scott, one of the lucky ones, vented his feelings. Captain Hardy, whose career followed Cockburn's so closely, made his own unique offering to his former captain by transferring *Barfleur*'s band, reputedly the best in the navy, to *Marlborough*.

George Cockburn had gained his promotion to flag rank at the age of 40. With more than 16 years outstanding service as post captain and commodore to his credit, his advancement, in a swollen wartime post captains' list, was well merited. Forty was not an unusually young age to attain flag rank – Nelson gained his at 38 – but it still gave him a five- to eight-year advantage over most of the other 20 officers similarly promoted.

Cockburn's advancement constituted the first rung on the admiral's promotion ladder. He would be the receiver of eight similar promotions before reaching Admiral of the Fleet. This first elevation would have given him the greatest pleasure.

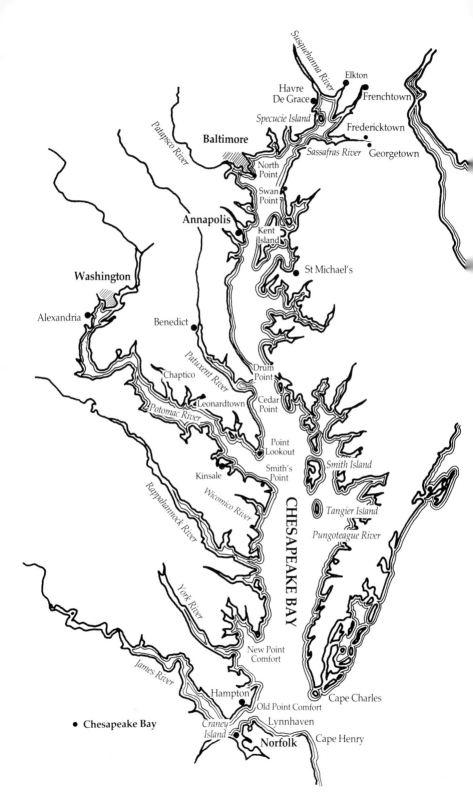

Susquehanna River
Elkton
Havre
De Grace
Frenchtown
Specucie Island
Fredericktown
Georgetown
Sassafras River
Baltimore
Patapsco River
North
Point
Swan
Point
Annapolis
Kent
Island
St Michael's
Washington
Alexandria
Benedict
Drum
Point
Chaptico
Patuxent River
Leonardtown
Cedar
Point
Potomac River
Point
Lookout
Smith Island
Kinsale
Smith's
Point
Rappahannock River
Wicomico River
Tangier Island
Pungoteague River
CHESAPEAKE BAY
York River
James River
New Point
Comfort
Cape Charles
Hampton
Old Point Comfort
Lynnhaven
● Chesapeake Bay
Craney
Island
Norfolk
Cape Henry

CHAPTER ELEVEN

Predator of the Chesapeake 1813

COCKBURN'S FLAGSHIP, THE *MARLBOROUGH*, a standard third rate of 74 guns under the command of Captain C B H Ross, sailed for Cadiz in convoy on September 23, but a south-westerly gale next day drove the ships into Torbay. When the wind backed south-east causing the ship to seek the relative safety of open waters, disaster nearly overtook her. Difficulty in weighing anchor caught the ship on the wrong tack; could she wear and clear Berry Head? In the emergency Cockburn took over from the captain. A *Marlborough* officer described what followed, 'the admiral decided at once there was room, put the helm up, and wore her in as short a space as was practicable; intense anxiety and suspense filled our breasts as she came to the wind. By getting the courses upon her, she looked to windward – it was however, "touch and go"; the lee yard-arms appeared as if they would graze the face of the beetling cliff; the angry waves as they rebounded from the rocks, dashing their spray over our lee-gangway, assisted in keeping us to windward. Her own breadth more to leeward, and I doubt whether any of us would have been left to tell the tale of woe'.[1]

The 39 ships in the convoy, scattered by the gale, slowly regrouped off Start Point, many showing a reluctance to leave Torbay even when the wind moderated. Cockburn complained to the Admiralty about the behaviour of one transport, the *Cora*, 'who showed no inclination to move in spite of the good weather'. Convoy work was never popular with serving officers.

There were other excitements. The frigate *Macedonian* picked up two French prisoners who had escaped from Dartmoor and were attempting to get away in a small boat. Then, when clear of the Channel, a French privateer schooner was found at daylight among the convoy! How this wolf came to be among so vulnerable a flock is obscure, but she was no match for the British armed escorts and wisely hauled down her colours. Cockburn reported her as the *Lenore* of 10 guns and 70 men, and left her in charge of the sloop *Dotterel* to be escorted to England.

The *Marlborough* accompanied the convoy as far as Cadiz where a state of relative peace now prevailed. During Cockburn's absence the siege had been lifted and Wellington's Peninsular army had gained everywhere apart from a recent retreat at Salamanca. Cockburn, reluctant to run down the defending force at Cadiz too quickly, particularly the gunboats, wrote a cautionary note to Admiral Martin, Commander-in-Chief at Lisbon, 'as the reverse of fortune which the army under Lord Wellington has lately experienced could not have been known in Lisbon at the time you gave your directions about the gunboats, and as HM Ambassador here has communicated to me an official letter from His Lordship stating that the two armies of the enemy opposed to him and Sir Rowland Hill are superior both in numbers and in composition, I have delayed executing your order to reduce the eight gunboats and am keeping them here in good order'.[2] Admiral Martin agreed with alacrity.

It was not long before Their Lordships decided that a more important job deserved a man of Cockburn's calibre; the war with the United States now in its seventh month had resulted in a number of humiliating reverses for the British navy. Individual frigate actions had shown that the better-built American ships could be overcome only by the concentration of a stronger British force in American waters. Operations from the main British base at Halifax, Nova Scotia, had been singularly ineffective. An aging Admiral Sir John Warren, well known to Cockburn from his Mediterranean days, commanded the Halifax squadron weakly, carrying out no vigorous offensives along the undefended American seaboard.[3] To inject new life, Cockburn was ordered to join Warren at Bermuda where he would be allocated a squadron to take the war into the American heartland. The *Marlborough* left Cadiz on November 23, arriving at Bermuda in the middle of January 1813.

Cockburn had gained great experience of the American scene from his visit in the *Phaeton* to New York some nine years earlier. Since then Anglo-American relations had steadily worsened primarily through rival interpretations of maritime law and the refusal of both Britain and France to allow America to trade freely. Napoleon's Berlin Decrees of 1806, and Britain's Order in Council of 1807, interrupted not only American trade with continental Europe but also the lucrative commerce between America and the West Indies. That year, 1807, America retaliated with the Embargo Act forbidding the departure of foreign ships from US ports without official clearance. Two years later, America strengthened that embargo by a Non-Intercourse Act aimed specifically against Britain and France. In the long drawn out Anglo-French struggle America inevitably suffered, but because of Britain's maritime predominance and the absence of a language barrier, America was more anti-British than anti-French. To acerbate that feeling, Napoleon artfully revoked the Berlin Decree.

According to the best estimate, some 2,500 British seamen annually were drawn into the American merchant service; on the other hand, about 1,000 seamen, supposedly British, but in large part American, were impressed from American ships by British warships every year. Perhaps the root of the Anglo-American quarrel lay less in rival interpretations of maritime law than in the problems of the western frontier where Americans hungered for land at the expense of the Indians and, sometimes, loyalist Canadians.

Ironically, a few days after the signed declaration of war on June 18, 1812, the British government took the positive step of revoking the offending Orders in Council realising that friendship was in the interests of both countries, but it was too late to prevent the conflict which, throughout, seemed to possess a quixotic quality – notably in the second half of 1812 when operations on land and sea bore results the reverse of those expected.

At the start of the war Britain's maritime dominance had persuaded Congress that the invasion of Canada was the most effective way of coercing Britain. Provision was made for a small standing army of some 20,000 men backed by volunteers to form a militia of 50,000. There were, however, in this still young country, deep internal divisions; the Federalists mainly in New England who gained from maritime trade and who still had a certain affinity with the country of their origin, were opposed to war and were not wholehearted in its prosecution; the north-eastern states continued to trade with Canada across an ill-defined border – a factor which never ceased to provide the British army with much needed provisions.

In July 1812, America was faced by 6,000 British regulars stationed thinly in isolated frontier outposts; they were supported by Canadian 'fencibles' recruited to serve only in the area in which they lived; and there were also the fiery Indian tribes of Upper Canada and the north-west – redoubtable allies of the British in the defence of their territories.

Superficially Canada was at a disadvantage with such a tenuous defence line of some 2,000 miles but she did possess an asset in the Great Lakes which formed a natural barrier from the outset. Throughout 1812 British control of the waters of Lake Ontario and Lake Erie remained intact thereby providing the most important single factor for American failure on land in the early stages. It was the vast expanse of Upper Canada surrounding the lakes which was most vulnerable; further to the east, the more populated area on the St Lawrence River between Quebec and Montreal certainly lay at the heart of the conquest of Canada, but Quebec along with Nova Scotia and New Brunswick presented formidable targets for a new nation not yet experienced in the finer arts of war. The most direct route north into Canada was the natural waterway formed by the Hudson River and Lake Champlain but General Prevost in command of the British forces was well prepared to resist an American invasion along this route, which in any case was inhibited by the attitude of New England.

Early American operations, therefore, had been concentrated in the west where advances from Detroit at the western end of Lake Erie, and across the Niagara frontier, seemed to offer the best hopes of success. Lack of co-ordinated effort and immature leadership failed to win any worthwhile trophies – indeed, the vacillation of General Hull and the loss of Fort Detroit in August established a nadir in America's military fortunes. The struggle was to be long and drawn out. The British had been unable to seize the advantage as they too suffered from mediocre leadership with the occasional exception, such as Major-General Brock. Prevost, commanding overall, did not inspire but he was supported in his cautious and defensive attitude by the British government which, under-standably, could guarantee few reinforcements while war with France continued.

The 1812 campaign ended with a tentative American advance northwards towards Montreal from Plattsburg on Lake Champlain in mid-November. It was late in the season for a serious endeavour and with troops badly equipped and led, it was rebuffed. In fact the attempt was counter-productive – damaging to American morale while providing the Canadian militia who opposed them with confidence in their own abilities. But the American soldier too, com-

● Admiral Sir John Borlase Warren,
Commander-in-Chief on the North
American station
(RN Museum, Portsmouth)

manded respect; Charles Napier, a young British officer later to
become a distinguished soldier, wrote, 'Yankees fight well and are
gentlemen in their mode of warfare . . . These Yankees, though so
much abused, are really fine fellows'.[4]

If the war on land had disappointed America, the reverse was
true on that other element, the sea, where Britain had every hope of
succeeding. Despite the disparity of naval forces available to the
combatants of mid-1812, the war was not to be a one-sided affair as
Britain was soon to discover at considerable cost. Britain's huge navy
was committed worldwide and the declaration of war by America
found only an inadequate British force at Halifax, Nova Scotia – the
main base of Vice-Admiral Sawyer, the naval commander-in-chief.
Sawyer had been on station since 1810 and in other circumstances
would not have been one of the Admiralty's chosen few for command in a war theatre. His ships, few in number and some in a state
of disrepair, were undermanned through desertion and sickness.
Attempts to redress the manpower situation by the activities of the
press gang in Halifax had been both unpopular and unsuccessful.
By contrast the small American navy and merchant marine were
magnificently manned by thoroughbred seamen who were all
volunteers; the maritime states had gained a deserved reputation for
ship construction – and, of course, the materials were plentiful.
Hundreds of merchant vessels when converted for privateering
found that they could outsail their British counterparts and reaped
a reward accordingly. America had forsaken an earlier intention to
build warships of the line (usually those carrying 74 guns or more),

on the score of expense; but their three largest frigates the *United States*, *President* and *Constitution* carried a punch little less and were vastly superior to the smaller English frigates.

Admittedly Sawyer had problems not of his own making. British licences for American ships to export goods from the United States prevented an effective blockade even if the ships had been available; indeed, he still had to operate under an Admiralty order which forbade his captains to sail within 15 leagues of the American coast and not to board any ships under the American flag.[5] Thus at an early stage in the war at sea the *President, United States* and other warships in company, were able to leave New York without molestation. In like fashion American privateers operated at will in the Bay of Fundy, the Gulf of St Lawrence and the Newfoundland Banks with such good effect as to capture 150 merchant vessels in those areas.

When the Admiralty became aware of the state of things, Admiral Sir John Borlase Warren was appointed to relieve Sawyer. They hoped that the more experienced man, as Warren undoubtedly was, could entice the American government to negotiate a peace agreement even at this late stage, but his feelers were unsuccessful. He lacked dynamism and did not prosecute the war with notable vigour or with greater success than his predecessor, although again it must be said his resources remained inadequate.

A series of individual frigate engagements in the autumn and early winter of 1812 reflected a state of incapacity in ships of the Royal Navy which has seldom been equalled in its long history. On an overcast day in August, the undermanned British frigate *Guerriere* met the *Constitution* 300 miles south of Halifax and in the ensuing action was overwhelmed. Two more American victories – by the *United States* over the *Macedonian* in October, and the *Constitution* yet again over the *Java* in December, had shocked the British. The *London Gazette* for years had been reporting successful single ship engagements in the long war with France and now, in a matter of months, three frigates had been beaten decisively in situations where the odds against them could hardly be all that great – or so it appeared. American sailors were more than making amends for their military counterparts on the Canadian front in this first phase of the war.

The naval news created consternation and much criticism in England and helped Warren in his demands for reinforcements. In November 1812 he was informed that his fleet would be augmented by three ships of the line, ten frigates and four sloops. One of these

● Nicolas Camillieri's painting of the US frigate Constellation in 1831.
(US Naval Academy Museum, Annapolis)

line ships would be the *Marlborough* which, as already related, had reached Bermuda in January 1813 with Admiral Cockburn onboard.

Cockburn was unable to meet Warren as agreed because of the *Marlborough*'s unseaworthiness. She urgently needed caulking in Bermuda Dockyard. Awaiting him there were orders to proceed to Chesapeake Bay, and take command of four third rates – *Poictiers*, *Victorious* and *Dragon* as well as the *Marlborough*, together with seven minor war vessels ranging from frigates, brigs and sloops to a schooner. In the Chesapeake he was to take charge of four more frigates – *Maidstone*, *Junon*, *Belvidera* and *Statira*. A new phase in the war afloat was about to begin.

Cockburn's orders included these directives:
To blockade the ports and river harbours in the Bay of Chesapeake and of the River Delaware in the most strict and rigorous manner according to the usages of war acknowledged and allowed in similar cases.
To capture and destroy trade and shipping off Baltimore and particularly in the Potomac, York, Rappahannock and James Rivers.
To obtain intelligence of the numbers of gunboats and state of the enemy's ships operating in the Chesapeake and elsewhere.
To procure pilots, taking black men if necessary for all Chesapeake rivers, the Delaware and Long Island Sound, endeavouring also to discover a place near the Chesapeake where the squadron can complete its water and its boats protected.

145

To ascertain the situation affecting the frigate Constellation and the best means of capturing her; also the defences and troops in the vicinity of the place and to report any additional force required.

To detach a force to blockade the Delaware but 'care to be taken for ships not to remain at anchor a moment longer than is necessary for accomplishing the particular object so as to subject the ships to an attack from gunboats, fire vessels or Fulton's machines'.

To allocate a small force to cut off trade in and out of Long Island Sound.

To maintain constant communication with the ships at their several stations so that they can be united in the event of a superior enemy force appearing.

To hold as little communication as possible with American inhabitants of the coast, pilots or others 'in order to avoid corruption, seduction, or the seeds of sedition being sown'.

To collect prizes and send them in convoy to Bermuda, prize crews of captured ships being then returned to their proper ships.[6]

Cockburn arrived at Lynnhaven Bay near the entrance to the Chesapeake on March 3, 1813, the passage from Bermuda against contrary winds giving him an opportunity to test his new squadron. The *Victorious* was censured for failing to observe a signal to take station astern of the *Marlborough* and to obtain the correct sailing order before nightfall. Even the firing of a gun to draw attention to the signal failed to have any effect. 'A ready and willing obedience to the orders of superior officers of the highest ranks are more particularly called upon to set example to the officers and men subordinate to them. . .' so opened the letter he sent to her Captain Talbot, 'detriment to HM Service will arise by captains merely permitting to be effected with loss of time, that which is within their power to execute in a few minutes by a little additional exertion', was how he concluded.

The weather was boisterous and the *Marlborough* laboured excessively; on one particularly arduous day Cockburn ordered, 'that such of the crew who have kept watch are each to receive in addition to their allowance, a gill of red wine mixed by the surgeon with a proper proportion of bark'. Expectation of high professional standards combined with concern for the welfare of their men, featured regularly in Cockburn's demands of his captains.

Admiral Warren joined Cockburn in the vast Chesapeake Bay ten days later on March 13 at his Hampton Roads base. From Cape Henry in the south to the Susquehanna River in the north lay 180 miles of navigable water surrounded by the states of Virginia and Maryland. Fed by innumerable rivers and interspersed by islands of

146

varying size, much of the area was uncharted and unsurveyed for which purpose the use of tenders and small craft was essential. At Chesapeake's northern end on the Patapsco River, prosperous Baltimore provided a hardy breed of seafaring men who manned their fine vessels and employed them as privateers to good effect; at the head of the Potomac and Patuxent Rivers, where they were almost confluent, lay the capital city Washington; and up the Elizabeth River near the entrance to the Chesapeake, more a tidal estuary than a river, rested Norfolk bordering on one of the finest natural harbours in the world.

Within ten days of Warren's arrival Cockburn wrote a comprehensive appreciation of the situation. Already he had amassed information which the resident frigates with more time at their disposal had failed previously to obtain. He established that Norfolk – which he hoped to attack – was well defended with a force of at least 3,000; the frigate *Constellation* – a prize target – had moved nearer the town, and was guarded by gunboats. To approach her he needed to negotiate an intricate channel by boat, but even if the navigation was successful, his squadron boats would have been no match in daylight for the American gunboats, each of which carried two 24-pounders. One attempt had been made by night under Westphal, the *Marlborough*'s first lieutenant. The attack coincided with the time the *Constellation* swung to the ebb tide, when her stern would be presented to the advance. The line of gunboats were to be attacked by one division of boats while another division, two of which were equipped with rockets, attacked *Constellation*'s stern. In the confusion *Constellation* might be captured and destroyed if the rockets failed to settle the matter. It was a well arranged plan. At ten o'clock

• **Mary of Norfolk was a typical Virginian pilot boat. (RN Museum, Portsmouth)**

the boats of the squadron assembled and began their five mile haul. Then it began to blow so hard that within a couple of miles of the *Constellation* the boats were unable to combat wind and tide. Lieutenant Westphal persevered overlong in hopes of a lull. The coming of dawn revealed them: *Constellation* promptly moved higher up river rendering further attempts fruitless.

As a consolation two pilot schooners, manned by *Constellation*'s officers and men, were captured by the British. These ships had been stationed near Cape Henry to warn their own countrymen against entering the Bay but it was also rumoured that they had been on the lookout for a French squadron expected to come to their assistance. These fine schooners were readily adapted by Cockburn for use as tenders to which were added later captures – notably the armed letter-of-marque *Cora* of eight guns and 40 men – reputedly Baltimore's fastest schooner.

Ships of light draught were clearly essential for continuing operations as was the need near the anchorage at Lynnhaven to buoy the shoals which the squadron's sailing masters swiftly accomplished. Cockburn felt that tactics hereon were for Warren as commander-in-chief to decide but if land operations were required, such as an attack on Norfolk, he strongly recommended that General Horsford, Governor of Bermuda, should provide a regiment to support the squadron's Royal Marines. 'The whole of the shores and towns within this vast bay, not excepting the capital itself, will be wholly at your mercy,' Cockburn wrote. In making this prescient comment he was unaware that two battalions of the Royal Marines and the 103rd Regiment were then preparing to leave England for Bermuda, although it says much for American intelligence that their papers already contained rumour of this. He completed his review by giving Warren an account of a successful assault up the James River by ships' boats under Lieutenant Westphal saying that, 'the capture of ships so high up one of their rivers and the possibility of similar excursions elsewhere has set the whole country in a state of alarm causing the continuation of hostilities with us to be now as unpopular in this area as it has been in other parts of the United States'.[7] He was, of course, referring to New England and other seaboard states where the war had been unpopular from the outset.

The exchange of prisoners of war was already beginning to pose a serious problem and would continue so until the end of hostilities and beyond. The long-established principle of reciprocal exchange was difficult because of the numerical imbalance: there was also a reluctance on the part of the United States to release prisoners considered by Britain to be *bona fide* British but about whom the Americans held a different view.

With the ever-increasing number of American prisoners from captured ships to be accommodated and fed, Cockburn was anxious to come to an understanding with Brigadier-General Robert Taylor, the officer commanding at Norfolk. He opened proceedings by returning to Taylor 'on principles of humanity, 28 American gentlemen and sailors by cartel who are not being treated as prisoners'. He regretted not being able to send the balance of confirmed prisoners until a regular exchange could be arranged. Taylor stalled by saying there was nothing he could do until officially informed by his government, but he flattered Cockburn with 'the humanity and generosity which my countrymen will receive at your hands whensoever they shall be fit subjects for the exercise of these sentiments'. Cockburn, perforce, had to act. On March 13 he ordered the *Acasta* to bring all the prisoners to Lynnhaven from Hampton Roads and arrange for their transport to Bermuda. The captain was told to take no chances, 'to put prisoners in the hold and to plank up around the hatchways and to take such other measures to prevent the possibility of them rising to attempt the capture of the ship during passage'. Cockburn, however, excepted Americans serving in British warships who could authenticate their American citizenship; he paroled them provided they declared that they would not bear arms again unless regularly exchanged.

These rumblings on a vexatious subject grew more vociferous in time.

While the *Marlborough* lay in Hampton Roads, Cockburn received an important letter from André de Daschkoff, the Russian minister in Washington. It had been sent under an American flag of truce and was delivered personally by his secretary. 'I have received the orders of the Emperor, my master, to offer his high mediation to the President of the United States for the re-establishment of peace between Great Britain and the American Republic. His Imperial Majesty charges me to propose it in a manner that cannot wound the national honour or pride of either party . . .'[8] President Madison had already been approached and had responded positively, claimed Daschkoff who now asked Cockburn's protection to a vessel which he wished to send with his despatches by way of Gothenburg to Russia. This was the first of many overtures from Daschkoff, and Cockburn was happy to grant the protection requested.

On April 1, the squadron – less those ships which had been deployed to blockade elsewhere – proceeded up the Bay. Next day five vessels, including four large schooners, were sighted off New Point Comfort and chased into the Rappahannock River. Unable to progress further in the shallow water, the squadron anchored off Windmill Point at the river's entrance. Boats were lowered and the chase continued by night in light airs. The following morning where the river formed a large bay, the schooners were discovered in battle array. A fierce engagement ensued in which Lieutenant Scott, later to become Admiral Cockburn's aide-de-camp, played a prominent part. At a cost of only two killed and 11 wounded, five open boats with one 12-pounder carronade, and 105 officers and men, succeeded in capturing all four schooners – the *Arab, Lynx, Racer* and *Dolphin*.[9]

The sequel is best told in Scott's own words, 'on the morning of the 5th our prizes were safely anchored with the squadron. On the same evening seven schooners and two brigs were seen to the north-north-east. The *Dolphin, Lynx,* and *Racer,* were immediately manned, the latter by the *Marlborough,* under our first lieutenant, and proceeded in chase. They were all first rate vessels of their class, fitted out without regard to expense, and sailed like the wind. By daybreak they were between the Potomac and Patuxent Rivers, with 36 sail of the enemy's vessels ahead of them. American colours and pendants were hoisted, and, sailing abreast of each other, they proceeded on. A pilot boat, recognising the vessels, stood towards them, and inquired if they wanted a pilot. A reply was given in the negative. "Have you seen anything of the Britishers?" – "Yes, they are coming up the bay." In a very few minutes the *Racer* had got upon the starboard beam of the enemy's vessels, the *Lynx* on the larboard, and the *Dolphin* in the centre. On attaining this position, the American stripes were exchanged for the English ensign, and the broadsides of the schooners opened out upon all around. The scene of dismay, confusion and indecision exhibited onboard the unlucky craft might be compared to the fright of a flock of sheep surprised by wolves leaping suddenly into the midst of them; one endeavoured to escape here, another there, but they were speedily stopped by the fire of their unmasked foes. The vessels were all captured and brought to anchor. A gale of wind in the night driving four or five of them on shore, they were destroyed; the remainder were conducted in safety to the squadron. The *ruse de guerre* completely succeeded; not one, it appeared, entertained the slightest suspicion of the truth till the English ensigns replaced the American'.

After this highly successful encounter, Scott was given command of the *Racer* as a tender. Admiral Warren in the *San Domingo* accompanied the squadron almost to Annapolis when Cockburn in the *Marlborough* was detached, taking with him the frigate *Maidstone*, the brigs *Fantome* and *Mohawk*, and the three tenders *Dolphin*, *Racer*, and *Highflyer* to penetrate the rivers at the head of the Chesapeake for which only vessels of light draught were suitable. Cockburn also had a specially selected detachment of 180 seamen and 200 Royal Marines forming a naval brigade for shore operations together with a few artillerymen lent by General Horsford at Bermuda.

In the Patapsco River area, off Swan Point, more prizes were taken which, when converted, replenished the squadron with the excellent water found there. The all important surveying of shoals which Cockburn never neglected continued so that in time the intricate waterways of the Chesapeake became as well known to them as to the Americans.

Cockburn started his offensive on April 28 by attacking Frenchtown on the Elk River where reputedly there was a large depot of military and other stores. The *Fantome*, to which Cockburn had transferred, anchored in the river, and at about midnight the naval brigade under Lieutenant Westphal set off by boat. Arriving at eight the following morning, they were warmly received by a battery of six guns. But the contest was unequal; the opposition was no match for Cockburn superintending his experienced, battle-trained professionals. By now an acknowledged master of amphibious warfare he had a quick answer. While the battery was carronaded by his launches, the naval brigade attacked the American right flank whereupon the militia fled. Frenchtown with its valuable military stores and merchandise together with five vessels lying nearby were destroyed by fire and the town's guns disabled. Cockburn paid for the cattle he took to provision his squadron. 'I shall give the owner bills on the Victualling Office for the fair value of whatsoever is taken but should resistance be made, I shall consider them as prize of war,' he told Warren. Nothing could be fairer.[10]

Cockburn's squadron set off for nearby Specucie Island to reform, but the over-confident townspeople of Havre-de-Grace, at the entrance to the Susquehanna, hoisted their colours and began firing. Cockburn reasoned that if it was worth erecting defences for the town's security, it was worth attacking. The boats were assembled by night, again under Lieutenant Westphal, alongside the *Fantome*

HAVRE DE GRACE

WAR OF 1812

HERE ON THE MORNING OF MAY 3, 1813,
BRITISH FORCES UNDER ADMIRAL
COCKBURN LANDED, SACKED, AND BURNED
THE TOWN. THE PRINCIPAL DEFENSES
WERE TWO SMALL BATTERIES ON
CONCORD POINT. THE "POTATO BATTERY"
ON HIGH GROUND, WAS MANNED TO THE
LAST BY JOHN O'NEILL.

MARYLAND HISTORICAL SOCIETY

● **The signpost says it all**

whose captain was entrusted with the command. Westphal's seamen and the rocket-boats led the van; Captain Lawrence brought up the rear with a Royal Marines detachment. The leading boats were discovered before dawn on May 3 and a heavy fire was opened upon them. So ably was this returned by the launches and the rocket-boats that the Americans were driven from their guns. Before Captain Lawrence could arrive with the marines, the town and several prisoners were taken; he had only to secure the conquest.

All was not yet over; Cockburn having forbade a pursuit, learned of the Principio Foundry, a nearby cannon factory reputedly one of the largest in the States. He led a small party and destroyed 51 large calibre guns and 130 stand of small arms. Five vessels in the Susequehanna were added to the tally as well as a considerable depot of flour.[11]

The attack, virtually without loss, had its lighter moments. Lieutenant Scott recounts, 'Havre stands on the high road between Baltimore and Philadelphia; the enemy had fled into the woods and, it appears, gave no intimation to their travelling countrymen of the change of affairs at Havre; for about noon the stage coach arrived from Philadelphia on its way to Baltimore, and stopped at the inn before the coachman and his affrighted cargo found they had fallen into the hands of the Britishers. Milliners with the latest fashions from Paris, merchants and tradesmen, were alike pretty considerably confounded, wondering how we had reached the high road between their two most flourishing and principal towns. The passengers got off in safety without loss, except a luckless milliner, of whose finery some had been purloined by an individual who ought to have known better, but who was deservedly mortified by the Rear Admiral obliging him to return the spoils *in propria persona* to the forlorn damsel, with an impressive rebuke'.

The next enterprise took place on May 6 as Cockburn, true to form, reported, 'understanding that Georgetown and Frederickstown, situated up the Sassafras River, were places of some trade and importance, and the Sassafras being the only river or place of shelter for vessels at this upper extremity of the Chesapeake which I had not examined and cleared, I directed last night the assembling of the boats alongside the *Mohawk*, from whence, with the marines, as before, they proceeded up this river, being placed by me for this operation under the immediate directions of Captain Byng of the *Mohawk*. I intended that they should arrive at the towns by dawn, but I was frustrated by the intricacies of the river, our total want of local knowledge of it, the darkness of the night, and the great distance the towns lay up it: it was unavoidably late in the morning before we approached them, when having intercepted a small boat with two of the inhabitants, I directed Captain Byng to halt the boats about two miles below the towns, and I sent forward the two Americans in their boat, to warn their countrymen against acting in the same rash manner the people of Havre-de-Grace had done, assuring them that if they did, their towns would inevitably meet with a similar fate. On the contrary, if they did not attempt resistance, no injury would be done to them or their towns; that vessels and public property only would be seized; that the strictest discipline would be maintained, and that whatever provisions or other property of individuals I might require for the use of the squadron would be paid for instantly to full value. After having allowed sufficient time for the message to be digested, I directed the boats to advance; regrettably I soon found the more unwise alternative was adopted, for on reaching within about a mile of the town, between two projecting elevated points of the river, a heavy fire of musketry was opened on us from about 400 men, divided and entrenched on the two opposite banks, aided by one long gun. The launches and rocket-boats warmly returned the fire with good effect. With the other boats and marines I pushed ashore immediately above the enemy's position, thereby ensuring the capture of his towns, or bringing him to a decided action: he determined, however, not to risk the latter; for the moment he discerned we had gained the shore, and that the marines had fixed their bayonets, he fled with his whole force to the woods, and was neither seen nor heard of afterwards. I kept my word respecting the towns, which (excepting the houses of those who had continued peaceably in them, and taken no part in the attack), were forthwith destroyed, as were four vessels lying in the river, and some stores of sugar, lumber, leather and other merchandise. Our small force was then re-embarked, and we proceeded down the river again, to a town I had observed situated on a branch of it, about half way up. Here I had the satisfaction to find that what had passed at Havre, Georgetown, and Frederickstown had its effect, and let these people to understand that they had more to hope for from our generosity than from erecting batteries and opposing us by means within their power; the inhabitants of this place having met me at the landing to say that they had not permitted either guns or militia to be stationed there, and that whilst there I should not meet with opposition. I therefore landed, with the officers and a small guard only, ascertained that there were no warlike stores, and having paid full value for any articles we stood in need of, re-embarked leaving the people of the place well pleased. I also had a deputation from Charlestown on the north-east river to assure me that neither guns nor militiamen shall be suffered there; and as all places in the upper part of the Chesapeake have adoped similar resolutions, and as there is now neither public property, vessels, nor warlike stores remaining in this neighbourhood, I propose returning to you with the light squadron tomorrow morning.[12]

Hostilities had been confined to the water hitherto, but Cockburn's 12 days before rejoining Warren on May 7 demonstrated the vulnerability of the surrounding shores. His small force, whose hardships were invariably shared by the rear-admiral, had shaken the inhabitants' confidence and revealed an exploitable weakness. The American press had heaped abuse upon him, and according to *Niles' Register* printed in Baltimore, 'a certain James O'Boyle, a naturalized Irishman, as he calls himself, residing at Pugh Town, Virginia, offers a reward of 1,000 dollars for the head of the notorious incendiary and infamous scoundrel, and violator of all laws, the British Admiral Cockburn, or 500 dollars for each of his ears on delivery'. Cockburn had conducted his war on foreign soil well within the accepted rules.

The squadron returned to Lynnhaven Bay and on May 17 Warren sailed for Halifax with 40 captured vessels, while another 30 proceeded to Bermuda under the convoy of the *Dragon*. No sooner had they gone than Cockburn received several flags of truce with various requests. Among them was another letter from the Russian Minister Daschkoff asking for a passport for General Moreau to take despatches from New York to St Petersburg in the transport *Hannibal*. According to Daschkoff, 'Moreau, at the pressing invitation of the Emperor of all the Russias, has accepted command of the foreign corps to be employed by His Imperial Majesty against the ruler of France'. Cockburn's reply displayed an ability to rival allcomers in diplomatic niceties, 'permit me, Sir, to offer Your Excellency my best acknowledgement for the sentiments you have been pleased to express respecting myself. I aid by every means within my power the views and wishes of the Imperial Government, the recent magnanimous conduct of which has so justly attracted to it the admiration, gratitude and confidence of all surrounding nations and the world in general, though, I believe, I may presume to add, of Great Britain in particular, whose actual close and happy alliance with Russia naturally occasions to her greater interest and participation in the gloriously successful efforts lately made to emancipate Europe and to shake a despot who has deluged the world with blood'. At this time, Napoleon's allies were dropping away one by one so that Daschkoff's request undoubtedly held merit.

It was now that the slaves in the surrounding countryside began to desert their masters and join the squadron. Invaluable for shore operations, particularly by night, because of their local knowledge, this first influx was well received. The militia and inhabitants naturally did all within their power to arrest the trend; on June 7, Cockburn received a letter from Colonel Addison of the 27th Regiment, Northampton County, requesting that one of his officers might be allowed to interview the deserters and those wanting to return should be allowed to do so, explaining also that, if they refused, they would lose their property. Cockburn conceded with alacrity but none of the negroes was persuaded. Two days later Addison sent a similar request showing increasing alarm at the daily desertions. Cockburn again agreed but could not see why the second attempt should succeed more than the first. His reply, made with human understanding, had a sting in the tail. It ended, 'permit me to seize this occasion to remove from you all scruple in addressing me on points of this kind. I cannot but derive the highest gratification in being at any time called upon to ameliorate the inconvenience and sufferings inseparable from a state of warfare, particularly for those who have not entered it, nor prosecuted it, with unnecessary or unusual rancour'.

Warren's departure on May 17 had left Cockburn with few ships to cover the wide waters of the Chesapeake and the Delaware River. A constant watch was necessary to prevent the escape of the *Constellation* from Norfolk, a requirement which denuded Cockburn of the *Victorious*, one his large ships, which accordingly maintained a station four miles off Old Point Comfort. On June 5, *Victorious'* boats found one of the powder machines commonly called Fulton's floating on the ebb. Designed as a floating mine, 'no doubt destined for the *Victorious* or some other of our ships here,' Cockburn warned his squadron, 'the American Government intending thus to dispose of us by a wholesale 600 at a time, without further trouble or risk, but as it is not likely their laudable efforts in this way have been confined to one machine only, I think it extremely probable others of a similar description have passed out to sea unobserved. As machines are as likely to come into contact with neutrals or American ships, everyone should be made aware so that the British are known to be blameless'.[13] Robert Fulton, a highly inventive American engineer of this period, was responsible for the development of submarine explosives besides being the constructor of the first submarine, the *Nautilus*.

In mid-June Cockburn received word of Admiral Warren's impending return from Bermuda with two battalions of Royal Marines, two independent companies, and the 102nd Regiment. Major-General Sir Sydney Beckwith had been appointed as commander of the land force with the object of capturing Norfolk. Before

● A Royal Marine of the period. (Royal Marines Museum, Portsmouth)

Warren arrived on June 19, Cockburn sensibly surveyed Crany Island whose batteries formed Norfolk's main defence. The trusted, indefatigable Lieutenant Westphal discovered a shoal running far out from the island. A landing here would inevitably ground the assault boats some distance from the shore; the attack required careful planning.

Cockburn submitted his findings to Warren and offered to co-ordinate the attack, but was turned down on the score that all plans had been completed before arrival, and that Captain Pechell of the *San Domingo* would have command. It was left for Cockburn to transfer his flag from *Marlborough* to the frigate *Barrossa* where he would at least be able to sail close enough to engage Crany Island's defences.

The attack took place on June 22 and was disastrous. The 102nd Regiment, mainly French prisoners recruited in England and known as Canadian Chasseurs, together with a battalion of marines were embarked in the boats to attack Crany Island. With no opportunity to rehearse and with too many contradictory orders, the boats grounded on the shoal under heavy gunfire. Those boats which had not been sunk retreated as best they could to their ships where the troops were re-embarked, but casualties had been heavy. Warren, in favouring his own captain with command, had erred badly on this, the first occasion, when an expeditionary force might have made a real impact on the course of this unfortunate war.

As though to show how it should be done, Beckwith and his troops embarked in the boats again on June 25, but this time under Cockburn's immediate command. They landed in good order a short distance to the westward of Hampton before daylight. Cockburn employed his now familiar and successful technique; the launches and rocketboats engaged the batteries while the troops marched towards the enemy. Hampton was carried but after keeping possession for ten days and obtaining the requisite supplies for the squadron, the batteries and ordnance were destroyed and the troops re-embarked. A subsequent court of enquiry investigated the disgraceful conduct of the Canadian Chasseurs who shamed British arms by plundering and killing a number of their captives. They were returned to Bermuda and never employed again.

Clearly if the British squadron was to continue in the Chesapeake, an island base would be necessary to serve as a rendezvous for prizes and provide a fortified refuge for slaves. Cockburn undertook surveys of Watts, Tangier and Smith Islands and corrected existing charts. He reported to Warren, 'there are few inhabitants on each island; they are very poor and living in much wretchedness and did not attempt resistance nor make the slightest difficulty about our people landing; nothing was taken from them without being paid for to its fullest value. Water is plentiful and anchorages are good'.[14]

The *Sceptre*, a 3rd rate of 74 guns, arrived in Hampton Roads for the express purpose of bearing the flag of Rear-Admiral Cockburn who shifted over to her, taking all his officers with him. A few days later on July 2 the *Sceptre*, in company with the troopships *Romulus*, *Fox* and *Nemesis*, in which about 500 of the 102nd Regiment under Lieutenant-Colonel Napier were embarked, sailed for Ocracoke Inlet, North Carolina, a valuable entry point for American ships hoping to reach Norfolk by inland navigation. On the passage south several vessels were captured, the small force arriving at the entrance to the inlet on the night of the 12th.

Lieutenants Westphal and Scott were despatched with a division of boats without delay to attack the armed vessels lying in the anchorage. Subsequently, Scott gave his own account, 'the passage was so intricate that we failed in discovering it till daylight, and at the same time our approach was observed by the enemy. An 18-gun brig and a letter of marque schooner opened their fire upon us but Westphal dashed on to board the brig. The resolution of the commander and his crew failed them; they cut their cable and submitted, after giving us the contents of her great-guns and small arms. The fate of the brig – the *Anaconda* – decided the schooner to haul down her colours. The former was, in outward appearance, a perfect model of beauty, and might have answered to the description of the *Water Witch* so admirably depicted by Cooper. She was near 400 tons burden, belonging to New York. The schooner – the *Atlas*, was a Philadelphia clipper mounting ten guns, and 250 tons . . . The troops in the meantime were disembarked; they took possession of Portsmouth and Ocracoke without any opposition, and, having paid for the supplies received, were re-embarked. On the 16th we took our departure with our prizes for the Chesapeake, and rejoined the commander-in-chief, three days afterwards, in the Potomac River.'[15]

Cockburn had been determined there should be no recurrence of the behaviour shown by the Canadian Chasseurs at Hampton. Before the start of the Ocracoke operation he left no doubt that offences would be severely punished. 'I command and direct all the officers and men under their respective commands on no account whatever to take from the individuals they may meet with, or the places they may visit, the smallest article of any description, nor on any pretence to separate from the officers, the boats, divisions, or stations in which they may be placed; and the officers in particular, are hereby required to use their utmost exertions to secure a due obedience to the spirit and intention of this order, and wherever they may find any person infringing it, they are hereby authorised to secure him or them as prisoners, it being the anxious wish of the Rear-Admiral to ensure the public notice and consequent punishment of whatever individual in HM Service shall so swerve from and forget his duty as to infringe herein.'

At the beginning of August the squadron moved up towards Kent Island, the largest in the Chesapeake, off the eastern shore. *Sceptre* and *Barrossa* anchored off the south end of the island, well ahead of the rest of the squadron. After taking soundings Cockburn decided to act ahead of the main body of troops under General Beckwith. His familiarity with the Chesapeake gave him the ability to assess any military situation, and the risks involved, with considerable accuracy. His action, therefore, was not so high-handed as might be thought, and in any case he had with him his trusted Royal Marines who were equally proficient afloat and ashore. The boats pulled in between island and mainland, cutting off communication between them. The Americans were thereby prevented from throwing in reinforcements and quiet possession was taken of the area.

Throughout the Chesapeake campaign thus far the Royal Marines had set a splendid example. Perhaps it was because of his additional rank of colonel in the corps that Cockburn held a special affection for them. On August 9, he wrote, 'the steadiness, zeal and integrity with which the Royal Marines under their commander Captain Dymock, have acted, during recent operations, has been observed by me and afforded me the highest possible gratification. I request Captain Dymock will assure the officers and men of the great credit which they must ever draw to themselves and their country by such behaviour and by their exemplary conduct which I shall not fail to report to the commander-in-chief'.

The force made Kent Island their headquarters for three weeks, sending expeditions to the surrounding countryside. One such was undertaken up the adjacent St Michael's River where an American force was prepared for the attack by ships' boats under Lieutenant Polkinghorne, first lieutenant of the *San Domingo*, but the destruction of a battery of six 12-pounder guns was successfully achieved before the boats returned.

As before, Cockburn dealt severely with looting, although among his men such cases were rare. Lieutenant Scott relates one incident of an unusual nature illustrating Cockburn's outstanding humanity. 'There was one poor American who lived at the north end of the island, whose house, standing alone, was attacked one night and

• George Cockburn as a Colonel, RM. (National Maritime Museum)

literally ransacked; the scoundrels had managed so well that we were never enabled to trace them. The poor fellow made his complaint, and I was despatched to the scene of spoilation. From several corresponding circumstances, no doubt existed that the plunderers belonged to us. The poor man had made his escape from the intruders. Every drawer and cupboard had been wrenched open, and their contents strewed about. I made my report. The injured man was sent for and questioned by the Rear-Admiral as to the amount of his loss. Jonathan guessed it could not be less than 350 dollars; that sum was immediately paid over to him from the private purse of the Rear-Admiral. This was only one of numerous instances of similar generosity by the man for whose head the Americans had offered a reward.'[16]

The squadron returned to Lynnhaven Bay on September 2. What was generally known as the 'sickly season' had arrived in the Chesapeake. The year 1813 had been one of unceasing activity for Cockburn's men; provisions had been erratic – there were never enough green vegetables available so scurvy made an occasional appearance. Now fever had broken out and was becoming progressively worse.

Warren decided to return to Halifax with the prizes so that Cockburn could go to Bermuda for a well earned break. The *Sceptre* sailed on September 6, arriving Bermuda on the 24th for a much needed refit.

There Cockburn stayed for the remainder of the year as the senior naval officer. The resident naval officer, Commodore Evans, who had responsibility for the dockyard, welcomed Cockburn's help in dealing with administrative problems. For example, Cockburn was disturbed by the primitive facilities for men requiring hospitalisation; patients were sent to an insanitary hulk called the *Goree* in an insalubrious area full of liquor shops. He promptly recommended the building of a new hospital on Tatham's Island.

During his absence from the Chesapeake, the command there devolved upon Captain Barrie of the *Dragon*, who kept Cockburn regularly informed. As a severe winter had set in no major event took place during this interval.

CHAPTER TWELVE

Scourge of the Chesapeake 1814

B Y THE BEGINNING OF 1814 Britain and her allies were on the borders of France for the first time since 1793. Russia, Austria, and Prussia were pressing from the east while Wellington's Peninsular veterans had all but driven the French armies from Spain. If the tides of war were rolling back in Europe nothing had come from the peace commission set up to resolve the Anglo-American conflict. The Czar's mediation had failed because Britain distrusted a third party's ability to settle maritime rights; on the other hand Britain was anxious that America should strengthen her negotiating team to accelerate agreed terms.

The new year opened with a letter to Cockburn from James Monroe, American Secretary of State. 'By a letter from His Britannic Majesty's Secretary of State for Foreign Affairs of November 4, 1813, I was informed that the Admiral commanding the British squadron on this coast would be directed to give the necessary protection to any persons proceeding to Europe, for the purpose of entering into a negotiation with the British government in consequence of the overture made to the President in that communication. The President having accepted the overture, and appointed Henry Clay and Jonathan Russell, Esqs, Ministers Extraordinary to repair to Gothenburg, to give it effect, I have to request that you will have the goodness to grant a passport to them, the Gentlemen, of their families and Attendants, as likewise for the vessel in which they sail. The corvette *John Adams*, at the port of New York, is appointed for this service.'[1] Cockburn replied without delay saying that although he had received no instructions from his own government, he did not hesitate in acceding to the request and granting the requisite passport.

Much as Britain wished to end the quarrel with America, she had no intention of waging the war any less vigorously. Instructions were renewed for a strict blockade to be enforced along the American seaboard, now made easier by the release of warships from the European theatre.

Bermuda saw the old year out with a magnificent ball given by Cockburn on the *Sceptre*'s departure. She sailed on January 3 and within a week encountered one of those sudden storms so common to the American coast at this period of the year. It was touch and go whether the *Sceptre* foundered; she began to take in water and the pumps were kept working continuously; the bread room flooded and 2,500lbs of bread jettisoned. On the fourth day, when things were at their worst, the gale began to abate. Cockburn duly reported to Warren how serious it had been, '. . . the seams all opened and the clothes and bedding of every officer and man in the ship were drenched with wet'. He referred to the ship's past record which showed the *Sceptre* to be a rogue in a seaway – she nearly foundered off Capetown in 1808 – and despite being largely rebuilt at Chatham, she had not improved; he intended transferring his flag to the *Albion*, 74, designed and built by Sir Robert Seppings, the Surveyor of the Navy, who had introduced a circular bow strengthening the ship's frame and giving added protection to the crew against raking fire from ahead. Small wonder that when Cockburn found the *Albion* lying off New London, Connecticut on his arrival there on January 29, he decided to transfer without delay, taking with him Captain Ross, for whom he had now developed a high regard, and all the key officers including Lieutenant Scott, shortly to become his aide-de-camp. Those officers joining the *Sceptre* in exchange had the unenviable task of sailing a lame duck back to Bermuda where she retired from the American war.

Cockburn's interest in New London stemmed from the presence of an American squadron there under Commander Decatur. Undertaking the blockade was his old shipmate Thomas Masterman Hardy, now captain of the line-of-battleship *Ramillies*. Cockburn knew that the blockade could be in no better hands despite the bitterly cold nights when the temperature fell to 10° below zero. Ships' boats rowing off the mouth of the river to maintain watch had a particularly gruelling time, with frostbite being common among the crews.

Decatur, with his local knowledge, was fully aware of the climatic peculiarities along this coast in winter; he knew that heavy rainfall frequently preceded severe and sudden frosts, and that he should make his bid to escape when he judged the sails of the British ships would be frozen so hard as to prevent their being spread. Although his timing was good he was not to know that the *Ramillies* and others had taken the precaution of covering their sails with white painted cloths to protect them from the wet and subsequent freezing. That was typical of Hardy's attention to detail, and meant that they were ready for Decatur with sails hoisted and anchors weighed when he attempted his break. Decatur had no recourse but to reverse course and take his frigates as high up the river as the tide would allow, where they remained inactive for the rest of the war.

The *Albion* sailed after Cockburn had made his dispositions for continuing the blockade along the coast; Hardy was given the onerous task of guarding the busy port of New York. En route south to re-activate the war in Chesapeake, Cockburn called, inter alia, at Block and Gardiner's islands, Sandy Hook, and the Delaware. At Block Island, he was visited by a Mr Gorton who presented him with a bill for the maintenance of an officer and 11 men who had been wrecked in their tender belonging to the *Albion* under her previous commanding officer. Although Cockburn could not himself validate the bill he despatched it to Captain Devonshire, now in the *Sceptre*, observing, 'the amount very much exceeds the normal cost of victualling, but as I conceive it to be just and necessary that it should be duly paid to ensure the same care and attention to any of our people who may meet with similar misfortune, I have to request you will take such measures as may appear equitable'.

At nearby Gardiner's Island he asked his ships to make no further demands upon the proprietor owing to the depletion of his cattle stocks which prevented him from keeping up his breeds. Further supplies, Cockburn said, depended entirely on Mr Gardiner informing them 'that he could spare such without distressing himself'.

On February 23, he was back in Lynnhaven Bay reporting to Warren (in Bermuda) that he now had a comprehensive understanding of the northern coastline situation and its demand on resources. This was important as Warren expected shortly to be relieved and in any transitional period Cockburn would take over. In the Chesapeake, the *Constellation* was still in her old berth in the Norfolk river protected by 22 gunboats, but as soon as the position allowed and with more warships at his disposal, he would take steps for 'the general annoyance of the enemy' as he expressed it.

So cold was it in March that operations could only cover blockading, intercepting and provisioning – especially with the abundant fresh water found at New Point Comfort. Cockburn's policy always had been to keep his men fully employed on the principle that idleness only fomented trouble; the punishment record of the *Albion* substantiated the truth of this in the uneventful and frigid months of February and March, with much drunkenness and mutinous behaviour. Spring, not far away now, would free his squadron to play the all-out role his nature demanded. On April 1 he learned of his promotion to Rear-Admiral of the White which was appropriately saluted by his ships. With those that could be spared, led by the *Dragon*, under the reliable Captain Barrie's command, Cockburn sailed again up the Chesapeake Bay to survey Tangier and Watts islands, sounding the channels between them and mainland, and buoying the shoals. Cockburn needed to confirm that Tangier Island was the most suitable operational base if activity was to be stepped up.

It provided an excellent anchorage for assembling prizes; and should yet more slaves desert then Tangier could act as their refuge where a regiment of black recruits might even be created.

For this the island would have to be fortified and Lieutenant Fenwick of the Royal Engineers started work on an advance redoubt and guardhouse. The fascines and stakes for these came mainly from the adjoining well-wooded Watts Island, but the fortuitous capture of a ship loaded with timber and shingles also helped.

Any long term plan for Tangier Island would require the commander-in-chief's approval so Cockburn wrote emphasising its strategic views of both sides of the Chesapeake and the entrance to the Potomac River coupled with a plentiful supply of fish and oysters. The reply bore the signature of Vice-Admiral Sir Alexander Cochrane who had relieved Warren in April, another whose strength lay in administration. Cochrane's terms of reference were wide to match his expected force which he was to use, 'in such operations as may be found best calculated for the advantage of HM Service and the annoyance of the enemy'. Although he had served but briefly in American waters, Cochrane had developed an almost manic hatred of all things American – referring to them contemptuously as 'spaniels', and insisting they needed a 'good drubbing'. But he had few ideas about how to conduct the war effectively.

Cockburn received Cochrane's answer on Tangier Island early in May with a rodomontade on the enemy. 'You are at perfect liberty as soon as you can muster a sufficient force, to act with the utmost hostility against the shores of the United States. Their government authorise and direct a most destructive war to be carried on against our commerce and we have no means of retaliating but on shore where they must be made to feel in their property what our merchants do in having their ships destroyed, and thereby be taught to know that they are at the mercy of an invading foe. This is now the more necessary in order to draw off their attention from Canada where, I am told, they are sending their whole military force. Their sea port towns laid in ashes and the country invaded will be some sort of retaliation for their savage conduct in Canada where they have destroyed our towns in the most inclement occasion of the year. It is therefore but just that retaliation be made near to the seat of government from whence these orders are enacted. You may depend upon my most cordial support in whatever you undertake against the enemy . . . Whenever the Americans may drive down cattle or other stock with the intention of drawing our people into ambush to fire upon them, you will take the earliest opportunity of retaliating upon them by the destruction and laying waste of whatever property may be near to the spot where the ambush was laid.'[2]

Cochrane postulated a magazine, provision store and hospital for Tangier as a matter for further discussion. Of more immediate moment was the raising of volunteers among the blacks to garrison the island. These would be formed into a Colonial Corps with the pay and clothing of Royal Marines, and a bounty of 20 dollars for each man. Ammunition, arms, and a uniform red jacket – 'red as their gay appearance may act as an inducement to others to come off' – would be supplied. Of the remaining negroes only those prepared to work in the naval yard should be sent to Bermuda and the residue to Halifax.

On paper it seemed plain sailing, but the protection of negro slaves posed problems not so much from putting them into uniform, but in the proclamation offering them the alternative of becoming free settlers in British colonies. Such a lure would bring in the numbers but for the wrong reasons. Cockburn could not encourage the idea of promising general freedom under British rule which he knew would be difficult to honour immediately let alone sustain indefinitely. However, with the proclamation already issued, the damage was largely done.

Increasing numbers of slaves with their women and children now fled from their masters expecting a utopia which could never materialise. Some, realising their bad exchange, wished to return to their owners; Cockburn allowed visits by the militia to take back those so inclined until the exchange became too difficult to control. Cockburn told Lieutenant General Gayle of the 61st Regiment, Matthews County militia, that it had to stop. Feeding them was never easy as, at times, even Cockburn's seamen were on short rations, and the negroes' diet of mealies, rice and fish had to be obtained as extra items. Their transportation to Bermuda also presented an unwelcome problem as ships could rarely be spared. In May Cockburn despatched the transport *Lord Collingwood* with refugees but had to detail a precious frigate as escort because 'their fate would be very sad indeed if they fell again accidentally into the hands of their old masters,' as he expressed it.

The small number which by the end of May had been specially trained and recruited into the Colonial Marines, performed quite admirably in their sorties from Tangier Island. They played a valuable part in a successful boat attack up the Pungoteague River in eastern Virginia. Captain Ross of the *Albion*, who commanded the expedition, reported, 'the newly raised black corps – the Colonial Marines – gave a most excellent specimen of what they are likely to be. Their conduct was marked by great spirit and vivacity, and perfect obedience'. They were also proving their worth as skirmishers, and made even deep penetration of the thick woods possible for landing parties.

As the year wore on, the sheer weight of numbers sent to Bermuda caused Commodore Evans, the resident naval officer, to write at length on the immense difficulties he faced in integrating them. Cockburn could offer no ready solution as his reply explains, but his dislike of Cochrane's proclamation which had so obviously backfired, is evident. 'With reference to the black emigrants from America lately arrived at Bermuda, in which you point out the inconveniences of this procedure, I consider it right to enclose the commander-in-chief's proclamation and orders which have been issued to encourage the people of any and every description to resort to our protection from the United States. From this you will observe that captains and commanders of ships are not only obliged to receive all persons so choosing to avail themselves of our protection, but are also enjoined to forward and facilitate as much as possible, their coming to us with no discrimination whatever as to age, sex and abilities of these persons. The commander-in-chief's proclamation having been widely diffused with much pains throughout all the counties bordering the American shores, we must keep faith in offering asylum until a change of policy is decided upon. The only question is how to dispose of these people under the colonial laws at Bermuda for Coloured People, and the inconvenience likely to arise from accumulating useless numbers. Some time back, the commander-in-chief directed me to send all refugees to Halifax but as there is now no direct communication with that place, there is no alternative but to send them to Bermuda despite your problems. At the same time, you should take every opportunity to send on refugees to Halifax where the laws are sufficiently liberal to enable Coloured People to earn their own maintenance by honest labour . . .' He ended the letter on a more optimistic note by saying how gratified he was to have relieved so many fellow creatures from slavery, and in having established from amongst them at little or no expense, a most efficient and useful corps which was now about 400 strong and constantly employed.

If the black colonials had a fault, it was their tendency to fall asleep at their posts. Cockburn devised his own punishment – lenient yet effective – of making defaulters wear their jackets inside out, and of stopping their grog.

The exchange of prisoners on anything like an equitable basis became a major issue by the middle of 1814. Thomas Barclay, the British Consul in New York, had the unenviable task of negotiating with his opposite numbers – General Mason, the Commissioner General for Prisoners in Washington, and John Skinner, the United States political agent. Barclay was everyone's whipping boy, his house in Haarlem frequently the target of angry mobs reacting to the 'illegal' seizure of American ships and their crews. Nor was he popular with the British naval command who considered him weak and vacillating.

In March, Barclay had informed Cockburn that he had been obliged to move his office to Bladensburg, (then a village near Washington), by order of the President on the score of easier communication. 'By my removal to this retired wretched village,' he said, 'I am totally deprived of doing my duty to the British prisoners.'[3] Stressing the one-sided aspect of the exchange of prisoners, he asked Cockburn to ensure that American prisoners were not landed from HM ships without an equivalent of British prisoners first being received. Captains of British ships had been lax in their interpretation of an enemy prisoner of war: on isolated duty it was far easier to assess a captured crew as non-combattant and land the men rather than have the inconvenience of guarding, feeding and transporting them.

Cockburn gave the necessary orders; but even he had been guilty – on strictly compassionate grounds – of returning schooners to their owners in circumstances where their retention would have caused great distress. The xenophobe Cochrane, unable to resist the opportunity to back up any tough line, also wrote to Barclay saying that he saw no reason for any further liberality towards American prisoners of war, and that all would be retained until the balance, heavily in favour of America, had been equalised. In the meantime he had made arrangements for 400 to be sent to England in the *Goliath*.

In June the celebrated case of Captain Jaboe of the American militia erupted.[4] *Albion*'s launch had been sent inshore under a flag of truce to obtain water and provisions for which payment was to be tendered. The lieutenant in charge was met on arrival by a colonel and other officers of the militia who understandably refused the request. The occasion was too much for Captain Jaboe who was among their number. With his musket poised against the defence-less lieutenant, he poured out a stream of offensive invective which, whatever the justification, was an insult to the etiquette observed under flags of truce. Jaboe's threat to the lieutenant to hang him up as a scarecrow, knowing full well that the lieutenant could not deliver a riposte, caused the latter to enquire on his return onboard whether Jaboe was known to any of the runaway slaves in the ship. 'Cappen Jaboe, him my massa, saar,' replied a young negro. Cockburn, having had the event reported to him, gave permission for the lieutenant that same evening to take a party of 20 Royal Marines and some colonials to attempt Jaboe's capture on the information provided. They found him in a house some eight miles from their landing place close to a militia encampment. Jaboe was discovered in his bedroom 'shivering in his shirt', in the lieutenant's words. Married but three days, his wife was in the bridal bed beside him; but the normally kind-hearted lieutenant, now without compassion, seized Jaboe together with his farm overseer and bundled them off, hotly pursued by the militia.

Jaboe was well looked after onboard the *Albion* and given the same privileges as the ship's officers but, according to Lieutenant

Scott, behaved cravenly in marked contrast to his previous swagger and insulting language. Cockburn received a special plea from General Mason at Washington, pointing out that Jaboe was not a regular soldier and that 'his wife has been affected by the circumstances of his separation in a manner peculiarly distressing'. Cockburn, normally so gallant whenever he could allay a lady's distress, remained unmoved. He informed Mason that he could not treat Captain Jaboe as a non-combatant but would release the overseer on parole 'in view of the special circumstances in which Mrs Jaboe is left'. Jaboe was sent to England.

Desertion under Cockburn's flag was rare despite the tempting ease with which it could be achieved when men were landed in open country. Towards the end of June when his resources were particularly overstretched, and daily boat expeditions provided suitable opportunities, an outbreak did occur. Cockburn acted swiftly. On June 21, he issued the following order, 'whereas Midshipman H Dickson belonging to HMS *Albion* did yesterday grossly neglect his duty by quitting the party of men sent under his charge to Watts Island on duty whereby to the disgrace of HM Service, eleven of the seamen of his party, some of them being drunk, were permitted to desert to the enemy. I do hereby direct that the said midshipman be disrated and borne as "ordinary", and that he be not permitted any longer to do the duty of a petty officer, and that this order respecting him may be made public throughout the ship'. The next day, the ship's log records that the squadron boats came alongside the *Albion* to witness the public flogging of Robert Waddle, seaman, who received 100 lashes for attempting to desert. Cockburn cautioned his men against desertion, and the situation improved.

All signs now pointed to the war in the Chesapeake intensifying. Since Napoleon's abdication in the spring large British forces had been released for employment elsewhere, and there was every prospect that a considerable proportion of them would be allocated to Cochrane. A new battalion of Royal Marines along with a company of marine artillery, formed at Portsmouth in March, was on its way in the troopships *Regulus*, *Melpomene* and *Brune*; after some training in Bermuda, they would be sent to Cockburn who, wearing his other hat as Colonel, Royal Marines, eagerly awaited their arrival. With a body of several hundred of highly disciplined 'sea soldiers' there was no limit to what could be achieved.

Even with the small squadron currently available life had been anything but quiescent. Admittedly, progress at Tangier Island – or Fort Albion as he liked to call it – had been slow owing to the constant separation of his ships, but he was still able to report to Cochrane the seizure of more than a million dollars worth of enemy shipping and stores in various forays, and all in a short compass.

Unable to protect the Bay's inhabitants, the American government decided to fit out some gunboats at Baltimore and place them under Commodore Joshua Barney. The flotilla consisted of the *Scorpion*, Barney's own vessel mounting eight carronades and a heavy long gun upon a traversing carriage, and 19 gunboats, each with a long gun in the bow and another in the stern, with crews of 40 to 60 men, depending on the size of gun carried.

Barney sailed from Baltimore at the end of May intending to join similar flotillas at Norfolk and in the Potomac. Then, with every chance of releasing the *Constellation* from blockade, a *tour de force* might be possible against Cockburn before reinforcements could arrive. The plan depended on Barney being able to escape the British watch over the waters between Tangier Island and Smith's Point on the southern side of the Potomac. He was out of luck for on June 1 he met the British schooner *St Lawrence* and a number of ships' boats under the command of Captain Barrie – that dependable officer who stood so high in Cockburn's estimation. Captain Barrie having left his own ship, the *Dragon*, the previous evening to reconnoitre to the north, was surprised to meet so unexpectedly the Baltimore flotilla of 25 sail including the lateen-rigged gunboats and a few sloops and schooners. Using his boats as a decoy, Barrie drew Barney ever nearer to the powerful *Dragon*, which by now had made sail. Commodore Barney had no option but to shelter in the River Patuxent nearby where a lengthy blockade started – from which, in fact, his flotilla never escaped. Barney was a well-known Baltimore Privateersman who had served as a Commodore in the French navy during the 1790s and in the American revolution.

Cockburn was delighted with the news and wrote Barrie, 'I am sorry the *Dragon* was not able to get up with the Baltimore flotilla before they housed themselves in the Patuxent. It is, however, of all the rivers in the Chesapeake, the best to have them in. I only hope you will be able to keep them there till we are strong enough to follow them up it with small craft'.[5] Barrie, of course, could not risk the 74-gun *Dragon* in the shallow waters of the Patuxent, but with the aid of the *Loire* and the *Jaseur*, smaller vessels which had now joined him, he was able to press Barney into St Leonard's Creek higher up river.

Many attempts were made to entice Barney from his well defended anchorage but with no success; but Barrie quickly realised that the Patuxent's fertile and undefended shores allowed for a diversion which might induce Barney to come to his compatriots' aid. Various landings made with 150 Royal and 30 colonial marines created havoc. Vast quantities of tobacco were taken and opposition easily overcome, but Barney ignored the bait.

Thinking that an invasion higher up the river might have the desired effect Barrie pressed on in the boats as high as Benedict where, in the middle of June, he found the town deserted – stocks of muskets and other military equipment suggesting a hasty retreat. Still not content, he went even higher to Marlborough whence he reported to Cockburn, 'Marlborough is near the seat of government. I thought an attack on this town would be a sad annoyance to the enemy and oblige the regulars and militia to try their strength with us, but I was deceived as both the militia and the inhabitants made off to the woods and we were allowed to take quiet possession of a town admirably situated for defence. Here we passed the night without molestation *though only 18 miles from Washington*'.[6]

The blockade of Barney's flotilla and the depredations of Barrie's squadron on the banks of the Patuxent disquietened Washington. Commodore Barney was ordered to destroy his flotilla, the Americans hoping that the British would then withdraw from their position so near the capital. The order was suspended only when an American colonel offered to drive the two British frigates from the mouth of St Leonard's Creek with artillery established on a ridge commanding the river. On June 26, a simultaneous attack by the American gunboats and the battery forced the *Loire* and *Narcissus* to retreat to Point Patience. The American flotilla moved higher up the Patuxent with the loss of one gunboat.

In early July Cockburn decided to assess the Patuxent situation himself. He reported to Cochrane that Tangier Island was secure enough to repel any enemy force mounted against it; the *Jaseur* would continue its guard with instructions that the inhabitants were to be under the captain's immediate protection and were not to be imposed upon or unkindly treated. Barney's flotilla was now so high up the Patuxent, he believed, that it no longer provided any threat;

its destruction could await the arrival of supporting land forces.

Scott who, as the admiral's aide-de-camp, knew Cockburn's inner thoughts better than most, mentioned at this time that, 'the rear-admiral had, from the commencement of his operations, always fixed an eye of peculiar interest upon Washington. It had been the concentrated object of his thoughts and actions; every measure he adopted was more or less remotely connected, conceived, and carried into execution, as affording preliminary steps to the final accomplishment of the grand ultimatum of his exertions'.

The enthusiasm with which ships' captains acted suggested that they, too, were privy to the plan formulating in Cockburn's mind. Captain Nourse, of the *Severn* – a fine frigate recently arrived – reported the consternation now existing in Calvert and St Mary's counties adjacent to the Patuxent, both virtually abandoned. 'In one of our expeditions an American told us he guessed we were the advance guard of a considerable force intended to land at Benedict and march to Washington. I wish with all my heart that the force was arrived, for Jonathan I believe is so confounded that he does not know when or where to look for us. . . It would require but little force to burn Washington and I hope soon to put the first torch to it myself. Horses may be procured in abundance.'

The *Severn*, drawing more water than ships previously making the attempt, gained Benedict without difficulty, her sailing master producing a river plan destined to be of the utmost value. Nourse found these higher parts of the Patuxent as deserted and defenceless as the lower reaches.

July 15 was a red letter day for Cockburn. Apart from the *Loire* and the *St Lawrence* which rejoined him with 14 prizes, it marked the arrival of the three troopships *Regulus*, *Melpomene* and *Brune*,[7] with the battalion of Royal Marines, now fully trained and raring for action. Other escorts arrived too – the *Asia*, 3rd rate, *Aetna*, a bomb vessel, and two sloops the *Thistle* and the *Manly*. With them came the news that they were being followed by Admiral Cochrane with 20,000 men.

Cockburn was confident that his trusted Royal Marines could cause mayhem everywhere; with additional troops of the strength forecast there was no limit to what could be achieved. Almost to the point of embarrassment the black refugees, too, had been streaming in although their training to fit them into the swelling colonial marine corps, of course, would take time. This led to a clever ruse, believed to have been invented by Commodore Barney, for selected

Americans to impersonate negroes by blacking their faces and hands to surprise any boat sent to fetch them, but it was never successful.

Early in July, Cochrane asked Cockburn for his views on operational possibilities. While the *Albion* lay anchored off Jerome Point he drafted a comprehensive reply. 'July 17 1814. I consider the town of Benedict in the Patuxent to offer us advantages for (landing) beyond any other spot within the United States. It is, I am informed, only 44 or 45 miles from Washington, and there is a high road between the two places which tho' hilly is good. It passes through Piscataway and is no nearer to Fort Washington than four miles, which fortification is 16 miles below the city of Washington and is the only one the army would have to pass. I most firmly believe therefore, that within 48 hours after the arrival in the Potomac of such a force as you expect, the city of Washington might be possessed without difficulty or opposition of any kind . . . The ships of the fleet would cover a landing at Benedict; the safety of the ships and the smoothness of the water in the river would render us entirely independent of the weather, an object of considerable importance when we recollect how fast the season is advancing . . . The army on its arrival would be sure of good quarters in Benedict, and a rich country around it to afford the necessary immediate supplies, and as many horses as might be wanted to transport cannon etc, which advantages might certainly *now* be obtained without the slightest opposition or requiring any sacrifice from us whatever, and as I have quitted the Patuxent and, on this account, do not intend again to visit it until you arrive with the army, or I hear further from you, I believe everything will remain till then in the neighbourhood of that river exactly as I have now left it. The facility and rapidity with which an army by landing at Benedict might possess itself of the Capitol, always so great a blow to the government of a country, as well on account of the Resources, the Documents and Records the invading army is almost sure to obtain thereby, must strongly urge the propriety of the plan and, the more particularly as the other places you have mentioned will be more likely to fall after the occupation of Washington than that city would be after their capture. Annapolis is tolerably well fortified and is the spot from whence the American government has always felt Washington to be threatened if at all. It is natural therefore, to suppose precautions have been taken to frustrate and impede our advance in that direction; add to which, Annapolis being fortified, a station for troops, and not to be approached by our larger ships on account of the shallowness of the water, it is probable the occupation of it might cost us some little time, which would of course be taken advantage of by the enemy to draw together all the force at his command for the defence of Washington, and enable the Heads of Departments there to remove whatever they may wish. Baltimore is likewise extremely difficult of access to us from sea; we cannot in ships drawing above 16 feet approach nearer even to the mouth of the Patapsco than seven or eight miles, and Baltimore is situated 12 miles up it having an extensive population mostly armed, and a fort for its protection about a mile advanced from it on a projecting point where the river is so narrow as to admit of people conversing across it, and this fort I am given to understand is a work which has been completed by French engineers with considerable pains and at much expense, and is therefore of a description only to be regularly approached, and would consequently require time to reduce which I conceive it will be judged important not to lose in striking our first blows. But both Annapolis and Baltimore are to be taken without difficulty from the land side; that is coming down upon them from the Washington road, the former being I think commanded by the Heights behind it, and Baltimore having no defence whatever in its rear, and from the moment of your arrival in the Chesapeake let the plan adopted be what it may, a small force detached to the Susquehanna will always prevent or impede the arrival of considerable reinforcements or assistance from the Eastern States. If Philadelphia is of greater importance than the places just mentioned, I should deem the landing at Elkton the most advisable mode of approaching it as the attack would thereby be masked till the army would be actually landed and on its march on the road from Elkton to Wilmington (above Newcastle), which is short and good, and does not offer difficulties or opposition of any kind. This movement need not prevent such ships as may be judged requisite, from proceeding up the Delaware to co-operate with the army as circumstances may require . . . if Washington (as I strongly recommend), be deemed worthy of our first efforts, although our main force should be landed in the Patuxent, yet a tolerably good division should at the same time be sent up the Potomac with bomb ships etc, to distract and divide the enemy, amuse Fort Washington if it does not reduce it, and will probably offer other advantages without any counterbalancing inconvenience as the communication between the Grand Army and this division will be easy and immediate in consequence of the very

176

small space between the Potomac and Patuxent. American guides will not be difficult to obtain when we have force to protect them and money to pay them. I have already one who has been ill-treated in his own country and seems extremely anxious to be revenged . . . I have therefore, now put him on regular pay according to the tenor of your directions, he being both a pilot for the rivers and a guide for the roads in this neighbourhood. Norfolk seems to be the only place where the Americans expect a serious attack; that place has been considerably strengthened of late, and I am informed eight or ten thousand men are collected there. It is not however, in my opinion worthy of primary notice, but you may deem it perhaps, Sir, worthy of attending to after others of greater importance have been disposed of.'[8]

On July 4 President Madison had faced up to the deteriorating situation so close to his capital by demanding of Congress an instant increase in the recruitment of men to defend their homeland, and to make arms available to them. Although late in the day, Virginia, and the shores of the Potomac River in particular, were readied to meet any British onslaught.

Since the river was strategically important in an attack on Washington, Cockburn decided that with the strong naval brigade and Royal Marine battalion at his disposal, this was the time to strike. Thus the *Albion*, accompanied by two troopships and other vessels, dropped down the Patuxent on July 17, leaving the *Severn* and the troopship *Brune* to continue blockading Barney's gunboats. Cockburn announced his intention of exploring the passage past the Potomac's Kettlebottoms shoals whose use was vital in any future operations; he would also destroy military stores wherever found. By this strategem he hoped to allay American suspicions of a more general attack and encourage the belief that no serious or permanent landing was contemplated.

From July 18 until August 12 Cockburn swept through the various Maryland and Virginia tidewater communities inside the Potomac: Leonardstown, Nominy Ferry, St Clement's Creek, the Machodic River, Wicomico River, Hamburgh and Chaptico . . . all were visited with similar results. Many prizes were taken and opposition was light. At Nominy the discovery of a bottle of poisoned whisky with glasses all set out as inviting Cockburn's men to slake their thirst, was considered a diabolical act well outside the accepted rules of warfare. On hearing of it, General Hungerford of the Virginia militia ordered a court of enquiry, but the conclusion convinced no one as there had been similar incidents previously.

On July 29, while at Wicomico, Cockburn wrote to Captain Skene of the *Asia* on guard duty at Lynnhaven Bay. 'I am now as high up the Potomac as I intend going this time, indeed as high up I believe, as a line of battleship can go. I shall steer again downwards as the whole country is now alarmed, and they are I daresay, beginning to feel uneasy at Washington, which for the present I would rather avoid occasioning.' As Cochrane was expected daily to arrive in the Chesapeake, it was important for Skene to be able to report to him the second in command's whereabouts and activities.

August 2 was a particularly successful day. Having discovered that large ships could navigate the passage through the Kettle-bottom shoals, Cockburn landed his men on the Virginia shore from the Yocomico River where they destroyed local ordnance stores. The American militia rallied on the heights at Kinsale and a hard-fought contest ensued. Cockburn reported the occasion in glowing terms. 'The penetrating with 500 men 10 miles into the enemy country at almost a run, and the skirmishing march back again surrounded by woods in the face of the whole collected militia of Virginia under Generals Hungerford and Taylor, added to the gallant manner in which the Heights of Kinsale were carried after such a march, will prove to you, Sir, how much the officers and men serving with me are entitled to my warmest praises.'

Cockburn's Potomac operations ended with two further visits – to the Coan River on August 7, and to St Mary's Creek on the 11th. Three days later, the *Tonnant* flying Sir Alexander Cochrane's flag, together with the frigate *Seahorse* and two transports, joined company; Cockburn wasted no time boarding the flagship hoping for Cochrane's approval of his cherished attack on Washington. The commander-in-chief's record of indecision suggested he would not find it easy. At least he could point to his activities over the past month during which, with only a battalion of marines, he had roamed wherever he liked. 'I express to you again the high opinion I entertain of the 2nd Battalion, Royal Marines, and of their gallantry and discipline . . . Although our marches have at times been excessively long and necessarily much extended in the thick woods of the country, and though our re-embarkations have frequently taken place in the night, yet during the whole of the operations neither a marine nor a sailor has been reported missing,' he wrote.[9]

CHAPTER THIRTEEN

The Patuxent
1814

ABOARD COCHRANE'S FLAGSHIP, *Tonnant*, Cockburn's restless activities had become something of a legend. One 15-year-old midshipman was later to report, 'it is almost impossible to depict my boyish feelings and transport when I gazed for the first time in my life on the features of that undaunted seaman Rear-Admiral George Cockburn, with his sunburnt visage and his rusty gold-laced hat'.[1]

As Cockburn stepped onboard the *Tonnant* it was but natural that this, his first visit, should stimulate interest; if he was the centre of hero worship he did not notice it, for he had more pressing business on hand but disappointing news awaited him in Cochrane's great cabin. Aware that the army being sent in support had been reduced from the original 13,000 men, now he received details of the regiments due from Bermuda. These would be the 4th, 44th, and 85th, totalling 2,814 veterans of the Peninsular War who, having embarked directly at Bordeaux, had not even visited their homeland in the interval. They would be supplemented by 1,000 men of the 21st Regiment who had followed from the Mediterranean providing a force of only some 4,500 inclusive of Royal Marines and trained naval personnel.

The reduction in the force's size now caused Cochrane to be over-cautious, so that Cockburn had to be at his most persuasive to obtain approval for his cherished attack on Washington. Cochrane was not the only hurdle; also onboard the *Tonnant* was Major-General Robert Ross commanding the troops. He too, having been warned by Earl Bathurst – the Secretary of State for War and the Colonies – 'not to engage in any extended operation at a distance from the coast', was understandably reluctant to commit himself.

Ross had been battle-hardened in the Peninsular campaign and although a firm disciplinarian he was much respected by his men. He possessed two admirable qualities; he never risked his soldiers unnecessarily, and always led from the front no matter how over-exposed. The latter was, of course, one of Cockburn's fortes and the two men quickly established a rapport which augured well. The following day Cockburn took Ross ashore to allow him to sample the tidewater country and to demonstrate the ease with which a disciplined force could move without hindrance. The artifice worked and converted Ross to Cockburn's plan to enter the Patuxent River, and land the army at Benedict as a springboard for possible future operations. Cochrane agreed temporarily to forsake his earlier choice of a landing further north at Rhode Island but was not yet prepared to approve an outright attack on Washington as it was not his nature to rush fences. On the other hand, the need to destroy Barney's gunboats was a purely naval matter affording him every justification to support Cockburn in that particular endeavour.

With perfect timing the *Tonnant*, *Albion*, and escorts made their way down the Potomac. As they entered the Chesapeake during the evening of August 16, the trooping fleet from Bermuda under full sail approached. In command and flying his blue rear-admiral's flag at the mizen-mast of the battleship *Royal Oak*, was Admiral Malcolm,

● **(left) Major-General Robert Ross (National Army Museum) and (right) Vice-Admiral Sir Alexander Cochrane (RN Museum, Portsmouth)**

a genial man perfectly cast for this particular role. Observers ashore had watched the fleet's progress through the Capes at the entrance to the bay, past New Point Comfort, and then on to Smith's Point where it was joined by the dozen or so ships under Cochrane. The spread of the ships across the water and the late summer haze made their counting difficult, but shoreside estimates averaged 51. The proportion of transports to other ships in that armada could mean one thing only to the experienced eye . . . invasion! The best horsemen were selected to undertake the 70-mile journey to Washington, there to inform President Madison and his ministers. The surrounding country was still defenceless despite the new military district recently set up for the area by the President, so every moment counted if preparedness was to be improved.

The final British briefing took place early next morning aboard *Tonnant*. With the assistance of Captain Codrington, a veteran of Trafalgar and now captain of the fleet, Cochrane outlined his plan. To safeguard the troops ashore, should they be cut off from their transports in the Patuxent, a small squadron under Captain James Alexander Gordon in the frigate *Seahorse*, would destroy fortifications along the Potomac River and create a diversion as far as Alexandria. Following another of Cockburn's recommendations, the frigate *Menelaus*, commanded by Captain Sir Peter Parker and

• **(left) James Monroe, US Secretary of State and (right) Commodore Barney USN. (both illustrations from the Royal Marines Museum, Portsmouth)**

accompanied by two schooners, would sail up the Chesapeake above Baltimore and interrupt communications with Philadelphia and New York. Gordon and Parker, outstanding frigate captains, had dash and resourcefulness, the precise qualities required for their tasks.

An hour later with all in high key the assorted ships got under way. By 9.15 am, Gordon was already in the Potomac with a well-balanced force comprising the two frigates *Seahorse* and *Euryalus*, a rocket ship, four bomb vessels, and a despatch schooner, while at the same time the main fleet had started its imposing but slow progress up the Chesapeake. Cochrane and his ships were anchored off the Patuxent by sunset, where Parker in the *Menelaus* was detached to pursue his special assignment.

Mention has already been made of the Patuxent surveys carried out by Captain Nourse in the frigate *Severn* during July and August while Cockburn was detached in the Potomac. With his special knowledge of the intricate river system, Nourse was the obvious choice to lead the fleet towards Benedict starting at dawn on August 18. The journey can be followed on the adjoining plan of the Patuxent, a copy of Nourse's original survey.[2]

The fleet's entry into the river between Cedar and Drum Points, led by the *Severn*, has been described as resembling a peacetime regatta with ships tacking across each other as they fought an adverse wind and tide. The first navigational hazard to be overcome was at Point Patience, some seven miles into the river where the

- **Old plan of the River Patuxent (Charpentier, Lithographer, Portsmouth)**

REFERENCES

A **Point Patience steep to**
B **Sandy Point must be given a wide berth**
C **Steep to**
D **C is as far as the *Severn* can go above which the Channel is very narrow and intricate.**

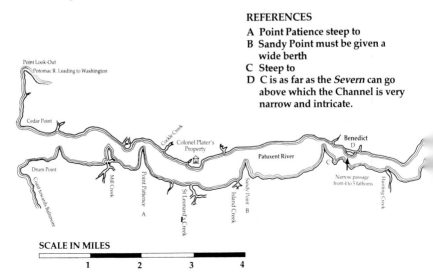

SCALE IN MILES

width was less than a mile. Here the tidal stream forced the fleet to anchor. The heavier ships with their considerable draught would find further progress difficult, so Cochrane wisely transferred the troops to the frigates and lighter vessels, shifting his flag to the frigate *Iphigenia*.

By afternoon with a flood tide under them, they passed St Leonard's Creek on the right bank where an unsuccessful attempt had been made to cut out Barney's flotilla. To their left was the well-known Colonel Plater's property, the target of earlier incursions. Here the large ships ended their journey. The lighter vessels reached Sandy Point to starboard, where Ross's assistant adjutant related his curious inpression of a fleet not sailing on water, but stalking through some primeval forest – so thick were the magnificent trees on both banks.

The narrow, steep-sided gap just before Benedict provided sea room for single file only, but by dusk the lead ships had anchored close to the town, the line extending ten miles down river. Progress so far had been uninterrupted and the British had seen little sign of human presence, despite the white cottages dotting the shore line.

The news of the British arrival at Benedict was known quickly in Washington whereupon the Secretary of the Navy ordered Barney to take his flotilla as high upstream as possible. Should the British approach he was to destroy his gunboats and help defend the capital. There were still doubts in the minds of many, including Armstrong, the Secretary of War, whether Washington was the target. He preferred to think that the move up the Patuxent was a feint for an attack on Baltimore. General Winder, in charge of the overall defences and a native of Baltimore, had different thoughts; Annapolis, which offered the British a base on the bay, was his choice.

The man whose views counted most, James Monroe, Secretary of State, held that Washington must be the prize above all others which the British sought. Besides being politically wise he had been, in his day, an oustanding cavalry colonel. He now decided to turn scout, select a few horsemen, and make for Benedict to find out for himself. Such positive action was rare among the American leaders at this moment of crisis, and Monroe's initiative was rewarded. He was able to keep in touch with British movements sufficiently long to be able to convince his colleagues that Washington was indeed the objective.

The landing of four regiments dispersed among so many troop-ships and transports, required considerable preplanning. Captain

Codrington's orders[3] give some idea of the detailed organisation required. The carrying capacity of the ships' boats varied; a launch would generally carry more men than a pinnace or barge, and they in turn would carry more than a cutter. Unopposed and in calm water the landings proceeded smoothly through the night of the 19th into the following morning.

After the men had been given time to rest and to gain their shore legs, they were assembled in the afternoon of the 20th in three divisions to start their march north towards Nottingham, about 20 miles upstream. Ross led the column along a road parallel to the Patuxent, while Cockburn kept pace up river with his miniature fleet; tenders, armed boats, and other craft crammed with seamen and Royal Marines – men who from repeated experience were by now expertly trained in this specialised type of river warfare. For his part, Ross wisely deployed skirmishers far ahead of his main body to provide ample warning of attack – a necessary technique recommended by Cockburn; but it was still rough progress for the troops despite the absence of serious opposition. The stifling heat, thick uniform clothing and heavy packs took toll of men who had spent weeks of inactivity on a sea voyage. After six miles' heavy going Ross decided they had had enough for one day and decided to camp for the night. A violent thunderstorm at midnight accompanied by torrential rain did little to improve their comfort, and at dawn on the 21st they were glad to be on their way again. At about five in the afternoon they marched into Nottingham to find Cockburn there and the prey gone. Barney and his flotilla had moved even further up the Patuxent.

So much for the British army's progress. On finding the bird had flown Cockburn reported to Cochrane on the night of Monday, August 22 from the tender *Resolution* lying off Mount Calvert, 'after parting from you at Benedict on the evening of the 20th instant, I proceeded up the Patuxent with the boats and tenders, the Marines of the ships being embarked in them under the command of Captain Robyns, Royal Marines . . . The *Severn* and *Hebrus*, frigates, and the *Manly*, sloop, were directed to follow us up river as far as might prove practicable. The boats and tenders I placed in three divisions, the whole under the superintendency and immediate management of Captain Wainwright of the *Tonnant*, Lieutenant James Scott, 1st of the *Albion*, attending as my aide-de-camp. I endeavoured to keep with the boats and tenders as nearly as possible abreast of the army under Major General Ross that I might communicate with him as occasions offered, according to the plan previously arranged, and about midday yesterday I accordingly anchored at the Ferry House opposite Lower Marlborough where I met the General and where the army halted for some hours, after which he marched for Nottingham and I proceeded on for the same place with the boats. On our approaching that town a few shots were exchanged between the leading boats and some of the enemy's cavalry, but the appearance of our army advancing caused them to retire with precipitation. Captains Nourse and Palmer of the *Severn* and *Hebrus*, joined me this day with their boats, having found it impracticable to get their ships higher than Benedict. The Major-General remained with the army at Nottingham, and the boats and tenders continued anchored off it during the night, and soon after daylight this morning, the whole moved again forward, but the wind blowing during the morning down the river, and the channel being exceptionally narrow, and the advance of our tenders consequently slow, I judged it advisable to push on with the boats only, leaving the tenders to follow as they could. On approaching Pig Point where the enemy's flotilla was said to be, I landed the Marines under Captain Robyns on the left bank of the river, and directed him to march round and attack on the land side the town situated on the point, to draw from us the attention of such troops as might be there for its defence and the defence of the flotilla. I then proceeded on with the boats, and as we opened the reach above Pig Point I plainly discovered Commodore Barney's broad pendant in the headmost vessel (a large sloop), and the remainder of the flotilla extending in a long line astern of her. Our boats now advanced towards them as rapidly as possible but on nearing them we observed the sloop bearing the broad pendant to be on fire, and she very soon afterwards blew up. I now saw clearly that they were all abandoned and on fire with trains to their magazines, and out of the 17 vessels which composed this formidable and so much vaunted flotilla, 16 were in quick succession blown to atoms, and the 17th (in which the fire had not taken), we captured. The Commodore's sloop was a large armed vessel, the others were gunboats all having a long gun in the bow and a carronade in the stern, but the calibre of the guns and number of the crew of each, differed in proportion to the size of the boat, varying from 32 pounders and 60 men to 18 pounders and 40 men. I found here laying above the flotilla under its protection, 13 merchant schooners, some of which not being worth bringing away I caused to be burnt; such as were in good condition, I directed to be moved to Pig Point. Whilst taking these vessels, a few shots were fired at us by some of the men of the flotilla from the bushes on the shore near us, but Lieutenant Scott whom I had landed for that purpose, soon made them prisoners. Some horsemen likewise showed themselves on the neighbouring heights, but a rocket or two dispersed them, and Captain Robyns who had got possession of Pig Point without resistance, now spreading his men through the country, the enemy retreated to a distance and left us in quiet possession of the town, the neighbourhood and our prizes. A large quantity of tobacco having been found in the town at Pig Point, I have left Captain Robyns with the Marines, and Captain Nourse with two divisions of the boats to hold the place and ship the tobacco into the prizes, and I have moved back with the 3rd division to this point to enable me to confer with the Major-General on our future operations. He has arrived safely with the army under his command at Upper Marlborough'.[4]

The letter provides a fitting conclusion to the Patuxent story. The success in effecting the destruction of Barney's flotilla belonged to Cockburn alone. It was his own careful planning in making the best use of his overstretched and meagre resources, which ensured that once Barney had committed his flotilla to the Patuxent, he was never to leave it. It was also Cockburn's foresight in having the river surveyed by the *Severn* that prepared the way for the final act; above all, it was Cockburn's fluency in arguing the case that persuaded Cochrane to approve the undertaking.

CHAPTER FOURTEEN

Target Washington
August 1814

THE EVENTS OF AUGUST 24 which followed the destruction of
Barney's flotilla found the small British force firmly ensconced
in the Federal capital as described in the opening chapter.
Cockburn's belief given to Cochrane in his secret letter of July 17 'that
within 48 hours the city of Washington might be possessed without
difficulty or opposition of any kind', had been vindicated.

In 1814 Washington had been the seat of government for only 14
years. Not much progress had been made in its development under
the expansive plan of Monsieur L'Enfant, and the work of surveying
the city under the able Surveyor General – Major Andrew Ellicott –
was far from complete. The city was dubbed with a number of
uncomplimentary titles by its residents including City of Magnificent
Distances, Wilderness City and City of Streets without Houses.
Much of the land to be developed was marsh, particularly in the area
surrounding the Capitol. Most Congress members understandably
preferred to live in the well-established district of Georgetown on
the fringe. The Capitol itself consisted of two wings – the House and
Senate Wings – with a makeshift wooden building joining them.[1]
Such other development as existed was spread around the Capitol
and the President's House, then the two foci as they are today,
which, linked together by a broad green mall, dominated the scene.

A census a few years after the British attack gave Washington a
population of 13,247 comprising 9,607 white, 1,696 free blacks and
1,944 slaves, with a total population of District Columbia rising to a
bare 33,000.[2] It is evident from these numbers that Ross and
Cockburn were under no direct threat from the civilian inhabitants
– not even from the few *franc-tireurs* who might have been amongst
them; but with Ross under specific orders not to undertake any

extended operations at a distance from the coast, neither he nor Cockburn could brook any delay in completing the task.

After a short rest from his labours of the previous day, Cockburn was astir before dawn on the 25th. Even more conspicuous on a white mare, he rode up Pennsylvania Avenue a second time to carry out his survey and thence to head towards Georgetown where the War Office containing the army and navy records was situated. He duly noted the smouldering ruin of the President's House dampened by an early morning storm and satisfied himself that enough had been done. A party of seamen under an officer was allocated the task of destroying the War Office which was somewhat remote from the main scene of activity and uncomfortably close to the heights above Georgetown where an American force was believed to be situated. With the arrival of reinforcements all went according to plan and without interruption.

The beautiful Government ropewalk and its adjoining stores, filled to the roofs with cordage, hemp and tar, was the next target. Scott, who was sent with another party of seamen to deal with it, was understandably reluctant to apply the torch, but Cockburn knew its logistic importance to the American navy and insisted on its destruction. The problem with ropewalks was to prevent fire, not how to create it. The highly flammable materials caught alight quickly and within half an hour the blaze, with accompanying dense volumes of black smoke, dominated the scene sufficiently to induce the American militiamen guarding the far end of the bridge across the Potomac to set fire to it from the Virginian shore.

Cockburn spent much of the middle part of the day on Capitol Hill in Dr James Ewell's house which served as a temporary operational headquarters. Ewell was a prominent citizen who had taken upon himself an entrepreneurial role of value to both sides. The burning and devastation of his city was as abhorrent to Ewell as to any other Washington native, but he felt that by mediating with Ross and Cockburn the usual excesses of an invading army might be largely prevented. Both British officers were markedly intolerant of looting and seven men were flogged for it. With victors and vanquished rubbing shoulders for most of the day, Ewell's assistance was greatly appreciated, and from the liaison a feeling of respect bordering on friendship developed between them.

The fort at Greenleaf's Point, where the Eastern Branch flowed into the Potomac, had been destroyed by the Americans, but the magazine remained. Shortly after midday a detachment of four officers and 200 men left the British headquarters on Capitol Hill with orders to remove the powder from the magazine and dispose of it suitably. Stifling heat and mounting cumulus gave warning of an approaching storm but for the moment all was calm and the party was anxious to complete the task before its onset.

A deep well close to the magazine provided the ideal receptacle and the barrels of powder were rolled into it with a will. Soon barrels and loose powder rested above the waterline which situation, in their haste to complete the job, went unreported to the officers in charge. A chance spark was the most likely cause of the horrendous explosion which followed although no one was certain. The effect was catastrophic – 12 were killed and the mutilated bodies of the 30 or more wounded were worse than anything seen on the battlefield at Bladensburg. They were removed gently to a makeshift hospital in an empty hotel near the Capitol.

Then came the storm or, in Scott's estimation, tornado. His account relates how 'trees were uprooted, plantations destroyed, and houses blown down, the conflict of winds setting at nought the industry and power of man'.[3] Roof tiles showered on the ground, and all those exposed to the storm were obliged to lie flat on the ground to escape its power. As an officer on horseback turned the corner of a street both were dashed to the pavement instantly. The storm was of brief duration, or the devastation of Washington would have proved of far greater magnitude than the mischief committed by the British.

As Cockburn sat in Dr Ewell's dining room in the late afternoon of August 25, convinced that every vestige of public property of use to the American government had been burned or destroyed, he realised that nothing was to be gained by prolonging his stay. That day the nearby townships of Alexandria and Georgetown had sent delegations to agree terms which would spare their houses, but General Ross had no intention of extending his small force further now that the main task had been accomplished. The two leaders saw eye to eye. Anything but an orderly and disciplined withdrawal would be dangerous. There were rumours that the American army was rallying above Georgetown and Ross's men were in no condition to fight a second battle so heavily outnumbered were they and so exhausted; the storm and Greenleaf's Point, too, had taken their toll.

For their own security, secrecy about their proposed retreat was paramount and the plan formulated by Cockburn and Ross to this end was masterly. Staff officers passed the word quietly to unit commanders to be ready to march after dark, a veil drawn over their intentions. Prying Washingtonians were misled and an 8 pm curfew made sure that they would all be indoors by then. Even Dr Ewell who, humanely, had agreed to minister to the wounded from Greenleaf's Point, had no clear idea of the next objective despite the intense activity around. Ewell was as good as his word; Cockburn wrote to him later, 'I lose no time in assuring you how much I consider my country in general, and myself in particular, to be indebted to you for the kindness and uncommon care and solicitude with which you appear to have attended our wounded when left in Washington, and I beg you to believe with what readiness and pleasure I would meet any wish of yours . . . I beg my best respects to Mrs Ewell and my acknowledgements to her for all she has said respecting the British Officers'.[4]

On Capitol Hill all seemed normal. British routine appeared to be following its customary course by the light of the camp fires, but in fact it was a charade. The protective camouflage enabled Ross's brigade in full marching order to steal silently away by night. Was it conceivable that their occupation of Washington had lasted little more than 24 hours?

Admiral Cockburn's report of August 27 to Sir Alexander Cochrane commented laconically on the return march, 'the general devastation being completed during the day of the 25th, we marched again at nine that night on our return by Bladensburg to Upper Marlborough. We arrived yesterday evening at the latter without molestation of any sort; indeed without a single musket having been fired, and this morning we moved on to this place (Nottingham) where I have found His Majesty's Sloop *Manly*, the tenders, and the boats; and I have hoisted my flag pro-tempore in the former. The troops will probably march tomorrow or the next day at farthest to Benedict for re-embarkation, and this flotilla will, of course, join you at the same time'.

It was, in fact, an epic march by men so tired that they barely knew where they were going and of its kind it was without parallel. They had marched nearly 50 miles into enemy territory, occupied Washington, burned the public buildings, and returned safely – all within 11 incredible days.

The attack on Washington and the burning of its public buildings was the cause for much recrimination in after years. That the burden

● The President's house after the fire in 1814 (RN Museum, Portsmouth)

of public feeling emanated in America is understandable but there were also many in Britain who regarded the destruction of the Capitol in particular as a Goth-like act – one of warring with the arts and sciences. In this context it is of value to bear in mind the opinion of Lieutenant Scott who was in the forefront of events. Scott's own career showed him to be independent, fair-minded and kindly. He had this to say some years later. 'I must do these persons the justice to confess that they were ignorant of the true state of the case. If a building is converted into a place of offence or defence, it loses its original character, and merges into that of a fort, and as such is liable to the laws and usages of war. It is folly to talk of this or that barbarism in such cases; war itself is barbarous, and though the issue may be regretted, the disregard by the Americans to the various parleys sounded by the General before our entrance, and the fire of concealed enemies, were the causes of the destruction of the Capitol and public buildings. Common sense should have led the authorities to sue for favourable terms for the city, instead of ensconcing a few hundred militiamen behind walls to impede our progress. Washington was, by such conduct, as completely at our mercy as any city taken by storm, and I believe the wiser and reflecting part of the Americans were grateful that destruction fell on the public buildings alone, and those houses converted into places of offence. The American writers have, generally speaking, done us more justice on this point than some of our own.'[5]

- **The Canadian frontier – War of 1812**

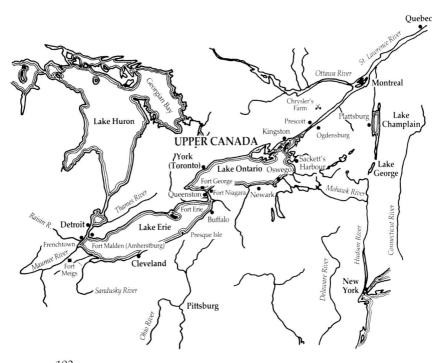

CHAPTER FIFTEEN

The Canadian frontier 1814-5

THE BURNING OF WASHINGTON brought the Chesapeake campaign to its climacteric. Sixteen months experience of this tidewater country left Cockburn in no doubt that swift follow-up action – if successful – would concentrate the minds of peace negotiators most wonderfully.

Little has been said about the main theatre of war on the Canadian frontier which, from the time of Cockburn's arrival in the Bay in 1813, influenced his actions. A brief resumé is appropriate towards an overall perspective.

It was obvious that America would pursue a vigorous offensive in Canada in 1813 to make amends for her failures of the previous year. The object, as before, would be to sever the St Lawrence and isolate Upper Canada but the precise point of attack and the timing of the main operation were matters which the American leaders found difficult to resolve. Kingston at the river's entrance into Lake Ontario was preferred as the primary target by Secretary of War Armstrong, and in February troops were assembled at Sackett's Harbor, the American base on Lake Ontario, to prepare for the advance, but the final plan was much delayed by Armstrong's indecision and the over-cautious General Dearborn in command. When Dearborn heard that the Kingston garrison had been reinforced and suspecting that the British General Prevost was himself planning an offensive against Sackett's Harbor, he decided on the less ambitious target of York (Toronto) at the western end of Lake Ontario and the capital of Upper Canada. As it had been an unusually hard winter, the opportunity of attacking the St Lawrence – before a thaw allowed the British to introduce men and supplies from the east into Upper Canada – had now been sacrificed by Dearborn for a more limited objective.

The American force arrived in their vessels off York on the night of April 26 and landed next morning. The British opposing them could muster only 700 regulars supplemented by a company of the colourful Glengarry Light Infantry Fencibles, Chippawa Indians and even a few dockyard workers. The American command was given to General Pike as Dearborn was in poor health; despite stiff opposition and a devastating magazine explosion, the town was taken. Pike was a casualty and later died.

Under the capitulation terms public property was to be given up but private property would remain untouched. Accounts vary on the conduct of the American troops but it does seem that some, at least, rampaged, looted and burned. The parliament house, official residences, barracks and printing presses were burned or destroyed and private possessions stolen. The truth will never be known whether excesses went beyond the accepted rules of warfare and the tenets of the time, but that it left an indelible impression on Prevost and other British commanders there can be no doubt. Retaliation was to be an unfortunate consequence in the Canadian war theatre and elsewhere. The scorched town was occupied for a week before the troops left for the Niagara River to capture the British forts in that region. While they were there and away from their starting base the opportunity was seized by Prevost to counter-attack at under-manned Sackett's Harbor; the British sailed from Kingston across Lake Ontario to find the smaller American force on the alert and ably commanded by a militia general. The attempt was unsuccessful and the British retired with heavy casualties.

Stalemate existed on the Niagara frontier in a cat and mouse game with first one side then the other gaining the initiative. In those summer months of 1813 the importance of the Great Lakes in ensuring mobility and tactical control became increasingly obvious. America had appointed Captain Oliver Perry of the US Navy earlier that year to command on Lake Erie and develop a fleet. Equally resolved to maintain the initiative the British had placed the Lakes under Admiralty jurisdiction, but the problems of supply and the manning of vessels from a distance made their task more difficult. They too, appointed a young naval captain – James Yeo – to command, but his role was intended to be mainly defensive with priority being given to the needs of Lake Ontario. Captain Barclay, a one-armed veteran of Trafalgar, was delegated to command on Lake Erie but the loss of materials intended for him, following the burning of York, made his task unenviable. He was also short of prime seamen and had to accept soldiers to bring his ships to an acceptable complement. The opposing forces met when Barclay had sailed to obtain provisions for which there was a desperate need. Perry won a hard-fought but decisive victory, and with the British land force retreating eastwards after abandoning Forts Malden and Detroit, the control of Lake Erie passed wholly to America in September. With the American general – Harrison – now hard on the heels of his British opponent Major-General Procter, the denouement on the Canadian side of Lake Erie could not be far away. Procter had been unable to decide whether to stand his ground to appease the Indian warriors fighting alongside him or to hasten his retreat to safety. When he compromised and faced his pursuers on the River Thames his demoralised force was scattered. Although British casualties were not heavy, 600 were taken prisoner and the Shawnee Tecumsah, the Indian leader of the British alliance was killed. Procter was court-martialled when the remnants of his army reached the Niagara frontier in October; he was sentenced to lose his rank but the gains so far established by America in Upper Canada were really of limited value.

Further east, Americans had been their own worst enemies. Disharmony among the generals, the inability to plan operations and keep to them and, in particular, the refusal of the north-eastern states to suspend trading with Canada, limited American successes. Provisioning the British army remained a perpetual problem and the Canadian population – ever under threat of starving themselves if overwhelmed – were reluctant to part with their own supplies. A vigorous and co-ordinated attack against Kingston or Montreal in that late summer of 1813 would surely have vanquished opponents who were handicapped by wholesale desertions without replacement, and the large number of French Canadians and American agents in their midst. It was a war full of anomalies with Briton fighting Briton on occasion. The British attempted to maintain a doctrine of 'inalienable allegiance' to deter British emigrants to the United States fighting for America in the same way that they applied the doctrine to seamen of British birth serving in American ships; men were tried if captured but it remained a contentious issue and one on which America reacted strongly as was to be expected.

The attempt on Montreal when it did come in October, by way of a two-pronged attack from Sackett's Harbor and Lake Champlain, was defeated at Crysler's Farm and severely damaged American morale. The American position on the Niagara frontier which had been favourable, also deteriorated. In December when abandoning

Fort George to return to the American side of the Niagara River, the Canadian village of Newark was burned with the unfortunate consequence that it stoked the fire for retaliation. It followed swiftly with the British destruction of the villages of Lewiston, Black Rock and Buffalo; yet again the Americans struck at Dover. It was an unpleasant way to end the year; America had gained little if anything after 18 months on Canada's frontier but Britain had rather more cause for optimism with the European war drawing to an obvious close and the likelihood of reinforcements.

In 1814 America maintained the offensive. After British failure to prevent American free movement on Lake Ontario, an attack was mounted at Sackett's Harbor in early July to attack the Niagara frontier. They had in command General Brown, an officer with an enhanced reputation. Brown's orders were to cross the Niagara River, take Fort Erie and then to advance against Fort George and Chippawa hoping eventually to sweep up the Canadian side of Lake Ontario. He succeeded as far as Chippawa where one of the hardest fought battles of the war took place with heavy losses on both sides. The expected reinforcements across the lake from Sackett's Harbor to support a renewed American offensive failed to arrive, and their army had no option but to withdraw to Fort Erie. The British were more fortunate but, although reinforced in August, their lengthy siege of Fort Erie was withstood and was abandoned on September 21. This battle of attrition in which neither side gained ended on November 5, when the Americans blew up the fort and withdrew from Canadian soil.

The additional British forces which began to arrive after Napoleon's defeat enabled Prevost for the first time to take the initiative. Even in this more favourable situation he was over-cautious but by the summer of 1814 the government and people at home were expecting results. The two options open to him were to attack Sackett's Harbor or Plattsburg. The former was likely to have supply problems for the British so preparation was concentrated on Plattsburg where, if successful, there was the possibility of an advance further south well inside American territory. Naval control and free navigation of Lake Champlain were essential ingredients for such a plan.

When all was nearly ready for the British to advance in August, Secretary of War Armstrong weakened the Plattsburg's defences by transferring a sizeable force to Sackett's Harbor to fulfil his oft-repeated wish to mount an attack on Kingston. Through his own inadequacies Prevost was unable to take advantage of this stupendous tactical error; having arrived at Plattsburg on September 6, he waited a week for his supporting naval force on Lake Champlain to begin its attack when he should himself have pressed on with his army. What to all militarists should have been an outstanding victory became a shameful reverse through uninspired leadership. The naval battle on the lake was won by Macdonough for America and Prevost ordered his troops to withdraw. For the many heroes of Wellington's peninsular army who were present, it was a shameful retreat and as an expression of their disgust there were many desertions.

At sea America was no longer able to continue her remarkable victories of the war's early months. With the arrival of additional warships in 1813, Admiral Warren could now make his blockade more effective – particularly by using ships of the line to support his frigates. It was impossible to establish a complete blockade with ports as far apart as Boston, New York, Charleston and Savannah, particularly so in bad weather. When American frigates did escape these watchful eyes they continued to show their remarkable qualities – notably the *President* and the *Constitution*. Privateers, too, continued capturing British merchant ships. The one outstanding reverse which America suffered happened when the frigate *Chesapeake* of 38 guns slipped out of Boston on June 1 to meet the British *Shannon* of comparable strength. The captains (Lawrence and Broke) and the crews of both ships covered themselves in glory before the *Chesapeake* finally succumbed.

When Admiral Cochrane relieved Warren in the spring of 1814, the ships at his disposal enabled the blockade to become more organised. A tighter control was exercised over the New England states where borders with Canada were ill-defined, and British raids along the coast from Passamaquoddy Bay to the Penobscot River in Maine met with little opposition. The object, in part, was to influence the peace negotiations taking place at Ghent.

It has to be said of Cochrane that he, more than anyone, appeared to be an exponent of retaliation. His support was readily given to Prevost when the request for it was made and he went so far as to obtain Admiralty endorsement to his proposals. There is a note of venom in Cochrane's directions to Cockburn on the subject given on page 167 which was alien to Cockburn's true character no matter how efficiently he carried out his orders.

CHAPTER SIXTEEN

The Patapsco
1814

TO REVERT TO COCKBURN'S OWN ACTIVITIES, after the troops had returned to the Patuxent River and re-embarked at Benedict into the transports on August 30, the squadron began its slow procession down river on the following day and by September 2 was back on the broad-bosomed Chesapeake.

With such a resounding success against Barney's gunboats and the capital, it was natural for Cockburn to assume that Cochrane would waste no time in attacking Baltimore. Cockburn had emphasized in his secret report of July 17 that after Washington it was important to strike quickly against Baltimore, primarily because of the defensive potential of Fort McHenry which guarded it. Even Cochrane had written to Earl Bathurst on August 28 that, 'Baltimore may be destroyed or laid under a severe contribution', and yet six days later in a letter to the First Lord of the Admiralty, he was contradicting himself. 'As soon as the army is re-embarked, I mean to proceed to the northward and try to surprise Rhode Island.'[1] So what went wrong and who was responsible for the temporary change of heart? As it happened Baltimore did indeed become the next target after much delay; it was British procrastination which, in the outcome, saved the city.

The true answer probably lies in a clash of personalities in the British high command. Cockburn, supremely confident and able to place an extraordinary reliance in his own abilities was bold without being rash, successful by design and never by accident; his whole make-up in sharp contrast to Cochrane's own. There seemed no enmity between the two but, had their characters been less antipathetic, all things should have been possible. It could have been that Cochrane smarted under Cockburn's 'blind eye' attack on

Washington. That he was upset seems reflected in his failure to allow Cockburn the customary honour of selecting the officer to carry home despatches of the event. Cockburn's nominee, without doubt, would have been his aide-de-camp, Lieutenant Scott who, in consequence, would have been given a well-merited promotion. But the choice fell upon Captain Wainwright of the *Tonnant*, an officer with nothing to gain and who visited the *Albion* to make his personal apology for the commander-in-chief's snub.

Ross made up the triumvirate. Of him Cochrane wrote to the First Lord of the Admiralty after Washington saying, à propos of Baltimore, 'as this town ought to be laid in ashes . . . some hint ought to be given to General Ross, as he does not seem inclined to visit the sins committed upon His Majesty's Canadian subjects upon the inhabitants of this state'. Apart from Ross's intransigence in not wishing to hit the Americans hard on their shores, the letter reveals Cochrane's own inability to be incisive or to direct the show. Cockburn manipulated Ross with far greater ease; when they were together Cockburn usually won any argument. Now that they were separated by water with Ross eating at Cochrane's table in the *Tonnant*, the rear-admiral was powerless to influence his friend.

Scott said of Cockburn, 'it was the rear-admiral's ardent desire that our success should be followed up by an immediate attack upon Baltimore, not 35 miles distant from Washington',[2] but the opposition was too strong for him to carry the day. Much play was made of the onset of the so-called Chesapeake 'sickly season' by those who were anti-Baltimore, but Cockburn knew from experience that its dangers were grossly exaggerated.

Decision seems to have been reached on September 4, when Cockburn received orders to take the *Albion* loaded with prize to Bermuda and then rejoin Cochrane at a secret rendezvous to the north. Admiral Malcolm with the transports was to go directly to the same rendezvous close to Block Island, leaving Captain Sir Thomas Hardy in the *Ramillies* as senior officer in the Bay.

Cockburn had sailed a bare eight miles when Cochrane signalled him to return and repair onboard the *Tonnant* where, much to his astonishment – and doubtful pleasure in view of the loss of valuable time – he learned that Cochrane had changed his mind and was to attack Baltimore after all.

The reason for Cochrane's *volte face* is not known. Perhaps it was news of the two diversionary expeditions under Gordon and Parker. The former's passage up the Potomac and his return downstream

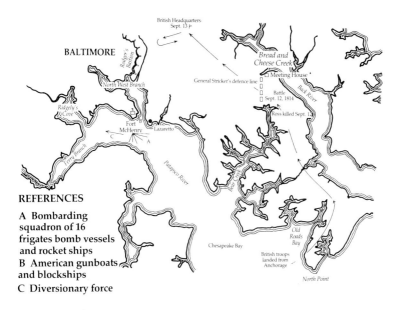

BALTIMORE

British Headquarters
Sept. 13

Bread and
Cheese Creek

Meeting House

General Stricker's defence line

Battle
Sept. 12, 1814

Back River

Ross killed Sept. 12

North West Branch

Ridgely's Cove

Fort
McHenry — Lazaretto

Ferry Branch

Patapsco River

Bear Creek

REFERENCES

A Bombarding
squadron of 16
frigates bomb vessels
and rocket ships
B American gunboats
and blockships
C Diversionary force

Chesapeake Bay

Old
Roads
Bay

British troops
landed from
Anchorage

North Point

- **The Battle for Baltimore**

with squadron intact – and 21 loaded prizes – turned out to be a minor epic. The *Menelaus* under Parker had sailed at random in the Patapsco off Baltimore, although the accomplishment had been marred by Parker's own death in action. Perhaps, again, it was a change of heart by Ross whose deputy quartermaster general – Lieutenant Evans – had always advocated attacking Baltimore.

Whatever the reason, the turn-round was effected with speed. By evening of September 9, the fleet had again anchored off the Patuxent. The following morning under a full press of canvas including studding sails, carried only in light airs, the 50 ships massing their way north presented a magnificent albeit disturbing sight to shore-side onlookers. The inhabitants of Annapolis worried lest they were the target; relief spread quickly as the fleet swept by. Baltimore it had to be. That city, in the 18 days of grace since the attack on Washington, had worked hard to improve its defences largely thanks to General Samuel Smith who had responded to the emergency with outstanding energy.

Smith had taken special precautions to guard the sea approach. The river split into two branches (see diagram), the right hand fork called the North-west Branch leading straight to the waterfront, the other fork dividing into the Ferry Branch and Ridgely's Cove, the latter within a mile of Baltimore. Smith sealed off the North-west Branch entrance with a barrier of cannon-bearing barges. On

201

Whetstone Point stood Fort McHenry rebuilt by French engineers and completed about 1800; it was the only permanent defence in the system and guarded the North-west and Ferry Branches on either side of the point.

Earlier Ross had transferred to the *Albion* to consult with Cockburn who favoured his well-tried and highly successful amphibious approach of mounting a direct attack in the tenders and ships' boats upon Fort McHenry, supported by land attacks on the flanks towards the city. Unwisely Cockburn was overruled; the troops would go ashore at North Point and advance as the main strike, while frigates and bomb vessels would close as near as their draught permitted, to assail the fort in support.

From an observation post of Federal Hill watchers could see the British ships approaching North Point through the heat haze during the afternoon of the 11th. Smith ordered Brigadier-General Stricker to move his 3,000 men in that direction; they quickly took up a defensive position at the Meeting House where a narrow neck of land divided Bear Creek from Bread and Cheese Creek.

Early next morning the ships anchored off North Point came suddenly to life; launches, barges, pinnaces and cutters crammed with soldiers were rowed ashore without hindrance. Once assembled they were led by General Ross, accompanied yet again by Cockburn. The admiral may not have won his way with the proposed frontal attack, but at least he would not be denied the right to be in the forefront with the naval brigade of some 600 seamen and marines. With a rousing call from the bugles the advance on Baltimore gathered momentum.

Stricker had been waiting with his untried militiamen in battle order at the Meeting House. At noon, fearing that a night assault upon his position might set him at a disadvantage, he sent out a scouting party of 250 of his best men. Suddenly they met an advance party of the British about 50 strong led by Ross and Cockburn, far ahead of the main British force. Cockburn had warned Ross of the danger they were in, but it was too late. In an exchange of shots Ross was hit in the chest and arm, fell from his horse and died shortly after. Cockburn wrote Cochrane three days later, 'it is with the most heartfelt sorrow I have to add, that in this short and desultory skirmish, my gallant and highly valued friend, the Major General, received a musket ball through his arm into his breast, which proved fatal to him . . . Our country, Sir, has lost one of its best and bravest soldiers.'[3]

The story is taken up by Lieutenant Scott, still Cockburn's aide-de-camp. 'Command of the army now devolved upon Colonel Brooke, of the 44th Regiment, who, closing with the advance, pushed forward. The enemy's forces, consisting of 7,000 men, were now discovered in an open space, and drawn up to oppose us; on perceiving the advance of our troops, they filed off into a wood on their right, and drew up behind a stout paling, where they appeared determined to wait our attack. (See General Stricker's defence line on page 201). As we debouched upon the open ground the enemy had just quitted, a sharp cannonade commenced from their field-pieces, which was replied to, with severe effect, by our artillery. Our troops on quitting the road, turned off to the right, and formed in line in front of the enemy. While the artillery were amusing themselves on both sides, the men were ordered to lie down and take what refreshments their canteens and haversacks afforded. This delay was to allow time for the detachment sent to turn the enemy's left flank. Previously to the commencement of the attack, the rear-admiral, who was well known to the enemy from his white horse and gold-laced hat, rode along the line from left to right, at a foot pace. The instant he was perceived, the fire of the enemy's guns seemed to follow him the whole length of the line; the shot might be seen grazing before, behind, under, and passing over his horse. I several times heard the troops, as he approached in front of them, jokingly exclaim, "look out, my lads, here is the admiral coming, you'll have it directly". The seamen trained to small arms formed the centre of the British line, and the admiral, not having any further occasion for my services at the moment near his person, kindly gave me the command of the *Albion*'s men. The light troops first advanced in open order, creeping along the ground under shelter of the smallest shrub or mound, which brought on a partial fire of musketry from the enemy. Our luncheon ended, we were impatient for the moment of action, for there is nothing so galling as being under fire without the power of returning it. The welcome note of the bugle sounded the advance, and the whole body started forward in steady quick time. While the Americans were ensconced in the wood behind a fence, resting their arms on the palings, and taking a deliberate aim, we had to move forward over an open space of five or six hundred yards, exposed to their fire. A roar of musketry opened out; it fell like a hailstorm around us; not a shot was returned till we were within 20 yards of the enemy, when they received a terrific discharge – our troops rushing on, scaled the palings. Their fire now became deadly on the flying foe, and would have told tenfold more severely but for the shelter afforded them by the trees; one of their guns fell into the hands of the bluejackets. It now became a regular chase and numerous Americans were taken prisoners. We popped upon one fellow, who impressed with the erroneous idea that he would receive no quarter, had determined to sell his life as dearly as possible. I observed him levelling his rifle, and called upon him to surrender. We were not half a dozen paces apart, but, instead of complying with my command, he fired, the ball grazed my left side cutting my flannel waistcoat, and unfortunately entered the breast of the young man close behind me, named Edmondson, who was attached to the *Albion's* party. While the main body of our troops advanced in front, the detachment sent to the right came up on the enemy's left and turned their flank. It was a second edition of the "Bladensburg Races". Here again we felt the loss of cavalry, and the effect of our previous fatiguing march; we were unable to pursue, and the scattered forces effected their escape, with a comparatively trifling loss in prisoners. Finding the pursuit unavailing, the bugle sounded the halt, and the whole army bivouacked at a short distance beyond the field of battle. Several soldiers were employed in filling their canteens, and Admiral Cockburn in watering his horse, when a volley of musketry was poured down upon us from above, killing and wounding several of the men. The volley was doubtless intended for the admiral's peculiar benefit; he however escaped unhurt, but his horse's shoulder was deeply grazed by a ball. The loss on our side in this action was severe. Our own wounded countrymen being provided for, the Americans now claimed our care: they were found in twos, threes, and sixes together; they shared with our people the aid of the medical men, and all the attention it was within our power to bestow upon their sufferings. The Meeting House, a place of worship, the only building near the scene of battle, was converted into a temporary refuge for friends and foes. At daylight on the 13th, the army moved on towards Baltimore, and before noon we arrived within two miles of the defences thrown up around the town. In the mean time the bomb vessels were busily employed in bombarding Fort McHenry. Captain Napier in the evening, with a detachment of boats, made a feint upon the defences on the river-side. The rear admiral in company with Colonel Brooke, reconnoitred the lines, and I was despatched to the commander-in-chief to state the supposed amount of the American forces, 15 or 20,000 militia, and the determination of the rear-admiral and general to attack the enemy at one o'clock in the morning, and to request that he would at that hour make a diversion on the sea front. On reaching the beach Sir Thomas Hardy gave me a passage off to Admiral Cochrane. After some time spent in discussing the matter of which I was the bearer, an open letter was delivered to me by the commander-in-chief, under circumstances precisely similar to those already related after the destruction of Commodore Barney's flotilla. That letter contained an order to the rear-admiral, in the following words, "you are on no account to attack the enemy, unless *positively* certain of success". I reached the headquarters about five or six o'clock in the afternoon, at the moment the rear-admiral and colonel were returning from a reconnoitring party. The former in high spirits thus addressed me, "well, Scott, have you delivered my message to the commander-in-chief? We have had an excellent view of their defences; before two o'clock tomorrow morning all that you now see (pointing out the lines on the Chincopink Hills) will be ours. What force is to assist us on the waterside?"

'In tendering the open letter of Sir Alexander Cochrane I observed, "I trust, sir, the contents of this despatch will not frustrate your's and the general's plans". The letter dispelled his animated smile of confidence and he handed it to Colonel Brooke; it was evident that there was a breakdown. The rear-admiral was still for proceeding in the execution of the arrangement for storming the works; but Brooke did not deem himself so authorised, after the communication of the commander-in-chief. It ended in a council of war being summoned by Colonel Brooke to which the admiral was invited, but which he instantly declined.

'The deliberations lasted till midnight, when the majority of the assembled officers decided upon a retreat; and at half past one in the morning of September 14, we commenced our retrograde movement. On the 15th, the whole returned to North Point, and embarked in the course of the afternoon, without seeing a man of the enemy, or having received an iota of annoyance on our slow return to the boats. It was a mortifying result after the brilliant success of the 12th; and we felt it to be doubly vexatious on acquiring the knowledge that, had the proposed attack been persevered in, it would have prospered, commissioners having been actually appointed on the part of the enemy to treat for the safety of the town. But it is a sad subject, and I will no longer dwell on unpleasant reminiscences.'[4]

Much of Cockburn's account subsequently sent to Cochrane is a repetition of detail already given. He stressed that he had stayed with Ross at the general's request until his death and had been unable to superintend personally the advance of the frigates, sloops and bomb vessels up the Patapsco to bombard Fort McHenry, but that he could not have had a more reliable deputy than Captain Nourse of the *Severn*. He referred to the excellent performance by the brigade of seamen comprising three divisions – each under the command of a ship's captain, and commanded overall by Captain Crofton of the *Royal Oak*; they had attracted the admiration of the army. He finished on an almost censorious note in saying that as Cochrane had himself accompanied the naval force against Fort McHenry, there was no need for his comment on that aspect. Certainly it is difficult to escape the feeling that Cockburn would have pressed home the seaward attack with much more determination had he been in command.

In fact, Admiral Cochrane transferred his flag to the *Surprise* shortly before the attack on Fort McHenry. Being a frigate of relatively shallow draught, she was entirely suitable as a command ship for Cochrane to direct the offensive. But – the rub – her captain was his own pampered son, Thomas Cochrane, who left much to be desired as a frigate commander. If not smacking of nepotism, the selection of the *Surprise* from which to control operations certainly seems to have been a case of unjustified favouritism. A transfer to the experienced Nourse in the *Severn*, or to the gallant Gordon in the *Seahorse*, would have made much more sense and with whom Cochrane might have mounted a more determined and persistent attack. As it was, he reverted to his old pessimism and indecision when battle was joined. His difficulties at Fort McHenry allowed him too readily to believe that the army had insufficient numbers to overcome a reported enemy force of 20,000 men without his support.

From Britain's point of view Baltimore was a disaster in its effects on the negotiations for peace then taking place in Ghent. The news of the earlier Washington success and Ross's own despatches reached London on September 27, and were instantly used as a weapon by Britain at the negotiating table to reach a favourable and early peace treaty. All went into reverse in mid-October when the Baltimore details poured in. The news was manna for tough and efficient American commissioners but it was the cause for the war to drag on for some months still to come.

Cochrane could only put on a brave face. On the 16th, his ringing proclamation to all hands praised their efforts in the 'demonstration and reconnaissance which it was deemed advisable to make upon the city of Baltimore'. His despatch to the Admiralty the following day either reflected complacency or camouflage of the real state of affairs. Brooke's advance was a 'decisive victory', and he excused the final withdrawal by claiming that the primary object of the attack had been accomplished. His private letter to Lord Melville, the First Lord of the Admiralty, written the same day was in quite a different vein; full of self-vindication it referred to bad tactics employed by the army and his consent given to the plan reluctantly only to preserve unity between the two services.

One person who had no doubts that Baltimore was an American triumph was Francis Scott Key, the Georgetown lawyer, who had witnessed the attack from a sloop bearing a flag of truce. He wrote a patriotic poem which was set to music; it became celebrated as *The Star-Spangled Banner*.

Before quitting Baltimore, Cochrane learned that an additional 7,000 troops from England would arrive in Jamaica towards the end of November. Already plans for attacking New Orleans were forming in his mind and, before sailing for Halifax on September 19, where he intended to finalise details, he gave his directions for the immediate employment of the fleet. Cockburn would be required to create a diversion to the expedition by blockading the coasts of South Carolina and Georgia after his overworked *Albion* was repaired in Bermuda. Malcolm was to remain in the Chesapeake in his flagship the *Royal Oak* together with a squadron of ships, and the troops were to resume raids on creeks and inlets before joining Cochrane for the attack on New Orleans. As the allocation of ships for the coastal blockade also came within Malcolm's jurisdiction, Cockburn asked him to send the frigate *Carron*, expected shortly from England, to Georgia to provide background information on the blockade required there, particularly the strength of Charleston, Savannah, Amelia Island and any other points used by American ships returning from long voyages.

All Cockburn's brothers had proved successful in their professions, particularly his elder brother James, now Governor of Bermuda. George's arrival there on October 6, in the *Albion*, if not quite affording him the delights of his own family hearth, found in his brother's household the next best thing. He was more fortunate than most for after the monotony and discomfort of weeks at sea, no greater relaxation existed than to quit shipboard life for a while. Cockburn, more than most, deserved a respite from his labours.

Bermuda in 1814 still had some way to go before the completion of its splendid 19th-century naval dockyard, but moves were already afoot to build some of the infrastructure such as permanent store-houses and a new hospital. Among the improvements was the acquisition of a house at Mount Wyndham for the station's commander-in-chief. Cochrane, in absentia, naturally wished to be kept informed of progress, and Cockburn duly obliged. His letters to Cochrane at Halifax reflect a pleasant domesticity.. Writing on October 9, he says, 'my brother is still taking advantage of the obliging offer you made him to occupy Mount Wyndham till Mrs Horsford (the general's wife), will allow of his getting into Government House. She is not yet in bed, though from her appearance, I should not suppose she can keep long out of one. I have delivered your asparagus roots to the gardener. He like everyone else on the island complains bitterly of the want of rain.'

A letter of October 24 continues the theme, 'the asparagus and everything in the garden now doing well in consequence of much wanted heavy rain which has recently fallen. I have taken up abode with my brother which is a good thing as it keeps the workmen up to the mark until Government House is available.' Cockburn ended with an interesting snippet of news on the peace negotiations at Ghent. 'A Mr Durnford who arrived here from New London, informed my brother that Mr Dallas – secretary to the specific commissioners at Ghent – had landed in America from an English cartel a few days before he, Mr Durnford, sailed and that it was stated in New York our commissioners having met the Americans in Ghent, the negotiations had commenced, but owing to differences had been broken off, and things seemed to be at an end. Lord Castlereagh passing through Ghent on his way to Vienna, had reconciled the differences and the negotiations were consequently resumed and generally expected to end in Peace.'

Finally on October 27, when Cochrane's preparations for the New Orleans enterprise were nearing completion, Cockburn advised, 'Mrs Horsford is at last brought to bed and has a fine daughter. You have therefore a chance of getting rid ere long of the present incumbents of your house. My ships will be ready for sea on Monday or Tuesday . . .'

If Cockburn's omission from participation in the Mississippi operations disappointed him he accepted it philosophically nonetheless. Reflectively he wrote to Colonel Brooke, still in command of the troops, 'it has been decreed that I am not to take part in your present expedition and it is perhaps for the best, for the longer I live the more I am convinced of the old adage that "too many cooks spoil the broth", and by my being kept away, you will at all events have one the less who, if present, could not possibly resist having his finger in the pie.'[5]

News was received from Admiral Malcolm that he had left the Chesapeake on October 14, to muster at Jamaica for the descent on New Orleans. Earlier, ships of his squadron had taken part in an expedition up the Coan River on the Virginia shore in which Captain Kenah of the *Aetna* had been killed. Cockburn grieved his loss. 'During the whole time he served with me,' he told Malcolm, 'I found in him always a ready, cheerful and able assistant in every expedition, and he was never so happy as when employed'. Glad to hear that Colonel Thornton had returned hail and hearty after the wounds he received at Bladensburg he commented, 'there are in my opinion very few like him to be met with'. He also thanked Malcolm for the 'Bat and Forage money' received for himself and other naval officers ashore in support of the army at Baltimore. 'I did not mind much about my own, not that I think I get a farthing too much from His Majesty,' he said, 'but I was very glad to have it in my power to give the officers theirs.' His concern for the welfare of his officers and men was ever uppermost in his mind.

Albion's refit dragged on until November 19. The ten-day voyage to the Chesapeake was uneventful and on the 30th she entered the Capes. Here Cockburn could collect his force and make his administrative arrangements. Captain Clavell of the *Orlando*, detailed for the defence of the Chesapeake, was warned that in preparation for the oncoming winter ships were to make canvas covers for any sails which were kept bent and exposed to the weather to prevent their being frozen to the yards, a precaution enabling ships to sail in chase at short notice.

The 3rd Battalion, Royal Marines, which had been on Tangier Island since the previous September, was now re-embarked in the troopships. Shortly before sailing, Cockburn was asked by Secretary of State James Monroe to provide a passport for a vessel taking despatches to the American plenipotentiaries at Ghent. Peace could not be far away but, until it came, Cockburn would not relax his efforts. So anxious was he to resume his task that he left the Chesapeake on December 18 independently of Captain Barrie in the *Dragon* and the troopships, with Cumberland Island as the ultimate rendezvous. Cockburn's intention was first to reconnoitre Charleston and Savannah and attack them if he could achieve an element of surprise. His hopes were frustrated by the tail of a hurricane which hit the *Albion* 300 miles east of Charleston; the ship was fortunate to survive and all hopes of contacting Barrie in the *Dragon* abandoned. It was not until January 14, 1815, that they were re-united at Cumberland Island where Barrie had arrived first having missed the hurricane. It was an unusual, indeed unwelcome, experience for Cockburn to find the landings already accomplished on Cumberland Island at the entrance to the St Mary's River; his captains had acted with initiative in putting the Royal Marines and the 2nd West India Regiment (which had also arrived), immediately to work.

Not to be outdone the rear-admiral promptly landed, took command of the force, and seized St Mary's, the frontier town of Georgia, gaining large quantities of military stores. On Cumberland Island itself he developed a fortified base from which his boats made frequent attacks up rivers and creeks, all this to divert attention from the New Orleans expedition and to hold down American forces. Disturbing news of failure at New Orleans largely negated his good work, but Scott's promotion to commander at this time pleased everybody. When Scott had been denied the privilege of taking home the Washington despatches which would have ensured his promotion, Cockburn took the unusual step of sending a letter of recommendation direct to the Admiralty instead of through Cochrane, the normal procedure. His private letter pulled no punches, 'if I have not the power of rewarding those officers by whose means I have been enabled to carry my plans into execution, I must beg leave to resign a situation so painful to my feelings,' it said. Only a big-hearted and generous man could express such sentiments and act upon them so fearlessly. He again wrote privately to the Secretary of the Admiralty saying how gratified he was by the promotion which had been fairly earned, excusing himself for not communicating through the normal channels owing to the time it would take![6]

News started to spread in early February that a peace treaty had been signed between Britain and America towards the end of December. To Captain Palmer of the *Hebrus* he wrote, 'little acceptable as is the news your lieutenant has brought me, nevertheless I thank you for the manner and promptitude with which you secured its reaching me. That Jonathan should have been so easily let out of the cloven stick in which I thought we so securely had him, I sincerely lament. The terms however, of the Treaty are tolerably disgraceful to him after all his vaunting, and this in some measure makes up for their not being quite so honourable to us as might have been obtained by a little more firmness, and a little longer continuation of the war with our present unfettered means.' Then two days later to Commodore Evans at Bermuda, 'a Swedish cruiser arrived here which sailed from Portsmouth December 28, bringing a paper *The Courier* of the the 27th, with an account of peace having been signed at Ghent on the 24th, and ratified by the Prince Regent the 27th . . . I have been very busy throwing up works to ensure to us the keeping of this island, after which I should have moved on Savannah. This peace, however, has knocked all my schemes on the head and I suppose I shall soon have official notification on this subject from Washington'.

Clearly Cockburn was disappointed with the treaty terms of which he was now unofficially aware. The negotiating teams had been locked in discussion at Ghent since August 8, 1814, and although each side had had its own ideas of the terms to be incorporated in any peace treaty, the progress of the war on land and sea, and the material advantages gained by the opponents in actual combat, were bound to influence that which the commissioners could achieve in hard talk. Although Britain regarded the American war as a sideshow, she still hoped to obtain territorial gains at the peace to include such things as exclusive possession of the Great Lakes, a guarantee for Indian lands, a cession of land in Maine and so on.

In early October news reached Ghent that Washington had been burned and that the future of Baltimore was in the balance. Added to these unpalatable facts was the expected victory of Prevost with his new army. Had Baltimore and Plattsburg gone Britain's way her bargaining position at the negotiating table would have been strong indeed. As it was, by mid-October, Prevost's retreat, the failure before Baltimore, and the inability of Britain to occupy any territory more important than a salient in eastern Maine, put new heart into the American team and enabled them to insist on retaining all their territory. As for the British negotiators they were content to ratify a peace treaty which allowed neither side the laurels of victory. Cockburn sent on this news to Cochrane by the fast sloop *St Lawrence* remarking, 'I shall continue to act as if no such intimation had been made to me, but should let you know of this intelligence with regard to operations you are arranging'.

Until Cockburn received official news of peace from England his position was unenviable. He wrote to Captain Clavell, still senior officer in the Chesapeake, ordering him to take onboard the *Orlando*, the garrison and stores on Tangier Island, but not to relax his vigilance. It seemed reprehensible that after two months since the signing of the treaty, no official word had come from home, yet Major-General Pinckney, Commander of the Sixth Military District of the US, was able to inform him at the end of February that there was no doubt of the treaty, or of its being ratified by the President. The two agreed to cease hostilities, Cockburn regretting his inability to evacuate Cumberland Island without orders.[7] At last, on March 6, the *Pylades* brought official notification and he started giving up the island in conformity with the terms.

The first article of the treaty required all slaves to be restored to their owners but, as so many had deserted their masters to achieve promised freedom and protection, the agreement seemed a British breach of trust. However, Cockburn had to interpret the article as best he could, avoiding distress wherever possible. He issued a fleet order, 'it is my direction that all the negro men, women and children of every description who have been received onboard the *Dragon* since her arrival on the coast of Georgia, be forthwith discharged into the *Albion* preparatory to an examination I have ordered to take place of the whole of these people now in the squadron, to ascertain if any or how many of them fall within the meaning and intent of the 1st Article of the Treaty lately concluded between Great Britain and America'. He told the *Orlando* that not a single negro was to be left on Tangier Island except by his own request if he had joined the British forces *prior* to the ratification. Cockburn was scrupulously fair, but it proved impossible to please all.

After completing the re-embarkation of guns and stores *Albion* sailed for Bermuda on March 18. There were some pleasant surprises, not least the division of prize money for which the prize agent came onboard. Best of all, perhaps, was the honour conferred on Cockburn 'in pursuance of the Royal Pleasure of the Prince Regent' as the ritual went, 'to assume the style and dignity of a Knight Commander of the Military Order of the Bath'. It was no more than he deserved.

Shortly before sailing for England on April 8, he issued his last order to the fleet. 'In taking leave of the several captains, field officers, commanders, other officers, seamen and marines lately composing the Force acting under my immediate orders against the enemy in Georgia, the Chesapeake, etc, I have the highest satisfaction in having the direction of the commander-in-chief to convey to them the entire approbation of their good conduct and of their invariable zeal and exertions in the country's service as set forth in my reports and to which he has informed me he will not fail to draw the notice and consideration of My Lords Commissioner of the Admiralty. Whilst promulgating this flattering testimony of the commander-in-chief's favourable consideration, I cannot refrain from making known to them also, that their invariably cheerful, gallant and steady behaviour was as gratifying to me as honourable to themselves, and for which I must therefore beg to offer them my warmest acknowledgements and to assure them how happy it will make me to have again the good fortune of acting with them in the event of our country calling for our mutual services at any future period.'

The journey home was uneventful. The *Albion* passed the Lizard light in the early hours of May 3, 1815 and reached Spithead two days later.

Cockburn went ashore after more than two and a half years absence from England on this occasion. How easily he could echo Admiral Lord Collingwood's sentiments of a few years before, 'my family are actually strangers to me. What a life of privation ours is – what an abandonment of everything to our professional duty, and how little do the people of England know the sacrifices we make for them!'

CHAPTER SEVENTEEN

Napoleon's keeper
- the long voyage 1815

SINCE HIS MARRIAGE IN 1809 George Cockburn had seen precious little of his wife and even less of his daughter, born in 1811 and now four years old. At last he could catch up with his sadly neglected private affairs and get to know his family. There was only one cloud on the horizon. Two months earlier Napoleon had reneged on his abdication and, at the head of 1,000 men, had arrived in France from Elba. The drama of the Hundred Days was already underway and no one knew how it would end. One thing was sure: should Napoleon abdicate a second time, a far more secure fortress would be required to house him. As far back as November of the previous year, the virtues of distant St Helena had been mentioned by the Powers.

For his first few weeks in England Cockburn was able to watch the development of the whirlwind campaign to contain Napoleon's ambitions with a degree of disinterestedness; but not for long. On June 18, 1815 Napoleon was defeated at Waterloo and ran; a second abdication was imminent and someone whom the British government could trust would be required to take him into permanent captivity. The minister responsible and the Admiralty Lords acted promptly. They took the first step by appointing Admiral Sir George Cockburn (the man they had in mind), as Commander-in-Chief of the Cape of Good Hope station, just three days after Waterloo. There was more in this appointment than met the eye. Although St Helena did not come within the naval command at the Cape – it was in the ownership of the East India Company – it was on the route to the Cape whence came most of such communication as there was with the island. It was logical, therefore, to nominate Cockburn as Napoleon's keeper when the need arose.

When in the early morning of Saturday, July 15 Napoleon and his suite surrendered onboard the *Bellerophon* cruising off Rochefort, plans were already well under way for their final disposal. *Bellerophon's* captain had been warned that if fortunate enough to take Napoleon he was to keep him under strong guard and return with all possible speed to the nearest English port.

Captain Maitland set *Bellerophon's* course for Torbay and the journey, which conveniently took more than a week to complete, afforded the British government time to finalise arrangements for Napoleon's exile.

Nothing, of course, could be done to prepare St Helena for his incarceration; all that lay within their power for the time being was to detail a squadron of ships to secure the long passage from the north to the south Atlantic and the personnel to guard him in the island. Already storing at Plymouth were a frigate and a number of sloops, the *Havannah*, *Zenobia*, *Icarus*, *Peruvian*, *Zephyr*, *Ferret* and *Redpole*; and at Portsmouth, two troopships, the *Bucephalus* and *Ceylon*, with the *Northumberland*, a third rate, earmarked to join them.

The *Bellerophon* duly arrived in Torbay and then, as ordered, sailed to Plymouth Sound where she remained for a while under the watchful eye of Admiral Lord Keith, Plymouth's Commander-in-Chief. The Corsican Ogre, as *The Times* called him, became a favourite exhibit for the boatloads of curious trippers as he stood on the *Bellerophon's* quarterdeck in two-cornered hat and green great coat. Strangely, the 'scourge of humanity' – according to the British press – touched an almost sympathetic chord among the visiting public.

In the morning of July 31 Keith's barge drew alongside the *Bellerophon*. He had come with Sir Henry Bunburry, Under Secretary of State, to deliver the British government's decision on Napoleon's future. It was straightforward enough but written in English which, for Napoleon's benefit, had to be translated laboriously. 'It would hardly be compatible with our duties toward our country and the Allies of His Majesty if General Bonaparte were left with the means or the occasion to again disturb the peace of Europe. For this reason it becomes absolutely necessary that he be restrained in his physical freedom, to whatever extent may be necessary for securing that first and paramount object. The island of St Helena has been chosen for his future residence. Its climate is healthful, and its geographic situation is such that he can be treated with more indulgence there than would be possible elsewhere, in view of the indispensable precautions that would have to be taken to restrain him.' The unexpected declaration, when understood, shocked and angered Napoleon. Only slowly did he regain his equanimity.

Meanwhile, the deputed jailer, Admiral Sir George Cockburn, had hoisted his flag in the *Northumberland*. From Spithead, during the afternoon of August 3, she quietly weighed and sailed west to rendezvous with Keith's flagship, the *Tonnant*, and the *Bellerophon*. They met off Berry Head on the Devonshire coast, well removed from the public eye, and there, for the first time, Cockburn met this important prisoner aboard the *Bellerophon*. Introduced by Keith, Cockburn addressed Napoleon in the manner in which he intended to continue, 'how do you do General Bonaparte?' he asked. Cockburn was not being deliberately discourteous by so addressing him; he realised that his tricky assignment required him to stamp his authority from the beginning. He then proceeded to inform the general of the government's instructions which produced another tirade: nothing like this had been expected; what was the objection to his spending the rest of his life in England?

But for the time being Cockburn's job was done and with his usual urbanity he enquired at what time on the following morning he should escort Napoleon to the *Northumberland*. The squadron was ready for its long journey. The 53rd Regiment of Foot under their commander, Colonel Bingham, had been embarked in the troop-ships before leaving Portsmouth; the Admiralty had directed two sums of 100,000 dollars each, to be placed onboard the *Northumberland* for use at St Helena and the Cape of Good Hope respectively, yet failed to instruct Cockburn how these monies were to be spent. Indeed, the whole question of accounting for the needs of Napoleon and his suite, and other exceptional expenses, was to cause Cockburn, lacking such guidance, permanent worry. In the urgency of the situation perhaps it is hardly surprising that the hastily drawn-up administrative arrangements and guidelines were inadequate. At least the government had chosen their man for the occasion wisely, knowing that he possessed abundant initiative and a flair for improvisation.

All Napoleon's luggage brought onboard *Bellerophon* from France had to be sifted and searched before transfer to the *Northumberland*. There was no vast amount of specie as might have been imagined but a small sum of 4,000 napoleons was found. This was left with Captain Maitland for forwarding to the government to be set against expenses, leaving Napoleon's followers with trivial sums for their personal use. This distasteful task completed, it remained only to demand the surrender of their swords.

Admiral Cockburn and Lord Keith arrived onboard the *Bellerophon* at 11 o'clock to escort the prisoner. Admiralty permission had been granted for a party of French who would not be accompanying Napoleon to take formal leave. A little group, headed by Lieutenant Colonel de Resigny, Savary and Lallemand, waited dejectedly on the quarterdeck and made their farewells, weeping unrestrainedly. Those who were to remain with Napoleon in exile had already transferred to the *Northumberland* – Le Comte Bertrand and Generals Montholon and Gourgaud. Mesdames Bertrand and Montholon and their children came too. In addition, Napoleon had Las Cases, his Secretaire du Cabinet, and 12 servants including loyal Marchand as his *valet de chambre*. Perhaps the most surprising member of the entourage was the Irishman, Doctor Barry O'Meara, *Bellerophon's* surgeon. Invited by Napoleon to accompany him as his physician O'Meara's appointment had been approved by Lord Keith who thought the doctor would provide a valuable source of information.

Now it was Napoleon's turn. He had already exchanged a few parting words with Captain Maitland of the *Bellerophon* graciously exonerating him from responsibility for the turn of events; he waved sadly to the officers and climbed down the ladder into the waiting boat, seating himself between Keith and Cockburn.

Chameleon-like his title and status had constantly changed. He had been First Consul, Emperor, or plain Napoleon. From the moment he stepped onboard the *Northumberland* he became General Bonaparte and thus would remain. 'Monsieur, I am at your orders!' was his laconic comment to Cockburn as he gained the quarterdeck, but neither he nor his followers were ever to find it easy to resign themselves to their new situation.

Bonaparte was taken to the wardroom where an old favourite of Cockburn who had captained his flagship in the Chesapeake, Captain Ross of the *Northumberland*, was introduced, followed by Colonel Bingham of the 53rd Regiment who would be responsible for Bonaparte's custody ashore.

The novelty of having such a notability onboard would wear off in the long days at sea, but for the moment all was excitement among officers and crew. The first evening at the wardroom table was convivial enough and Napoleon showed himself a lively conversationalist. Eager to explain his past successes and failures, he fascinated his audience with an account of the Russian campaign: the villages of fire for which the Russians themselves were responsible; the intense cold which caused half his own guard to freeze to death; the inevitable pillaging by the French troops, and so on. Cockburn was delighted with Bonaparte's ability to unwind until the end of the meal when all ended abruptly. Bonaparte was not inclined to share the port and linger as was the British habit. Instead, he made a bold attempt to secure the wardroom as his own study for the voyage – a brash request brashly refused. He then retired to his own cabin where his valet Marchand had already set up a camp bed. Here for more than two months he would live, read and dictate his memoirs in between exercise on deck. Later that summer evening *Northumberland* and her escorts weighed anchor.

The start was tantalisingly slow. Twenty hours later the *Northumberland* was still lying off Plymouth although the wind was fair. An essential element of the squadron – the storeship *Weymouth* – was completing and not yet ready to join. However, it provided *Northumberland's* captain with a welcome opportunity to strike down the enormous quantities of baggage and equipment embarked in such haste. The last-minute wants of their distinguished detainee could also be attended to before all contact with the shore was lost; at Bertrand's request 20 packs of cards, a backgammon board, and a domino table were conjured up.

On Wednesday, August 9 Cockburn and his miniature armada were close to Falmouth. A boat was sent inshore with last despatches, including letters written by the general and his followers. From now on Cockburn would follow his instructions which laid down that all correspondence – sent or received – would pass through his hands. Censorship was not the object: outgoing letters would invariably be sent in parcels to Earl Bathurst, the Secretary of State for the Colonies, to enable the government to keep its own watchful eye on their contents.

Cockburn seized the opportunity to report to Mr J W Croker, the Secretary of the Admiralty, the first of a series of letters about matters affecting Bonaparte and anything else of interest for the benefit of the Admiralty Board. After only two days with the Frenchman, Cockburn observed, 'I find General Bonaparte and all his suite drink great quantities of claret which my present stock will perhaps not be adequate to maintain, and supply his first wants on arriving at St Helena. I have thought it advisable to order the *Peruvian* to Guernsey to procure 60 dozen for me and to follow. The remains will be put in Bonaparte's house when he lands'. The lack of positive instructions on accounting for such an unusual expense was concerning Cockburn even this early. 'I have given without hesitation,' he said, 'a draft on my bankers Coutts feeling full confidence that Their Lordships will not permit my *private* account to lie entrenched upon to answer these unavoidable demands . . . Previous to my leaving London, Lord Melville gave me reason to hope I might expect a letter from the Board to authorise my drawing additional allowances for myself during the continuation of my command at St Helena.'[1] The total bill at this stage came to £1,964 for special items purchased in London, Portsmouth and Plymouth. Strangely, although a commissary general had been appointed, presumably to overcome such problems, no authority had been given to Cockburn to draw bills through him.

Next day, August 10 the Lizard stood about 17 miles to the northeast, and at noon the squadron lost sight of land. There were moments when Bonaparte seemed increasingly reconciled to his fate. His mood was variable – sometimes sullen, at others almost ebullient. At this time Cockburn noted in his diary, 'it is clear he is still inclined to act the sovereign occasionally; but I cannot allow it and the sooner he becomes convinced it is not to be admitted, the better'.[2] While in the *Bellerophon* everyone in Bonaparte's presence on deck removed their hats in respect. Cockburn's refusal to allow this to continue piqued the general severely.

His absence from dinner one day when there was a heavy swell suggested that he was not immune from its effects, but the close company and routine of a sea voyage soon broke his reserve – borne out by Cockburn's comment that he usually retired to bed 'as much at ease as if he had belonged to the ship all his life'.

He was happy to chat with Cockburn over dinner, how for example he had planned to amass a fleet of 100 sail of the line to attack England, making use of Irish agents in the attempt; he confirmed his correspondence with Tippoo Sahib in which he proposed taking India after the conquest of Egypt; and, on a matter particularly close to Cockburn's heart, of how he had been prepared to lend ships to President Madison in America's fight with Britain, a request which never materialised. Madison had declared war too late was his opinion.

In general, Cockburn judged Bonaparte's manner to be bombastic, uncouth and disagreeable. He played chess with General Montholon – his ADC at the battle of Waterloo – with an obvious lack of prowess but had to be allowed to win. If the cards did not favour him at *vingt-*

et-un, a game of chance, he sulked and retired to his cabin.[3]

For two days of typical Biscay weather nothing was seen of the French party. On their recovery, further conversation examined the unpopularity of the Bourbons which gave Bonaparte his excuse for the break out from Elba and the Hundred Days. King Ferdinand of Spain, whose escape from France Cockburn had attempted to engineer, was dismissed by Bonaparte as both fool and coward. He predicted – correctly – that Spain would lose all her American colonies through Ferdinand's bigotry.

By August 14 the squadron was off Cape Finisterre where earlier Cockburn had maintained his watch in the *Minerve*. How different it all was! No watch for strange sails on the horizon; no chase with the men at the guns ready to open fire; not even the constant altering of course and sail trimming to gain on an enemy. Now it was a leisurely journey southwards surrounded by a cordon of minor war vessels. Even the weather was in stark contrast to the storm-wracked days of 20 years before.

The prisoner's spirits were low at this period and Cockburn's diary explains that Bonaparte 'was inclined to assume again improper consequence and I was purposely more than usually distant with him; exchanged common salutations and high looks, but nothing passed between us'.

August 15 was another fine day. It was also Bonaparte's 46th birthday and he showed a readiness to enjoy the event. Indeed it was a turning point and there was a noticeable improvement in his spirits which seemed to coincide with a toast to his future health. In the evening he reverted to his pet subject – the invasion of Britain – one no less absorbing to his listeners. He was convinced that, if the build-up at Boulogne had gone to plan, the British fleet would have been deceived and unable to prevent a massive landing of 200,000 troops within 24 hours in the vicinity of Chatham. And then Pouf! London was but a short distance by road. He maintained his admirals had failed him by their disobedience. As for Admiral Villeneuve, Nelson's opponent at Trafalgar, there was nothing suspicious about his subsequent death as the British were inclined to believe: he took his own life.

Bonaparte made no attempt to emulate the Royal Navy's habit of rise and shine. He rested until ten or eleven o'clock when he breakfasted on meat and wine. He remained *déshabillé* until three or four in the afternoon, ate too much and took little exercise. Cockburn feared for his health.

He continued to reserve a topic at dinner each evening. On one occasion it was the escape from Elba, with reflections on his officers and men. He had a poor opinion of the former, whose *sauve qui peut* attitude at Waterloo proscribed all hopes of victory, and a high opinion of his troops who remained loyal and firm. Had they won, a truce might still have been possible. Cockburn coldly told Bonaparte that no British government would have placed any reliance on his word.

On another day Bonaparte talked egotistically about his career – of how he had risen to the chief command of the French army at the age of 24, had conquered Italy at 25, and had risen from nothing to be Consul at 30. In attempting to draw a parallel with Britain's own hero, Lord Nelson, he claimed that if only he had been killed after the entry into Moscow, his military career and fame would have been unequalled. Dwelling on the races of Europe it was his opinion that the Russians and Poles were decidedly braver than others – except, he said, as a quick afterthought, not wishing to offend his listeners, the French and the English!

The squadron was now nearing Madeira where the ships would replenish water and provisions. For security Cockburn wanted minimum delay so sent the *Havannah* (Captain Hamilton) ahead to procure requirements at Funchal. Bonaparte's obvious lack of knowledge of the islands they were approaching – Madeira, The Canaries, Cape Verde Islands – shocked him. As a seaman perhaps Cockburn should have made allowance for Bonaparte's ignorance which he recorded as being 'quite wonderful!'

Having spent 1,155 dollars obtained through the Commissary General at Funchal (Mr Ibbetson) on wine and other items on August 23 for Bonaparte's party, and made arrangements for despatches to England, the squadron soon resumed its journey. Cockburn's report to the Admiralty recorded only their arrival adding that, 'Bonaparte and his suite have preserved their health and appear as much reconciled, and submit to their fate with as good a grace as I could have expected'.

As so often happens on long voyages, tedium depressed Bonaparte when the journey resumed; the weather changed for the worse and for days the warm, sultry and moist sirocco wind that blows from the African desert encouraged lassitude. Little was seen of Bonaparte for the next three weeks.

On September 6 he appeared on a rain-swept deck with some of his followers ill-dressed for their promenade. Cockburn watched with bemused interest. Count Bertrand tried to persuade the general to go below but Bonaparte, to prove his toughness, replied that the weather would not hurt him more than the sailors. His bravado was shortlived.

In the evenings he occasionally opened up in discussing with Cockburn matters of mutual interest: he was, for instance, inordinately proud of Cherbourg harbour's fortification which had been his particular brainchild (at a cost of three million napoleons!) When asked why, he answered that he had always been apprehensive of a British *coup-de-main* from the nearby Channel Islands. His intelligence from England was invariably good thanks to information provided by smugglers whose activities were endemic throughout the war; Irishmen who travelled through London also made valuable contributions.

Crossing the Line was duly observed: King Neptune and Queen Amphitrite were welcomed onboard in usual fashion and all novitiates duly enrolled as members of His Most Turbulent Majesty's Kingdom. Bonaparte enjoyed the occasion and asked permission to give the seamen 200 napoleons. Cockburn would not entertain it – so large a sum was simply courting cheap popularity.

'I told him,' Cockburn said, 'that the custom in ships of our nation was for those whose rank and station authorised them to look for indulgence on these occasions, to send a bottle of rum to the seamen'. An offer to Bonaparte that he could give the equivalent of about five napoleons if he wished but no more, was ill-received. In the end he gave nothing.

For a fortnight the squadron progressed slowly on calm seas beneath an overcast sky. All were now hoping for a quick end to the journey but, as so often happened when vessels under sail were almost in sight of their landfall, wind and current failed them. 'Restless Frenchmen with a foul wind make but unpleasant messmates,' wrote Cockburn. However the long sea journey proved beneficial; according to Cockburn Bonaparte was looking better – and fatter! – than when he first came aboard.

On Sunday, October 15, 1815 after 72 days at sea Cockburn alerted his charge, who was on deck, that St Helena was close at hand. With an eye to his field glass, the prisoner's gaze was rewarded; there, projecting 2,500 feet above the sea, was the formidable solid mass with its forbidding brown and grey walls of volcanic lava. A later description of the island given by a Frenchman, 'the most isolate, the most inaccessible, the least attackable, and the most unsocial place in the world,' probably reflected Bonaparte's thoughts, too.

The *Northumberland* anchored off the island's capital, Jamestown, in the afternoon. Cockburn had first to tell Colonel Wilkes, St Helena's Governor, of the service with which he was charged, and make arrangements to call upon him next day. Paramount was the need to remove foreign ships from the anchorage without delay and to set in motion compliance with Earl Bathurst's instructions. 'I am commanded to signify to you the pleasure of His Royal Highness the Prince Regent, that measures should be immediately taken to prevent ships of every description from touching at St Helena with the exception of their belonging to HM service or to the East India Company. In the event of any ships being in distress from want of water or provisions endeavouring to touch at the Island, they may be permitted to receive such supplies as can be afforded without inconvenience provided crews are not allowed to communicate with the shore. After a sufficient period shall have elapsed for a public notice to the above purport to have had effect, any intercourse with the Island is to be wholly prohibited except for HM or East India Company ships.'[4]

Cockburn ordered two of his sloops to patrol St Helena's waters – the *Icarus* (Captain Devon), to the east, and the *Ferret* (Captain Stirling), to the west. Their detailed instructions warned them to be particularly on guard at dawn each day to scotch clandestine night operations. Every 48 hours the warships were to close the land to read any necessary signals; they were to carry out regular soundings and establish the flow of currents around the island and ensure that no ship could anchor or escape undetected. In fact, the deep waters surrounding St Helena virtually ruled out such a possibility, but nothing was left to chance.

Cockburn now turned his attention to Bonaparte's safe keeping ashore – by far the more difficult and exacting half of his assignment.

CHAPTER EIGHTEEN

Napoleon's keeper
- St Helena 1815-6

ON MONDAY, OCTOBER 16 Cockburn ordered his barge for a preliminary interview with Governor Wilkes of the East India Company. The boat came alongside the few steps cut out of the steeply rising rock which afforded the only practical landing place on the leeward side of St James's Bay. Nothing had changed since his last visit nine years earlier when the *Howe* called on her way back to England. He walked through the sally-port and the enceinte into the small straggling town set at the base of a huge crevice in the rock. Its small colonial-style houses in their claustrophobic setting between the rock faces offered little inspiration.

He was escorted to Plantation House at the end of the valley where the Governor resided. With 20 well-appointed rooms, surrounded by 220 acres of parkland, it was a palace compared with other island habitations. In the beautiful reception room he and the Governor concentrated on where to house Bonaparte. Plantation House was large enough for the whole party but that was clearly out of the question; in an island as small as St Helena, only ten miles long and eight miles wide, a quick survey on horseback could be readily undertaken. It took little time to decide that, of all the options, a house called Longwood, occupied by Lieutenant Governor Skelton and his wife, was the best available. Skelton could move elsewhere without trouble.

Cockburn wrote to the Admiralty endorsing Longwood's virtues, 'I visited with the Governor the different houses and estates throughout the island and he fully concurred with me that Longwood was not only the best, but the only place in the island calculated to answer for the future residence of Bonaparte'.[1] It was well separated from the inhabited parts and most distant from the coast,

- **Jamestown, St Helena (John Murray, London)**

so that boats could not possibly remove Bonaparte by a *coup de main;* it was surrounded by level, open ground facilitating the work of sentries; and it was suitable for equestrians and walkers alike. Admittedly small, it was equal in size to any other dwelling in the island except Plantation House; however extensions could be built using the *Northumberland's* own carpenters together with local workmen to make it more commodious. He hoped the French would be in residence there the following week.

Bonaparte had to be landed quickly for not only would his morale deteriorate rapidly if kept onboard overlong, but his presence would increasingly embarrass officers and crew now the ship was anchored. A house belonging to Mr William Porteous (later referred to by Count Bertrand as the Hotel Garni), had been earmarked to accommodate Bonaparte and his followers temporarily. On Tuesday evening, October 17 the party occupied the furnished rooms and spent a miserable night in their new surroundings. The accommodation may have been somewhat *infra dig* for an ex-emperor but there was no alternative.

Cockburn was astir betimes the following morning to take Bonaparte on a quick visit to Longwood, some five miles from Jamestown. Count Bertrand joined the party which made its way on horseback up the steep narrow path to the plateau above, slowly negotiating hairpin bends which provided glimpses of the town nestling below. When they had climbed to 1700 feet and reached the level ground of what is still called Longwood Plain, a sudden drop in temperature accompanied a noticeable change in the flora. They had travelled, in a relatively short distance, from a sub-tropical vegetation of date palm and exotic plants in the Jamestown valley to grassy slopes of broom, tamarisk and scattered pine, a phenomenon effected by strong south-easterly trade winds and the cold waters of the South Atlantic current.

A little way on, having passed through dramatic scenery with a green valley to the right and a contrasting rock-strewn declivity to the left, they turned off the road and approached Longwood through an avenue of mulberry trees. The old pink-washed farmhouse with its green-painted shutters was not displeasing to the eye, nor was Bonaparte's first reaction unfavourable. Cockburn conducted him round the five small rooms and adjoining annexes explaining, as they progressed, the various extensions he had in mind to accommodate the officers and servants. The sun was shining and in that early southern summer all seemed benign. Winter winds and rains would show it in a different light as Bonaparte would discover.

Two miles from Jamestown, on the way back, Bonaparte spotted an attractive red-roofed house on a slope by a waterfall. Here the vegetation had reverted to Mediterranean lushness with an abundance of evergreen trees and colourful flowers. Cockburn knew the house which belonged to Mr Balcombe, an East India Company agent – 'a respectable inhabitant' as he called him when reporting to the Admiralty that he had engaged him to obtain essentials for Bonaparte. All that the general and his party had brought were 'a small service of plate and another of fine china'. Furniture, linen and all else would have to be bought as best they might in the island to provide the standard 'usually enjoyed by one of general's rank', as Cockburn expressed it.

Mr Balcombe showed Bonaparte round both house and garden where geraniums grew in profusion. Facing the building stood an unusual pagoda-like erection on rising ground which caught Bonaparte's eye. It had only one main room with a garret above and was used by the Balcombe children as a playroom. Despite its obvious limitations Bonaparte urged that he be allowed to stay here until Longwood was ready; the homely environment of The Briars, as the house was called, was infinitely preferable to the Jamestown hotel. It was a concession the admiral was only too happy to make.

Cockburn's forecast, that Longwood could be occupied by the

French party the following week, was wildly optimistic. Despite daily landings by the *Northumberland's* carpenters and seamen it was to be seven weeks before the required alterations and additions were completed. The work was severely handicapped, and occasionally held up, by the island's lack of suitable timber.

Thus Bonaparte's stay at The Briars was longer than expected, giving rise to a letter of complaint from Count Bertrand on behalf of his master. It was iniquitous, he wrote Cockburn, that the emperor as he insisted on calling him, had but one room in which to sleep, eat, work and stay in all day, with only Las Cases and his son occupying the small room upstairs. After such a long voyage, it was desirable for Bonaparte to bathe which was not possible at The Briars; he was surrounded by sentries and neither Bertrand nor any other member of the suite could communicate with him without being accompanied by a British sergeant. He asked for horses to be provided for all and that they should be allowed to ride or walk without constraint. He observed that escape was practically impossible as the rocky shore prohibited any vessel's approach. If necessary, he urged, sentries should be posted on the shore for added security. He complained that their existence was not consistent with that afforded ordinary prisoners of war and that, at the very least, mem-

● **The Briars caught Bonaparte's eye (John Murray, London)**

bers of the suite should be provided with lodgings close to Bonaparte to keep him company.

There were other pinpricks to their pride such as: a guard tent pitched in the garden of The Briars to enable an officer and two sergeants of the 53rd to maintain a constant watch. Nevertheless some of Bonaparte's happiest days in St Helena were spent close to the domestic life of the Balcombe family. He remained in the house or garden almost all day, inviting himself to join the family party in the evenings for whist with the ladies of the family, playing for sugar plums until his usual bedtime.

Having made the best ad hoc arrangements within his power Cockburn was stung sufficiently by Bertrand's contumely to reply immediately on November 5, 1815, 'you oblige me officially to explain to you that I have no cognizance of any Emperor being actually upon this island, or of any person possessing such dignity having, as stated by you, come hither with me in the *Northumberland.* With regard to yourself and the other foreigners of distinction who have accompanied you here, it has been, and will continue to be, my most anxious study to render your situations as little irksome and disagreeable as possible under the existing circumstances, and I can only further assure you that I very sincerely lament to find my endeavours on this head seem hitherto to have proved so unsuccessful. It is incompatible with my instructions to permit of your passing beyond the established line of sentries without your being accompanied by an English officer or non-commissioned officer. I beg of you to accept the assurance of high respect and consideration . . .'

The admiral felt it wise to record this correspondence with Earl Bathurst so that the government should be fully aware of the preliminary difficulties connected with Bonaparte's detention. His own covering letter commented that, 'General Bonaparte inhabits his present temporary residence *wholly and solely* in compliance with his own urgent and pointed request after looking at it, and the only English officer stationed there is the one in attendance upon the General agreeably to my instructions on that head . . . Since my arrival at this island I have not ceased in my endeavours to render these people as comfortable as their situations and the existing circumstances would admit of, but I am sorry to say I find their requests and complaints, particularly those of M Bertrand, but increase with every favor and attention shown them'.[2] This was certainly true for he had already arranged the purchase of a carriage for Bonaparte through Governor Wilkes and had written to Messrs

Nourse, Christian & Co at Capetown to buy a pair of horses to draw it since none was available in the Island. Collection and delivery by warship had to await a convenient opportunity.

There were three main problems facing Cockburn in these early days at St Helena: first and foremost the island's security to leave no possible loophole for Bonaparte's escape; then the need to provision the island consonant with its new role and vastly increased population; and thirdly, communication with the outside world (particularly with the Cape of Good Hope), to ensure the attainment of the first two desiderata.

Cockburn now reported to Admiralty that as Ascension, then unoccupied and a mere 600 miles away from St Helena, could be used to assist in Bonaparte's escape, he had taken steps to prevent its occupation by any other nation. This was no fantasy. It would have been feasible for a foreign power to place a force on this unowned island to ease the general's escape. In October he had sent the *Peruvian* (Captain White), to examine vessels arriving there. Water was short in the island so that when the *Peruvian* was duly relieved by the *Zenobia*, the latter ship carried water reserves to facilitate the keeping of a permanent watch on shore. Thirty tons in cask were placed near the anchorage under tent and guard thus avoiding the depredations of rats which infested Ascension. To protect the casks from the heat they were payed with a coating of pitch mixed with earth. *Zenobia*, in turn, was relieved by *Havannah* whose crew landed provisions and erected wooden sheds. Slowly a presence was created on the island.

Meanwhile Admiralty had asked Cockburn to comment on Ascension's permanent occupation: he did not consider it would become a settlement of value, post-Bonaparte, as it was barren and waterless. St Helena, a mere three days sail away, was far more productive and adaptable to cultivation, having regular traffic with the Cape of Good Hope where supplies were plentiful. He recommended a more respectable force should be sent for the duration of Bonaparte's captivity; in the interim he would map the island and take soundings.

Before Cockburn's report arrived – a letter could take six months to be sent and the answer received – the government acted unilaterally; in early March, 1816 he was told by Earl Bathurst to occupy it. Clearly the government felt Ascension might well affect Bonaparte's security. Cockburn promptly proceeded to augment Ascension's occupying force. He pointed out that a permanent force could become discontented in such isolation, doing as little work in a year as the crew of a sloop stationed there would achieve in three months. He therefore intended to send 65 seamen and Royal Marines, volunteers all – the complement of a sloop of war – to serve on Ascension under his Flag Lieutenant, William Roberts, 'a most deserving officer who distinguished himself throughout the American campaign'.

His appointment of Roberts as Governor read formally, 'I have received orders to take necessary measures for the occupation of Ascension Island. I hereby appoint you Acting Commander and Covernor of the island of Ascension and direct you to take possession of and hold . . .' The detailed orders given to Roberts listed, as top priority, the prevention of Bonaparte's escape through a foreign intervention, although there was much else of interest in steps to be taken to develop the island. Cockburn showed a naturalist's interest in the preservation of the turtles which landed to lay their eggs, and referred also to the pasture, a 'nourishing kind of purslane' as he called it, being suitable for the rearing of sheep and pigs.

On St Helena everything was done to enhance security. Off the south-west coast the small but vulnerable Egg Island represented a weak link in the defence system. Ships were ordered there to help the army strengthen it and provide a guard boat to prevent foreign approaches by sea. Understandably Cockburn frowned on any laxity. A message was sent to all ships on November 2, 'it appearing to me that there must have been considerable neglect on the part of the Officer of the Guard or the Signal Officer of the flagship in having suffered a boat from a strange vessel to reach the town this morning *after daylight* instead of intercepting . . . Any such dereliction of duty in future will result in court martial'.

A major scare developed when a passing merchant vessel reported that the man-of-war *Minden,* due to call at St Helena on her way home from the Cape, had onboard a number of people lately involved in a conspiracy to seize Mauritius in the Indian Ocean for Bonaparte. This island had been in British possession since the recent Treaty of Paris, prior to which it was French under its more familiar name of Ile de France. A possible coup to regain it had to be taken seriously. Cockburn wrote to the *Minden*'s captain, 'having received information . . . that the *Minden* is likely soon to arrive here on her way home having onboard a number of persons who have been lately detected in a conspiracy to seize and hold Mauritius for Napoleon Bonaparte; I hasten to despatch this letter to HM Sloop *Icarus* that her commander may deliver it to you previous to your closing with this anchorage, to acquaint you the said Napoleon Bonaparte with many of his followers being now detained on this island, I consider it of the highest importance persons of the description mentioned should not stop here under the existing circumstances'. It proved a false alarm and the *Minden* was allowed to call and anchor, but only the guard boat was permitted to communicate with her.

Nothing could be left to chance. The loyalty of some of the soldiers and East India Company personnel was open to question; Cockburn sent 72 of them 'who from the tenor of their behaviour should be sent away', as he expressed it to Lord Charles Somerset, the Governor of the Cape of Good Hope colony, asking that they should be replaced by trusty men, and 16 Light Dragoons sent to escort Bonaparte whenever he rode.

Limited local resoures, particularly of building materials, delayed work at Longwood throughout November. Provisions, too, ran short: the *Northumberland*, which had met the requirements of the smaller sloops, now had but four day's rum remaining on the 11th of the month. Fortunately storeships from both England and the Cape were expected hourly.

If Bonaparte and his followers were discomforted by their cramped lodgings, so too were the men of the 53rd Regiment who were still under canvas. The French party complained about the meat so bruised, they said, as to be unfit to eat, and the quality of claret unfit to drink. As Cockburn reported to Admiralty, the claret bought in Guernsey on the outward voyage to meet their needs was consumed at breakfast, dinner and supper by the party – ladies and children included. While perhaps non-vintage it must have been drinkable! He recommended that the next ship bound for St Helena should embark a few casks at Bordeaux for them.

At the end of November the arrival of the storeship *Hyaena* from the Cape did much to restore morale. Such supplies were better, fresher and cheaper than those which came from England. Cockburn recommended that only salt meat should be sent from home in future.

On Sunday, December 10 Longwood was ready, except for a few detached rooms still being erected close by for Count Bertrand and his family. Cockburn escorted Bonaparte from The Briars up the familiar track and across the windswept plateau. It had been raining but the sun emerged to greet the general as he crossed the threshold. No one could pretend the house was well furnished but Cockburn had done his best by buying second hand from local sources at some expense. The house itself was at least functional and just large enough to accommodate the prisoners. Before moving in, secretary Las Cases had commented to Bonaparte, 'Sir, here we are in a cage. There we'll be penned up'. A fair assessment, but the best the island could offer barring Plantation House. By the time the valet Marchand had tidied the rooms and hung a few pictures, Bonaparte declared he was well pleased.

Now he could walk at leisure not only in the small garden immediately adjoining the house but also inside the walled pale which extended four miles beyond. Sentries from the 53rd Regiment were posted at regular intervals along this limit; at sunset they moved nearer the house. There was also a 12-mile enclosure where Bonaparte could ride if he wished. Here the fixed sentries were

- Bonaparte's Longwood home on St Helena (John Murray, London)

replaced by mobile patrols to check his movements ceaselessly.

When Bonaparte moved to Longwood, Cockburn appointed Captain Poppleton of the 53rd Regiment to reside with the general and keep the admiral well briefed. 'Be so good as to inform me once in the morning and once in the evening whether all is well with them, and at other times intimate to me their movements, particularly whenever any of them pass (although properly attended) the cordon of sentinels,' were his written instructions.[3] Even this was not enough; Cockburn introduced a system of telegraphic signals for use by the various signal posts to alert military patrols, their commanding officer Colonel Bingham, and Governor Wilkes as well as himself should any of Longwood's people absent themselves improperly.

If Bonaparte wanted to visit parts of the island other than his own defined area of free movement, he could do so subject to Poppleton's approval who would then normally accompany him; members of his suite were treated similarly except in their case any commissioned British officer could replace Poppleton.

It was not long before Cockburn had cause to define the rule in greater detail, as his letter of December 18 to Poppleton explains. 'Understanding a French officer under your immediate charge passed yesterday the cordon of sentries accompanied only by Doctor O'Meara; I intended the word 'officer' as in my last letter, to signify either a general officer, a field officer, a captain or subaltern of the army, or an admiral, captain or lieutenant of the navy and *no other*. Inform likewise the commanding officer of the 53rd Regiment'. As O'Meara was a member of Bonaparte's suite, he was *persona non grata* for this duty, indeed a naval surgeon then was not a commissioned officer.

Where Cockburn could modify the rules and make them less oppressive, he did; an order issued at the end of December permitted the servants at Longwood and attendant seamen lent from the *Northumberland* to visit Jamestown once a fortnight if provided with a pass, subject always to Poppleton's discretion. Certainly he was justified in reporting to Their Lordships after taking these security measures, 'I feel very confident not only of it being quite impracticable for the general or any of his followers to escape from Longwood, but even for them to have communication with any person whatever without my sanction'.

The first three months at St Helena had confronted Cockburn with a logistic problem. Although his squadron arrived somewhat denuded of provisions, there were few replacements to be had from the East India Company resources, and then only at a price. As senior officer Cockburn was also responsible for the feeding of the eight companies of the 53rd Regiment whose numbers exceeded the static population of the island.

Governor Wilkes was helpful. In October, 61 acres of good pasture land was offered for rental, and 25 cattle and 252 sheep were bought by the Commissary for 'the very moderate rate of £15 per bullock and 25 shillings per sheep' to provide fresh meat for current needs.

In the longer term Cockburn had to look to Capetown 2000 miles and 14 sailing days away. He wrote to Sir J Brenton, the Cape of Good Hope Commissioner, and Mr Johnson, the Agent Victualler there, receiving helpful replies from both. Brenton reported, 'fresh provisions, bread, calavances, wine and flour may be had in great abundance and at a moderate price'. He also listed other advantages possessed by Simonstown, then being developed as Capetown's alternative naval base and dockyard. It offered splendid ship repair facilities, and could accommodate 100 patients in its hospital. If Cockburn could organise a store depot at St Helena, Brenton would send an allocation of cordage, sails and so on for each ship, and a storekeeper clerk to look after them. Understanding there was a shortage of grazing on the island he was having hay bags made from canvas which, when filled with pressed hay, should make a useful contribution together with the casks of oats and barley he intended to send. The Agent Victualler replied in similar vein saying that there would be no problem in supplying live animals which were 'cheap and wholesome'. As the *Hyaena* storeship was particularly well adapted for conveying cattle and other provisions, Cockburn decided to retain her exclusively for this purpose, and so informed Admiralty.

As a result, supplies at St Helena became almost plentiful so that Cockburn was able to approve the issue of fresh meat to seamen and soldiers three times a week instead of the regulation two. On Christmas Day additional fresh beef and wine or spirits were allowed. The convenient arrival from England of a transport named appropriately *Admiral Cockburn* with some early prefabs, wooden 'moveable houses', provided much needed storage.

Once Bonaparte and his followers were acquainted with their surroundings, and the security net which contained them, they became disenchanted with Longwood. General Montholon replaced Bertrand as chief complainant. On December 21 he wrote at length to Cockburn, a letter concocted it must be assumed with Bonaparte's encouragement – if not his co-operation – in its drafting.

Symbolising themselves as enduring the lives of martyrs and declaring that posterity would regard the British government's treatment as totally unjust and against the rights of nations, Montholon proceeded to complain on many counts; the harsh security regulations, the desolate surroundings in total isolation, and the lack of furniture and bedding in the house which they were forbidden to supplement from their own money. He had asked only the day before if they could be given back their guns to shoot the wild goats and partridge which roamed the confines but had received no satisfactory answer. Finally, the emperor was ill, upset by the smell of the new oil paint and they all wanted to move to a more agreeable and healthy part of the island.

Cockburn replied promptly answering Montholon's points seriatim,

1 He expressed ignorance of such a person called Emperor Napoleon.

2 He took exception at the intemperate language against the British government. He would not answer future letters if couched in a similar strain of invective. In fact the British government's and his instructions 'breathe throughout the same moderation and justice which has characterised the whole conduct of my government towards you which will no doubt obtain the admiration of future ages'.

3 They all had permission to visit not only the town but every part of the island except fortifications, provided they were accompanied by a British officer whenever they went beyond the Longwood boundaries – but Doctor O'Meara did not qualify as an accompanying officer.

4 Visitors were not forbidden to Longwood subject to permission being given by the Governor and others nominated.

5 On the general complaints about the regulations he had amended and would continue to modify them whenever possible.

6 Longwood was the most pleasant as well as the most healthy spot of 'this most healthful island', and all pains had been taken to make the house as comfortable as possible in very short time. General Bonaparte was contented with it when he, Cockburn, had accompanied him and perhaps views may change with the arrival of better weather – it had of late been rainy beyond precedent.

7 It was quite incorrect for Montholon to say they could not buy items with their own money. Mr Glover his secretary, with whom there was an arrangement, had been misrepresented.

8 He had agreed to the use of fowling pieces which would be kept out of the house but available when wanted. 'This being however, the season at which it is contrary to the laws of the island to shoot,' he said, 'no further discussion is necessary.'

He finished the letter in a hurt tone. 'I have now followed your letter to its conclusion though not without the pain natural to a person upon discovering his constant and unremitted exertions likely to fail in one of their principal objects but I hope, at least, to prevent any future misconception.'[4]

There was an interesting sequel. In informing Earl Bathurst of these exchanges he revealed that Montholon had acknowledged that his letter was written *in a moment of petulance of the General, who has been long subject to paroxisms of such nature*. Montholon was aware of the reproaches to which he subjected himself by writing it; he considered the Longwood party, in point of fact, to be vastly well off, except for the restrictions on Bonaparte's travelling unattended. Cockburn could not agree to the latter and would continue to forbid it until the island's new Governor, Sir Hudson Lowe, arrived.

Lowe was expected daily but Cockburn was being over-sanguine, the government making no arrangements for Lowe's passage until it had heard that Bonaparte had arrived safely. Cockburn's letter of October 15 contained this information written on the day of arrival, and despatched home immediately in the sloop *Redpole*. Allowing for the time on passage, it is unlikely that the news would have been received in London until towards the end of December. An Admiralty letter was written on January 9, 1816 acknowledging the information and saying, *inter alia*, that Lowe was taking passage in the frigate *Phaeton* (Cockburn's earlier command). On Lowe's arrival at St Helena, Bonaparte was to be put in his charge. In fact, the *Phaeton* did not sail until the end of January: allowing a normal passage, she could not be expected until April.

Once Lowe had accepted responsibility for Bonaparte, Cockburn expected to return home. It came as a shock to receive news from the Admiralty, at the turn of the year, proposing his transfer from the *Northumberland* to the *Jupiter* as commander-in-chief, Cape of Good Hope, an unjust and unfeeling proposal. He replied without delay 'that having clearly and perfectly understood from Lord Melville previous to my quitting Town that an admiral destined to command here upon the Peace Establishment would come out to relieve me in the *Jupiter*, I of course, counted thereupon . . .' Having embarked in the *Northumberland* at short notice he had left many private affairs undone and for the sake of his health he was entitled to and needed a break. He asked Their Lordships to supersede him as early as consistent. Melville's promise as First Lord was honoured in due time by the appointment of Rear-Admiral Malcolm to relieve Cockburn who had to wait another three months for his arrival.

Cockburn's relationship with Governor Wilkes of the East India Company had been excellent from the outset. Wilkes was quick to recognise Cockburn's unusual assignment, waived protocol and was friendly and respectful. Plantation House had offered a room whenever Cockburn needed to remain ashore. At the end of January Cockburn expressed his appreciation in a letter, "how very much I consider myself indebted to you for the cordial, candid, and efficacious co-operation which since the first moment of my arrival here, I have so invariably experienced from you'.

Less clear was the position of Doctor Barry O'Meara, Bonaparte's Irish medical adviser – and the intended spy in the camp at Longwood. O'Meara had added little to Cockburn's knowledge. The doctor wrote at some length in January on the question of his emoluments which had never been clearly defined. He provided the background to his unusual appointment, how, previous to leaving the *Bellerophon*, an offer of 12,000 francs and free living had been made on Bonaparte's behalf if he went to St Helena. He refused but had agreed to go with Their Lordships' approval if they would decide his salary, leaving him the option to resign if he so wished. He pointed out the special circumstances of St Helena – the high cost of living which was double that of the United Kingdom, the remoteness under which he lived justifying a liberal salary for such a sacrifice. He had also given up a permanent professional job in England and therefore hoped that at least the salary offered to him by Their Lordships would equate with Bonaparte's original proposal. If not, he wished it to be understood that the option was open to him to resign or retain the situation as he pleased.

Cockburn's proposal was to enter him on the books of the *Northumberland* and 'as his table is found for him at Longwood, if he be allowed in addition the highest proportion of pay given to surgeons afloat, I consider it would be a full and just remuneration for him . . . notwithstanding the nature of the family in which he has placed himself'. O'Meara was dissatisfied, but if he were paid the sum, believed to be £500 per annum offered by Bonaparte in addition to his free table, Cockburn believed he would be well paid by naval standards.

O'Meara remained on the island under Lowe's governorship until their relationship deteriorated when he returned home, one example of those who could get along with Cockburn but not with Lowe.

Longwood was now running smoothly. Montholon and Bertrand still had lingering complaints but the sting of their position had largely been removed. Montholon moaned about bad claret, lack of coffee, water shortage and poor beef in much milder terms. Cockburn was equally conciliatory in his reply. There literally was no coffee to be bought in the island but he had managed to collect three pounds from the purveyor which he would lose no time in handing over with what remained from his own stock; claret would be provided from a different 'house' and he hoped it would prove better; he would remedy the water situation, 'but with the ten English servants I have sent to assist you in addition to the 12 French, with the horses also at your command and the water not 500 yards from the house, I cannot help flattering myself from the known energy of your character, that you have not suffered any serious inconvenience through the neglect of the Chinese labourer to deliver a double ration on Saturday to cover Sunday's requirement'. As regards the beef, meat would be sent as soon as the animal was killed, which should improve its quality.

At Count Bertrand's request Cockburn sent English and French newspapers. As regards mail for Bonaparte's household there could be no deviation from his right to read letters from Europe prior to delivery and vice versa. It was necessary for Cockburn to know about complaints and to be able to rebut, discuss or act upon them in good time. Letters must remain unsealed.

The storeship *Hyaena* collected mules from Rio de Janeiro to improve mobility on St Helena's wretched roads and tracks. 'An acquisition beyond price,' Cockburn considered them.

The settling of accounts and the method of dealing with them worried the admiral throughout his stay. Almost his last letter from St Helena addressed Admiralty on this subject, 'as no plan nor instruction on keeping accounts was given to me previous to my quitting England nor sent to me since, I have been forced to adopt a mode for myself, and not being much accustomed to these matters I look for the indulgence of Their Lordships and the government should these accounts not be kept according to the precise manner or forms they might have wished. I feel however, some confidence that they will prove at least satisfactorily clear and accurate'.

He was not only inconvenienced by the lack of instructions but was also put to considerable personal expense through the lack of any allowances. The 4,000 napoleons set aside for Bonaparte and his suite were soon expended, although Bertrand and others seemed to expect a never-ending stream of benefits to result from this small sum. Cockburn had drawn the attention of the Admiralty to the lack of instructions for Bonaparte's maintenance immediately he arrived at St Helena, saying that he would adopt such measures as appeared advisable until he heard from the government. As Bonaparte's followers were possessed of no private funds Cockburn felt they were entitled to a small allowance besides their board and lodging, but no satisfactory answer was ever provided from London.

When the Navy Office wrote about some trifling expenditure and peremptorily demanded repayment from his private resources, it was the final straw. 'I consider the harsh and dictatorial behaviour of the Navy Office towards me to be as little merited on my part, as considerate or necessary on theirs, and that although the Commissioners have passed the periods of warfare so very differently in quietness and comfort by their firesides in London, yet I feel they might have brought themselves to have entered rather more liberally into the difficulties which attend mine.'

On Easter Sunday *Phaeton* anchored off Jamestown whereupon Bonaparte called for his carriage to watch proceedings from the crest above Longwood. Cockburn viewed his old frigate with affection – and some relief – as she furled her sails and he repaired onboard to welcome the new governor. 'I have regularly delivered over to Lieutenant General Sir Hudson Lowe the charge of General Bonaparte,' he reported to Admiralty.

But it was not until early June that the *Northumberland* flying Cockburn's flag sailed for home, arriving at Spithead on August 1, when he wrote, 'arrived this day in the *Northumberland* in conformity with Their Lordships' order of April 13, 1816, having duly delivered over to Rear-Admiral Sir Pulteney Malcolm the command of

HM ships on the Cape of Good Hope station and given to the Rear Admiral every possible information . . . I propose proceeding to Town to wait upon Their Lordships to afford them of further information they may wish relative to the services I have had under my charge'.

Four days later a courier arrived onboard carrying a letter[5] for Admiral Cockburn.

Downing Street, August 5, 1816.

'Sir, I have the honour of conveying to you, by the command of the Prince Regent, his most gracious approbation of your conduct during the time you had the person of General Bonaparte under your custody you have discharged a very delicate trust with great zeal and judgement. You have not allowed yourself to be imposed upon by the authoritative tone, deceived by the misrepresentations, or cajoled by the flatteries which have occasionally been practised upon you; and yet you have not been unmindful of that tenderness and respect which adverse fortune, however merited, has ever a right to claim from the generous and humane.

'It gives me great satisfaction to have this opportunity of doing justice to your conduct; the more so because I felt how much was necessarily left to your discretion in the instruction which I had the honour of addressing to you. Bathurst.'

● The old Town Hall, Portsmouth (Portsmouth City Library)

CHAPTER NINETEEN

Political interlude - Portsmouth 1820

COCKBURN HAD MISSED THE PEACE CELEBRATIONS at home in 1815. Now it was his turn to enjoy a well-earned rest and to plan his future knowing that he was no longer at instant recall. Although active service appointments for admirals in peacetime were difficult to come by, Cockburn was still young and in robust health; his contribution to the victory had been outstanding both as seaman and diplomat and his temperament, ability and love of hard work were qualities which earmarked him for higher office even in a diminishing navy.

He had set up his permanent home at Wallsgrove, High Beech, a delightful and spacious late Georgian manor house on the edge of Epping Forest in Essex – now part of the London borough of Woodford – a short ride from town. Here he was able to experience life with Mary, his wife, and their five-year-old daughter, Augusta.

The war had left Britain debilitated and in the throes of recession. Unemployment was inflated by the discharge of a third of a million ex-servicemen. There had been recent food riots in East Anglia not far from his home; corn laws had been introduced to protect home growers with a corresponding increase in the price of bread; and in the midlands and the north Luddite disorders had destroyed textile and other machinery. Minor troubles plagued the kingdom but, most disturbing of all to a man of Cockburn's background, was the spread of radical thought embracing even revolution to achieve party ends. Six acts were passed to repress agitation: 'to prevent delay in the administration of justice in cases of misdemeanour; to prevent the training of persons in the use of arms and the practice of military evolutions; for the prevention and punishment of blasphemous and seditious libels; to authorise justices of the peace, in

243

certain disturbed counties, to seize and detain arms; to subject certain publications to the duties of stamps upon newspapers . . . .; and for the prevention of . . . seditious assemblies.'[1]

Gunsmiths' shops in London were attacked and perhaps most alarming of all was the arrest of a gang in Cato Street – a turning off the Edgware Road – whose intent was to murder all the cabinet at a dinner party and seize the Bank of England. Economic distress and social misery walked arm in arm throughout the land.

Politically, the tories – although not all would acknowledge such nomenclature – held power, more resistant to the principles of revolution than their political adversaries. Most men of independent mind, and those of substance, shared a tory outlook; Cockburn was one of them as were many of his friends – the highly influential Wellesley family, for example, and Lord Melville, a fellow Scot and First Lord on the Navy Board. Cockburn had too many recent memories of revolutionary Spanish juntas to sympathise overmuch with current concepts of reform, subscribing to the tory view that this was the first step on the road to cataclysm; in any case his naval career, which he now wished to advance, endowed him with the innate conservatism so deeply rooted in that service.

When peace came the navy had been ruthlessly reduced in ships and men and indeed in political importance. A bare 13 line-of-battle ships remained with only 20,000 men available to fulfil all commitments. There was little to be pared after the 1816 and 1817 naval estimates had made their inroads. Jobs for promising admirals on the active list were rare but a vacancy for a junior Lord Commissioner of the Admiralty – or 'Commissioner for the Discovery of Longitude at Sea',[2] as the post was still archaically called – then appeared. Cockburn was well qualified, available and rich in influential backing. He gained this appointment to the Admiralty Board where his political sympathies were in keeping with the government in power, a position he could enhance by being returned as a Member of Parliament. This would enable him to answer questions in the House of Commons and act for the good of the navy. The custom of senior serving naval officers standing for parliament had been practised for many past years and would remain for some time to come.

Cockburn's opportunity came in the June, 1818 general election when he contested Portsmouth whose tradition it was to return a naval member. In the past Admirals Vernon, Hawke and Hood had represented the port. Cockburn's local influence was considerable and his reputation high thanks to his outstanding war career. The townspeople favoured him and he could call on the support of many local naval friends and business acquaintances, some of whom qualified as electors. The limited franchise of that time varied from county to county and from one borough to another.

In the 1818 election three candidates, two of them whigs, were proposed and accepted for the borough's two vacant seats. The first, John Carter, a wealthy local barrister whose father had represented Portsmouth over many years, looked a certainty for one seat. The other candidate was Admiral John Markham who had been an Admiralty Commissioner as far back as 1801, and Portsmouth's Member of Parliament a year later; he had been a notable henchman – if not hatchetman – of Admiral Lord St Vincent and, in the pursuit of harsh reforming policies in the dockyards, had won few hearts for self or master. An unimpressive figure alongside the much younger and more renowned Sir George Cockburn, he retired from the contest to avoid an embarrassing and expensive defeat whereupon John Carter and Sir George were elected unopposed.

Office, and the demands of the House of Commons, kept Cockburn at full stretch for the next 18 months. In the House retrenchment and economy were the recurring themes and Cockburn with difficulty prevented further inroads on the navy's slender resources. In April 1819 the number of commissioners on the Admiralty Board was under attack. With such a reduction in the administrative requirements of the peacetime navy why three naval and three civil lords on the Board? Cockburn's questioners were not convinced by his reasoned defence but were given ample proof of his ability as a debater. When asked about his own job as a junior lord on the Admiralty Board, he was able to satisfy them that it was no sinecure. As Hansard reported, 'he could say most conscientiously, that from the day of his appointment up to the present time, he had not had any cessation from business and had sometimes not had an hour's walk for ten days in succession'.[3]

George III died at Windsor on January 29, 1820 after a reign of 60 years. Parliament could continue for six months after the death of a monarch but Lord Liverpool, the prime minister, plumped for an early election on March 9. The nominations for Portsmouth were as they had begun in 1818: Sir George Cockburn, John Carter and Admiral Markham again the candidates. Although no actual contest had taken place for 40 years because candidates had been returned unopposed, on this occasion it was to be a fight. Before the reign of Charles I, Portsmouth had been an open borough whose local householders enjoyed the franchise. A new charter granted to Portsmouth in that reign altered the title of the corporation from 'the Mayor, Burgesses and Inhabitants' to 'the Mayor, Aldermen and Burgesses', the inhabitants thus losing their vote. It was considered that their interests would be well guarded by a Guild of Merchants to which the majority of leading citizens belonged. Almost automatically, therefore, the aldermen and burgesses would take note of the Guild's preference in candidates for election and vote accordingly. With the passing of time, and through non-usage, the corporation lost sight of their responsibilities as trustees of the people; aldermen and burgesses voted as their own consciences dictated ignoring inhabitants' wishes.

As election day approached, Portsmouth's inhabitants demonstrated where their sympathies lay. Some 2,376 house holders in favour of Cockburn signed a petition which was delivered to the corporation. Couched in respectful, reasonable terms it pointed out that Sir George was the fittest person to be their representative and had exerted himself in every way for their well-being. A corresponding declaration signed by 217 people in Admiral Markham's favour was also lodged but the town had made its wishes clear. The radicals however, although few in number, made their presence felt in several ways; handbills and placards defaming Sir George and attacking his professional character were distributed widely; one burgess with radical sympathies actually displayed some in his shop front until compelled to remove them.

The whigs, with a numerical superiority in the corporation, had been active in other ways well before election day. Appreciating that the votes of burgesses were critical they had set about increasing their number, most of whom were not even resident within the borough. Thirteen had been enrolled on one day alone and their additional votes ensured Mr Carter's and Admiral Markham's success. Sir George 's popularity with the people and their own wishes thus counted for nought.

When Sir George entered town a few days before the election, a large body of inhabitants met him at the Half-way House. Removing the horses from his carriage, they drew him through Portsea to the George Inn where Nelson had spent his last evening in England before Trafalgar.

The election took place in the town hall which was full and its doors closed long before the proceedings started. The adjoining streets, too, were thronged with Cockburn's well-wishers. The peace officers had the greatest difficulty in preventing some from breaking into the hall, and on Sir George's arrival he was received with rapturous and continuous applause.

After the usual formalities John Carter addressed the constituents briefly. He defended his stance in the late short parliament relating to the Six Acts. In particular he referred to the Bill introduced to regulate public meetings organised to express grievances. He had opposed the Bill as he considered it to be an infringement on the long-established privileges of the people.

On being proposed and seconded, Sir George Cockburn rose to loud and continued cheering. If it was a sin to have a bias in favour of His Majesty's government, he said, he now stood before them a far greater sinner than when he had last addressed them: His Majesty's present ministers had the strongest claims to their support for having honourably and triumphantly carried us through an unending contest against France. They had added tenfold to these claims by hazarding their lives, (the Cato Street Riot), to save the country from anarchy and civil war. He had supported the Six Acts because he considered the country's peace and welfare required them. Liberty was dear to every Englishman but it had to be a *rational liberty* respecting and securing the rights of all. The bill for regulating public meetings, opposed by Mr Carter, had received the support of Lord Grenville, who usually opposed the government, and of Lord Wellesley. Sir George said that he had not been inattentive to Portsmouth's interests as even those members of the corporation who were opposed to him politically would bear out. His efforts in this respect had been invariably successful in the House of Commons. Disapproval had been voiced at naval officers having seats in the House but, despite his short experience, he was convinced this was essential. What better than for the first naval port of the kingdom and of the world to be represented by one? He provided examples of occasions when his special knowledge had been indispensable without consideration of party, but hoped he would be forgiven for remarking that Mr Carter invariably divided against the government on such occasions – or on any other when great national objects were at stake. His speech was applauded long and loudly.

Admiral Markham was proposed and seconded. (Loud hissing.) He bore witness to the professional and private character of Sir George but disagreed with his political principles. As for himself, he had represented Portsmouth for 17 years but it formed no part of his ambition to be returned again. It was the *electors* of Portsmouth who had called him from his retreat to represent them and he felt he ought not to refuse. He did not subscribe to the doctrine that a member should go to parliament to benefit the particular town he represented. Private interests were to be abhorred and his chief object, if returned, would be to act for the whole community – to preserve the privileges of the people and to lessen the burden of taxation.

An eloquent speech from Sir John Hippesley followed, delivered much in the manner of a judge's summing up, which was appropriate for one who sat on the Bench. He assessed the merits of each candidate and claimed his special right to undertake this duty in view of his *free and unshackled* position as a burgess of the town, which was more than could be said of the majority of the corporation. He reviewed the peculiar circumstances affecting voting rights in Portsmouth and left no one in doubt that he favoured Sir George for the same reasons as the citizens at large.

Mr Callaway, the town clerk and last speaker, appealed to his fellow burgesses to consider the merits of the candidates fairly and without political bias. If not, the people would consider they had been treated with contempt and disrespect, and would react.

Feelings ran high and the meeting degenerated into noisy confusion. When order was restored, the mayor called for a show of hands to indicate the favoured candidates. Sir George won handsomely with Mr Carter a poor second, but this had no legal standing. Admiral Markham knew it and demanded a poll restricted to the mayor, aldermen and burgesses when John Carter received 53 votes, Admiral Markham 37 and Sir George Cockburn 22.

Before the poll's close many complained to the mayor, saying that they had come to the hustings to tender their votes as local householders but had been refused. One, Mr Winkworth – Sir George's agent – then objected to four aldermen and 22 burgesses who had joined the corporation illegally from places outside the borough, including Admiral Markham himself. Their votes alone had denied Sir George a considerable majority. This objection and the claim of the inhabitants were duly inserted in the poll book, the mayor adding that both would be the subject of legal enquiry.

After the newly elected members had returned thanks, Sir George said he would ever be mindful of the kind and friendly manner in which he had been received and would continue to promote

Portsmouth's interests notwithstanding. He was conducted back to the George Inn by an immense throng and, responding to their calls, addressed them yet again. Finally, he asked them to disperse quietly and to give no-one the opportunity to complain of their conduct, hitherto impeccable.[4]

Investigations into the legal aspects of the poll began in June 1820 when a parliamentary select committee tried to establish how the various charters granted to the townn affected voting rights. A complicated subject was not helped by a loss of certain corporation books. Committee work, involving elaborate and lengthy evidence taken from many witnesses, dragged on for a long time without, so far as can be established, any final ruling being given.[5]

But the Portsmouth affair had provided a classic example of the abuses prevailing in the choice of members to serve as Members of Parliament, and probably influenced the extended franchise provided by the Representation of the People Act a few years later. To this extent, Cockburn had every reason to feel that the hornet's nest he had disturbed in 1820 was an act of liberalism far exceeding anything the whigs had achieved.

Sir George had made passing reference to invitations from other places in his main speech to the Portsmouth electorate. Among these was Weobley, a 'rotten' borough in Herefordshire where he was elected unopposed to represent that borough in the new parliament. If not what he wanted, and certainly less prestigious than his first choice, it was a seat nevertheless. As a junior lord at the Admiralty he could now continue to wield his influence on the navy's behalf in the House.

• **Weobley, Herefordshire as it is today**

CHAPTER TWENTY

America and West Indies 1832-6

THE NORTH AMERICA AND WEST INDIES STATION, the most important overseas command in 1833, was also the most lucrative for its officers, not least the admiral commanding. Rules for conveying treasure, enacted in 1819, permitted warships to earn freight money by carrying specie belonging to the Crown and other commercial interests; usually two per cent of the value of each cargo was divided between the admiral, the captain of the ship involved and the Hospital at Greenwich. Benefit was not necessarily one way as officers were responsible for making good any loss or damage.[1] The wealth of the Caribbean and the West Indies was the source of a high proportion of world trade; nothing was safer than a warship to convey the profits of gold, silver and jewels accruing from it, so that the lure of freight money made naval service on that station attractive.

Financially Sir George had every reason to be pleased with this appointment but more important was his release from the 'fag of Admiralty' as he liked to call it. Once again – and for the last time as it transpired – he would have command in an important operational area, shouldering responsibility without the need for consensus or discussion in committee as had been his lot for the past 14 years.

The two most important bases on the station, Bermuda and Halifax, possessed dockyards with repair facilities. Jamaica, a close third, was set in an area where Spanish influence predominated and strategically important for that reason. Barbados also acted as a base for maintaining a division of ships for service throughout the Leeward and Windward Islands.

Cockburn's fleet in 1833 consisted of seven frigates, nine sloops or brig sloops and eight schooners. The smaller vessels, speedy and manoevrable, were particularly suitable for anti-slavery patrol, combatting piracy, and the occasional embryo brush-fire war as ships of the line were inappropriate for these duties. Even Cockburn's flagship, the *Vernon*, a 50-gun hybrid, had been selected mainly to accommodate the commander-in-chief and retinue.

From Newfoundland and Canada in the north to the Caribbean in the south, 20 British governors administered the numerous colonies and islands. Cockburn's task was to maintain a good relationship with them all and act in their support when required. These sought-after posts were filled mainly by army generals. Only Newfoundland, because of the importance of its fisheries, could boast a naval officer – Admiral Sir Thomas Cochrane – as its governor. So striking was the imbalance that it caused Cockburn to write to a naval friend at home, 'I do not think our officers have too much to look forward to as compared with officers of equal standing of the army who have commands, regiments and government, out of number. In France they give the government of their island colonies only to officers of their navy to put them on a par with the army in such matters'.[2]

Cockburn hoisted his flag on January 29, 1833 and sailed from Plymouth Sound the same day. In bad weather the *Vernon* laboured to Madeira where Cockburn reported on the ship's poor sailing qualities and general unworthiness to Sir James Graham, the First Lord. 'I do not think that any other ship I have ever been in would have suffered at all in similar circumstances,' he wrote. 'The ship by the extraordinary manner in which she pitches, very soon carried away all that was done to her head at Plymouth. She plunges into the sea and now leaks in every part of her. I have been the more particular in laying the statement before you because from a conversation I had with Captain Symonds before I left Town, I know him to be impressed with an idea that the breadth of this ship's bow at the waterline, must protect her from pitching deeply.'[3] The ship's only virtue was that in light winds she sailed moderately well and Cockburn asked that Captain Symonds, her designer, should be informed tactfully of her shortcomings. It was a delicate matter since only recently had Graham appointed Symonds as Surveyor of the Navy to replace the old School of Naval Architecture which, in the opinion of many, had operated unsatisfactorily and unscientifically.

The *Vernon* was not Cockburn's only problem. The station had been without a commander-in-chief since the death of his predeces-

● Cockburn reported adversely on HMS Vernon's sailing qualities (National Maritime Museum)

sor, Admiral Colpoys. On arrival at Bermuda, Cockburn found that command had been assumed by the senior captain – Farquhar of the frigate *Blanche* – who had been granted temporary rank as Commodore First Class and was reluctant to lower his broad pendant and thus lose his entitlement to freight money. He argued with Cockburn beyond all reason but there was no alternative. 'The longer we live the more we find we are all doomed to meet our share of annoyances in this world from one quarter or another,' Cockburn wrote to his old friend Thomas Hardy who had succeeded him as First Sea Lord. Shortly after, Farquhar was withdrawn.

Bermuda had changed little from Cockburn's earlier experience of it during the American war, although slowly the dockyard was developing into a base of consequence. For the first time he visited Halifax; the cool climate of Nova Scotia enabled his wife and daughter to spend their time agreeably between Bermuda and Halifax according to the seasons.

Jamaica posed the greatest problem; England's move towards the emancipation of slaves was likely to cause more upheaval in that island than in any other colony. In reporting his arrival there to Sir James Graham, Cockburn said 'he was glad to find tranquility prevailing in lieu of the late excitement of which I had heard so much in England previous to my sailing… Many of the principal merchants of this place having called upon me, I was much pleased to find them generally to speak of their situation in a mild and softened tone. None of them appeared to speak upon the subject as if they

253

contemplated an immediate measure of emancipation, but rather as if they now at last saw the propriety – if not the necessity – of making some enactment in their Assembly more in accordance with the views of the English government'. Cockburn discussed with Jamaica's Governor, Lord Mulgrave, the potential danger if news of emancipation reached negroes prematurely, and made arrangements to concentrate a strong naval force should circumstances demand.

Cockburn agreed with the colonists who 'seem to be impressed to a man that (emancipation) would produce their decided and immediate ruin, and cause also the destruction of the negroes themselves.' It was essential to emancipate the slaves by degrees. Local views influenced the British government; those whigs who urged the abolition of slavery at one stroke had to give way, and on August 7, 1833 the House of Commons introduced a system of apprenticeship as a means of freeing slaves by stages. At the same time a sum of £20 millions was voted as compensation for the planters. The decision depressurised a volatile situation; Cockburn informed Graham immediately of his impression that 'the Government measure will prevent any necessity to use force against any class. I feel sure the planters will find the grant of 20 millions and the 12 years given to bring about general emancipation, far better than anticipated'. That concern should have been shown for the white planters by awarding them such generous compensation may seem odd, but the key role they were expected to play in maintaining stability was vital.

While Britain busily emancipated the slaves in her West Indian colonies, the drive towards suppressing their illicit trading continued apace. Most European countries had introduced laws prohibiting slave traffic but there was no uniformity in their approach to the problem. Thus Britain had separate treaties in force with Holland, Spain, Portugal and France as no simplistic formula which might be generally adopted could be found. While Britain's neighbours tended to follow her lead, Cuba, Brazil and even the southern United States reacted quite differently.

Cuba in particular, selfishly exploited by Spain, was a hotbed of slavery. The traffic from West Africa, and from its neighbouring islands, was vast. Cockburn's anti-slavery patrols did their best but, with limited resources pitted against such a highly organised and profitable illicit trade, success was rare. Most notable were the achievements of Lieutenant Bolton of the schooner *Nimble* who, over a period of 20 months, took six heavy vessels having onboard a total of 1902 negroes. His schooner came to an untimely end by being wrecked in the Bahamas Channel in 1834. Another outstanding affair was the engagement of the schooner *Skipjack* of five guns with the slaver *Martha,* three times as large and carrying a formidable armament of six 18-pounders and two long 12-pounders, with a crew to match – as well as 445 negro slaves. The occasions when slavers submitted without struggle were rare.

In response to a report from Charles Mackenzie, the British consul in Havana, that slaves were being imported openly, Cockburn placed a ring of cruisers round Cuba at the end of 1833 in an attempt to contain the situation. But, as he pointed out to Mackenzie, 'so long as higher authorities share in the profits they are bound to wink at the proceedings, and it is impossible for our ships to put an entire stop to it and we can only do the best we can with the few small vessels at our disposal'.

Cockburn's difficulties were made no easier by the French who still had a considerable ex-colonial interest in nearby Haiti. Reviewing the anti-slavery measures for the First Lord's benefit Cockburn commented, 'I am sorry to observe that the French have put such limits to the positions in which they have agreed to a mutual right of search. It must tend to defeat the value of the arrangements except on the coast of Africa'.[4]

The British were suspicious of French motives throughout the century. It was not unnatural, therefore, for Cockburn to take a particular interest in a French squadron of four large frigates and several corvettes under the command of Admiral Mackau which sailed from Martinique to Carthagena in Colombia to demand satisfaction for alleged insults to the French consul. Their intervention could result only in distress to British subjects in Colombia and upset commercial interests. Luckily the affair was settled amicably.

Life had its lighter moments. A regatta was organised at Bermuda and Cockburn accepted an invitation to be present. 'I have no doubt,' he said, 'that much good sailing and boat management will be displayed. I beg you to have the goodness to insert my name as a subscriber of 32 dollars... and if the Committee decides to have a "ladies purse" for one of the prizes, Lady Cockburn requests her name to be inserted for 12 dollars, and Miss Cockburn for six dollars.'

Equally a letter to Admiral Sir Richard King, commanding at The Nore, provides a good insight into life as experienced by Cockburn. 'I find this command extremely pleasant as compared with the office fag that fell to my lot for so many years, and although the command is no longer the profitable thing it was, it still does rather more than cover my Mess and Establishment which is so far good. My wife and family have enjoyed excellent health since our arrival on the station and they manage to pass their time agreeably enough between this place (Bermuda) and Halifax – the latter as the Town House with much visiting and parties, and this quiet place as the Country House... The Spanish Americans in the former Spanish colonies of the Continent are still fighting one party or faction against another for temporary supremacy, and they seem determined to go on much like the Kilkenny cats until they shall have eaten one another up. We continue to trade with them as convenient to us and meddle not in their internal broils. My friend Jonathan is at present very quietly and friendly disposed *towards us* but involved in some difficulty in his domestic policy in consequence of some late arrangements of the currency which has occasioned many bankruptcies.'[5]

A new addition to the Fleet reflected the changing times. The steam vessel *Rhadamanthus,* a wooden paddle sloop, completed in Plymouth Dockyard in 1832, acted as a despatch vessel, embarking the Governor of Jamaica and others whenever they required passage. Steam brought attendant problems. Engineers and mechanics were required to service machinery sometimes involving excessively severe work in a trying climate; and coals had to be taken onboard at frequent intervals causing heavy wear and tear on clothes. There were no rules to guide Cockburn so expediency had to play a part: extra pay for repairs, fresh beef daily when in port to recompense for the climate, and the hiring of civilian labour to assist on those days when the ship received coals. But Cockburn enjoyed the novelty of steam, and appreciated its crucial role. 'I was pleased to hear that you had put the power of the *Rhadamanthus* to surmount the opposition of a strong sea breeze to so good and early proof, and that the result was so satisfactory,' he wrote her commander.

The mail service to and from England improved. Warships now only supplemented the regular and reliable packet service between England and Bermuda, calling at Halifax and Boston en route, and provided under a contract with a Mr Samuel Cunard. Passengers paid £5 from Halifax to Boston, or £7 10s on to Bermuda. From this early initiative the Cunard company became legendary as an

Atlantic steamship operator.[6]

Cockburn was an outstanding supporter of exploration and surveying work, and counted Captain Francis Beaufort – the Hydrographer of the Navy – among his intimates. Of particular interest to him beyond the northern limits of his station were the attempts to discover a north-west passage. He received charts from Beaufort showing Captain Ross's recent discoveries in that area, as well as a copy of the new *Nautical Almanack*. In acknowledging the present, he gave detailed professional comment and his views on the then unknown northern boundary of the American continent. Public funds for voyages of discovery were limited and much of the financial support was provided privately with the encouragement of the Royal Geographical Society. On this occasion, as on so many others when there was a worthwhile cause, Cockburn offered a generous subscription as well as his advice for further exploration.[7]

Cockburn could not reconcile himself to his flagship *Vernon*. Her many imperfections grated on his professionalism and after carrying out extensive trials with the tender *Fly* on different points of sailing, he wrote again to the First Lord on the subject. 'I hope the details will give you a better practical proof of what the *Vernon* really is than anything deduced from theory. I firmly believe that in smooth water and a good breeze, she will beat anything that swims upon the sea especially to windward; but the moment she is opposed by a sea ahead she becomes more than can be believed . . . and I can compare her to nothing but a child's rocking horse constantly moving up and down without advancing a step.' Admiralty decided to replace the *Vernon* by the *President*, a fourth rate completed in Portsmouth Dockyard in 1829. 'If she is (as she was ordered to be) an exact copy of the American *President*, she will be a fine frigate and good ship which must make up to me for the inconvenience I may be put to for want of room,' Cockburn replied philosophically. The *President* arrived at Bermuda in July 1834 whereupon the unlamented *Vernon* sailed for England. His new flagship fulfilled expectations and sailed remarkably fast on passage to Halifax under Captain James Scott,[8] her new commander, a firm favourite with Cockburn as was Scott's predecessor, Westphal. Always there existed between Cockburn and his captains a two-way loyalty similar to that held between Nelson and his band of brothers of earlier days.

Shortly after the *President's* arrival at Halifax in August, cholera broke out in the town and spread so rapidly that the Rifle Corps stationed there was forced to encamp some distance away in the country to reduce the spread of the disease. Similarly, Cockburn dispersed his ships leaving only the *President* in Halifax at an isolated anchorage. Despite these precautions there were more than 400 deaths before the epidemic subsided at the end of September. Cockburn's good sense kept naval casualties to a minimum; he, himself, sensibly visited the Nova Scotia interior with his family, a break that was much enjoyed. 'We have taken advantage to ride and drive about this wild and in parts beautiful country,' he informed Ussher, Halifax's Captain Superintendent.

Cholera apart there was little to worry about. Some British merchants in the island of Anguilla were found to be sending cargoes of slaves to the Danish island of St Thomas; and prompt measures were required to restore order at St Kitts and other neighbouring islands. Invariably the assistance of the navy was requested by the governor concerned, and an unfailing response maintained a remarkable stability in what otherwise could have been a troubled area. Even Jamaica, for long regarded as the Achilles heel, remained quiet despite occasional angry outbursts in the local Assembly.

The ability to administer justice, and for it to be seen to be done, was undoubtedly the prime reason for this happy state of affairs, as this letter from Cockburn to an administrator in Bermuda reveals. 'The very attentive and willing manner in which I have observed the two convicts – Thomas Humphries and Richard Collins – perform their labours, added to the extremely good character I have received from their immediate superintendent, has induced me to listen to their request for mitigation of punishment. They are both under condemnation for life but as an encouragement to such good behaviour as evinced by them, Lord Melbourne may not be indisposed to admit my recommendation to change their present hopeless lot to 14 years transportation.'

Naval discipline was maintained by a notable absence of punishment. Those ships able to send the commander-in-chief a nil quarterly return of punishment received Cockburn's commendation for the 'good and steady state of discipline'. His view was that the volume of punishment related directly to the quality of the officers awarding it.

His comment, to Admiral Sir William Parker serving at the Admiralty, reflects his thoughts on one aspect of discipline. 'No man can be more anxious than I am to keep down corporal punishment. The best method is to encourage rather than to restrain the discharging from the navy of refractory and ill-disposed men. They cannot be flogged into good behaviour.'[9]

Cockburn left Halifax in November 1834. He had been watching closely political events at home where there were signs that whig dominance in government was waning. In the previous June, Sir James Graham, the competent First Lord, had resigned and was replaced by Lord Auckland. This unexpected event was not to be interpreted, so the newspapers reported, as one which would shake the whig government off its intended course. But Cockburn with burgeoning optimism viewed it differently; as he expressed it metaphorically to a political ally at home, 'I cannot help viewing it as the first bright gleam that has broken through the dismal, black, threatening cloud which has for the past few years been hanging over us, and that it opens a hope for fairer weather and better days. It will fall upon us to endeavour after such a reckless storm to right the good old vessel now so shattered and on her beam ends and to save her from entire destruction'.

His assessment was correct in one respect since that distinguished politician Sir Robert Peel had recently returned to England from Rome and was revitalising tory policies. A new name was creeping in for the tories described by Peel in this manner, 'I presume the chief object of that party (tory), which is called Conservative, will be to resist radicalism and to prevent those further encroachments of democratic influence which will be attempted, as a natural consequence of the triumph already achieved'. Cockburn agreed wholeheartedly with this maxim as he was a firm believer in temperate and constitutional government.

While in early 1835 Cockburn was visiting Barbados, Antigua, Trinidad, and other areas inaccessible to mails, events were taking place at home of which he was officially unaware. The 'bush telegraph', however, foretold the dissolution of parliament and Melbourne's replacement as prime minister by Peel. Such a change *could* entail Cockburn's early return to England to take up duty as First Naval Lord. Though he had no wish for the post, his sense of duty would compel his acceptance should the invitation come. In fact, Peel *had* formed a new administration and Cockburn's appointment was virtually automatic, so highly were his talents valued.

'Conceiving it would be an act of great injustice to recall this excellent officer from so important and lucrative a command,' Sir

John Barrow, Secretary of the Admiralty, noted in his autobiography 'I waited on Sir Robert Peel to take his opinion whether he considered it absolutely necessary that he should at once be recalled to assume his seat at the Board, or would suffer him to remain a little longer. "By all means," Peel said, "write to him to say in my name that there is no occasion for his turning over the command, and that I will let him know when he is wanted here". It was fortunate that I stopped him; for had he come home on seeing his appointment he would have found his seat occupied by some of the whig party. Sir Robert Peel's government having ceased in April 1835, Lord Melbourne became a second time the premier.'[10]

Cockburn, appreciative of Barrow's intervention, replied in May, 'I am most truly obliged for the kind and flattering consideration towards me so fully manifested by everything you have decided and done'. His relief was evident from other correspondence exchanged at the time; to have inflicted recall would have been like asking a schoolboy to return to school in mid-vacation.

He was unprepared for it in another important way. He had represented Plymouth as a member of Parliament since 1826 and in anticipation of a general election in 1835 pressure had been placed on him by local supporters to stand for election. But he felt it was all too difficult to stand *in absentia* and had replied to the invitation, 'if through the influence of my former staunch friends and others there acquainted with me they should be induced spontaneously and during my absence, to elect me as their representative, I should feel most truly proud of it and most highly gratified, but it is not my intention or wish to press myself forward to the notice of the constituency of Plymouth or any other place'.[11] It was not to be.

Cockburn returned to Bermuda from the heat of Jamaica in February 1835 to enjoy the Spring. He invited the Bishop of Nova Scotia, with whom he had struck a friendly family relationship, to take passage in the *Racer* and stay *en famille* in Admiralty House. The bishop accepted, arriving conveniently on Easter Day. He returned to Halifax after an enjoyable break, and consequent upon the fall of Peel's government in April, 1835 after only a few months in office, Cockburn wrote to the bishop, 'you will have heard of the destruction of the Conservative government. I shall not say more respecting it than that I have felt much disappointment by that event, but find my present duties far more healthful and I am glad I have not been obliged to return to England to join the Board . . . I grieve on account of the proof it affords of the almost impossibility of any government now preserving its existence if it will not run at a speed with the vicious appetite of the times by going hand in hand with the destructive radical combination. Our only hope must still be in Peel . . . and a more sober feeling generally pervading the country'.[12]

In August, the *President* was again at Halifax. 'I take the opportunity of everything being quiet and safe to go to Quebec which I propose to do immediately,' Cockburn reported to the Admiralty. His reliable deputy, Captain Sir Thomas Ussher, remained at Halifax during Cockburn's two months' absence. The Cockburns embarked in the *Forte* and sailed up the St Lawrence. By the time of his departure from Halifax in November, Cockburn had already arranged with Lord Auckland, the First Lord, to be relieved at Bermuda early in 1836. He was now at the end of his commission; the most relaxed and enjoyable three years of his long service life. He was on his last round of official duties at Bermuda and the *President* was being prepared for the journey home. Coincidentally his younger brother Sir Francis, Governor of Honduras, was also due to return home. Cockburn offered his brother a passage in a minor warship provided he did not incur any public expense on the journey to Bermuda. From there they could have the pleasure of each other's company in the *President*, but the offer was not accepted as Sir Francis was able to arrange a direct passage home.

The *President* arrived at Bantry Bay in Ireland to take refuge from the weather at the end of May after a stormy passage. Cockburn reported his arrival there to Admiral Adam, the First Naval Lord, saying that, 'The Board will confer upon me a great kindness if you will send an order to meet us at Portsmouth directing the *President* to proceed to Woolwich for as I have a great accumulation of things onboard, and as my house at High Beech is within 10 miles of Woolwich, it would very materially help me getting them home'.

Adam swiftly agreed to this reasonable request. No arrival home could have been more pleasantly or conveniently arranged.

CHAPTER TWENTY-ONE

Admiralty Board
1818-30 & 1841-6

FOR CONTINUITY OF SERVICE on the Admiralty Board, Sir George Cockburn had no equal; after the Napoleonic Wars he occupied a seat on it for 17 years. The minutiae of transactions during his long period in office are more fittingly recorded in naval archives as Sir George was first and foremost a man of action, but he possessed an outstanding intelligence and an eye for detail which made him a natural choice for conducting the navy's affairs from its highest office.

In the first half of the 19th century the navy's administration was too tightly controlled by statesmen lacking knowledge of how to manage it. Any naval officer aspiring to serve on the Admiralty Board needed to be elected as a Member of Parliament so that he could influence events. That in turn involved a political affiliation which, later, was found to be undesirable for officers on active service. For 14 of his 17 years on the Admiralty Board, Cockburn served in the House of Commons, representing Portsmouth, Weobley, Plymouth and finally Ripon as a staunch tory. He was appointed a junior naval lord on March 25, 1818, which was also the date of his return to active duty after Napoleon's incarceration at St Helena. He had been rewarded a little earlier with the Knight Grand Cross of the Order of the Bath and additional armorial bearings for his distinguished services, and in the following year was promoted to vice admiral of the blue, all of which indicated the government's continuing need for his active employment.

Equally gratifying was his election to the Royal Society. That learned and ancient institution appreciated his considerable professional support for expeditions in search of the North-West Passage for which public funds were inadequate.

Each year Cockburn played a prominent part in the debate on the navy estimates in the Commons: when arguing his case he was usually the target of Mr J Hume, a whig with strong radical tendencies who had gained a reputation for being the guardian of the public purse. Every item came under Hume's prolonged scrutiny and Cockburn's life was made difficult by his forever insisting on a direct vote. Sir George, overworked, was particularly sensitive to his inquisitor's attack on the need for six commissioners on the Admiralty Board – three naval and three civilian. Hume's insistence that a total of four would suffice stung Cockburn to reply, 'if the gentleman opposite could find any individual who could, without injury to his health, attend at his office from nine o'clock in the morning until four in the afternoon, and then be in his place in this House from four in the afternoon until two in the morning, to answer such questions as might be put to him I, for one, would have no objection to let you instal him in this office'. Hume knew that it was not unusual for Cockburn to work such a demanding routine, and his amendment was defeated when the vote was taken.

In 1822 Hume also resisted a move to increase the strength of the Royal Marine Corps to 8,000 men.[1] The advantage in recruiting marines was that they served on a regular engagement which the seamen, as yet, did not. Cockburn, recently promoted Major-General in the Royal Marines and with memories of the Corps' gallant support in the Chesapeake, pleaded their cause. When the House divided Hume was again defeated.

Of greater national interest was the funeral of Queen Caroline who had died in August, 1821 while King George was at Holyhead, about to start on a state visit to Ireland. The story of Caroline's unseemly behaviour and her estrangement from the king is a matter of history, but the Admiralty became involved because of the queen's wish to be buried in Brunswick. The king and prime minister Lord Liverpool hoped that the body could be conveyed without fuss down the Thames and then by warship to its destination – primarily to avoid popular demonstration if the cortege passed through the City. The Admiralty preferred Harwich as the point of departure and a route through the northern outskirts of London was chosen as a means of avoiding the crowds and the City. It was a forlorn hope. The radicals were out in strength manning the barricades and in the inevitable clash two civilians were killed and the cavalry escort met with brickbats. Those in charge gave way and redirected the cortege through the City and on to Harwich. In the subsequent enquiry Cockburn contributed the naval reasons why the Thames route was discarded in favour of Harwich; the narrow arches of London Bridge allowing passage only for half-hour periods at slack water, the impossibility of ensuring a strict timetable along a river crowded with boatloads of spectators, and the danger of an accident involving the waterborne coffin.[2] Most unpredictable of all, in the strong westerly gales then prevailing, would have been the transfer of the coffin to the waiting frigate in open waters.

This unfortunate event left the public conscience disturbed for some time. The following year in the House the matter surfaced again, 'that the respect and solemnity which by ancient custom have been observed at the funerals of the Queens of England . . . have been unnecessarily and indecorously violated'. The navy's participation could not be faulted, and even Mr Hume supported Cockburn with a commendation of the navy's conduct which he had witnessed personally at Harwich.[3]

In 1825, Cockburn was promoted vice-admiral of the white; everything stood in his favour of reaching the summit of his profession. Well known and respected among the *haut ton* he was a fashionable figure of the London scene; through the Carlton Club he maintained close social contact with the political cognoscenti. At the general election which took place in 1826 he preferred Plymouth, a town with naval ties, rather than to seek re-election at Weobley. His success there made amends for his defeat six years previously at Portsmouth; in the following year he received a political accolade from the king himself by being enlisted as a privy councillor.

Until this moment Cockburn had served at the Admiralty under Lord Melville, who had held the post of First Lord since 1812. While personable and friendly, Melville was a man of moderate talents[4] who, in his long stint, had failed to prevent the navy's decline in national regard. When Canning became prime minister for a brief period in 1827, a strange constitutional experiment was decided upon involving Melville's replacement by the Duke of Clarence as Lord High Admiral. The revival of this ancient office, which had been in abeyance for more than a hundred years, was politically expedient to occupy Clarence who was not without naval experience, having risen to the rank of post captain in the previous war. The navy's administration would be run by a new Council replacing the Admiralty Board, with Clarence in a supporting role. In practice it did not work. Apart from Clarence's frequent failures to consult his Council when taking important decisions, there was a clash of personalities between the Duke and Cockburn – now head of the Council. Unfettered by restrictive practices some of Clarence's reforms were beneficial, but too often he acted unilaterally with hare-brained ideas, such as his introduction of military scarlet to the collars and cuffs of naval uniform with no understanding of the psychological upset it would cause officers. A final break with his Council came over the setting up of a committee on gunnery over which Cockburn had not been consulted. An angry exchange of letters ensued and a feud developed requiring Wellington – now prime minister – to intervene. Wellington refused Clarence's demand for Cockburn to be dismissed but felt obliged to refer to the king for his verdict. George IV supported his prime minister and wrote to his brother, 'it is with feelings of deepest regret that I observe the embarrassing situation in which you have placed yourself. You are in error from the beginning to the end. You must not forget, my dear William, that Sir George Cockburn is the King's Privy Councillor, and so made by the King, to advise the Lord High Admiral.

'What becomes of Sir George's oath, his duty towards me, his Sovereign, if he fails to offer such advice as he thinks necessary to the Lord High Admiral? Am I, then, to be called upon to dismiss the most useful, perhaps the most important naval officer in my service for conscientiously acting up to the letter and spirit of his oath and his duty? The thing is impossible . . . you must give way, and listen to the affection of your best friend and most attached brother.'[5]

The Duke of Clarence duly resigned and Melville returned again to the post of First Lord of the Admiralty that he had filled previously for so many years. Cockburn became senior naval member and thus at the age of 56, after 42 years of active naval service, reached the pinnacle of his profession. Clarence, a kindly man free from malice, probably never forgave Cockburn for causing his resignation. Fortuitously, there was little opportunity for their paths to cross when Clarence acceded to the throne as William IV; Cockburn was in the West Indies for most of William's short reign, and as a tory was out of office for the remainder. Sir Robert Peel's high opinion of Cockburn as the mainstay of the Admiralty and Wellington's friendship undoubtedly helped Cockburn to weather the storm. James Briggs, then a young clerk at the Admiralty, provides a subordinate's view of the man. 'Sir George Cockburn was a highly educated gentleman, gifted by nature with a powerful intellect. He could pen a despatch like a Secretary of State, and dispute a point of law with almost the ability and acumen of his talented nephew, Sir Alexander Cockburn (later to become Lord Chief Justice of England) . . . In the House of Commons he could defend the navy estimates in a manner that proved his powers of debate were of no ordinary character. He was a man of the world and was very kind, humane, and the friend of all naval officers in trouble and difficulty; and invariably took the lenient view of every case submitted for decision. He was a true friend to the widow and orphan and lavish in the distribution of his charities.'[6]

Cockburn's attitude towards the impressment of seamen for naval service was unequivocal. Along with his opponents in the House he recognised that it was – to use his own words – 'repugnant to humanity', and that resort to it should be made only in wartime. But until it could be replaced safely by another system he would not endanger national security. Peacetime manpower requirements were helped by better service conditions, including a much improved daily food ration which encouraged volunteers. Many now preferred the navy to the merchant service; if this policy could be stepped up therein might lie the solution – so Cockburn thought, an empirical approach which achieved its reward in time. A Register of Seamen[7] a few years later, leading to regular long service engagements some time after, eventually killed impressment.

As with impressment so with flogging.[8] Cockburn understood well enough the objections to this degrading punishment but felt the time was not yet ripe for its abolition. Strongly supporting the discharge of incorrigibles, he let it be known that credit reflected on captains restricting the use of the cat.

His approach to these social problems dissatisfied his radical opponents in Parliament but Cockburn remained unaffected by political considerations: what was best for the service was all that interested him. Nor was he deflected by those who tried using influence to obtain naval appointments. In 1830, Captain Dillon – socialite, diarist, and close friend of the Duke of Sussex (Clarence's younger brother) – thought he had secured the command of the Ordinary (the ships out of commission) at Portsmouth. Even royal intervention failed to obtain this plum job for Dillon when, in Cockburn's view, there were more deserving officers – with better qualifications – in line for it. He wrote diplomatically to the Duke of

Sussex, 'I lament extremely not having been able to meet your Royal Highness' commands by obtaining employment for him (Dillon) and having thus candidly laid before your Royal Highness the real state of the case, I humbly but confidently look to your forgiveness'[9]. According to Dillon the Duke was furious, uttering 'a stream of abuse that cannot be repeated'. Even a second approach did not shake Cockburn's resolve. It was suspected that Cockburn's clashes with the royal family effectively blocked the peerage his close friends had confidently anticipated.

Towards the end of 1830, after Clarence had become William IV, a general election took place. The whigs, out of office for nearly 50 years, now formed the new government. The Admiralty Board had to change its membership to conform with the transfer of party power and influence; Cockburn was relieved by his lifelong friend Sir Thomas Hardy who also had matured in Nelson's shadow. Their long naval association, covering some 35 years in which Hardy had always been subordinate to Cockburn, provided an amusing anti-climax when Cockburn received his appointment of Commander-in-Chief, West Indies. According to custom he waited upon Hardy who was understandably diffident. An onlooker observed, 'he felt in Cockburn's presence exactly as he did when serving as his old first lieutenant'. Cockburn's old-world charm removed embarrassment. 'My dear Hardy, I have come to receive your instructions. As you know I am now under your orders.' Sir Thomas invited Cockburn to make any corrections to his orders to which the latter replied with a smile, 'it is not for me, Hardy, to make corrections, but merely to offer any *suggestion* that may occur to me for your better consideration'.[10] And so it was agreed that Sir George should take the instructions home with him to pursue at leisure.

The reforming zeal of Parliament, culminating in the great Reform Act of June 1832, extended the voting franchise and during the next few years reorganised public administration. The Admiralty did not escape its effects. Under its highly competent new First Lord – Sir James Graham – the Board's powers were increased by bringing the civil departments, formerly known as the Navy Office, under its control, and economies were achieved by the abolition of sinecures and redundant posts. Fortunately for Cockburn he was in the West Indies while the reorganisation took place, too far away to be worried. By the time he returned in 1836 the civil offices, previously at

Somerset House, had transferred to Admiralty in Whitehall where they were working comparatively smoothly.

With the whigs in power no vacancy existed for Cockburn since the only position open to him was as First Naval Lord. The possibility of another election in 1837 after the death of King William IV could interrupt Cockburn's sabbatical. Old friends urged him to fight the Portsmouth or Plymouth seats, but he was reluctant to proceed without proof that the unfortunate circumstances of the 1820 election would not be repeated. As no positive assurance could be given he withdrew his candidature from both.

While the whigs continued to govern Cockburn enjoyed the benefit of an Admiralty 'grace and favour' apartment at 4 Whitehall as well as his High Beech house. With his elder brother Sir James, the eighth baronet, living in Harley Street, and his younger brother Francis recently back from Honduras, in Stratton Street, family social life featured strongly for a change. Even his mother, the dowager Lady Cockburn, was close at hand at Southbank, Regent's Park, until her death in 1837, the same year in which Cockburn was promoted to Admiral of the White.

Cockburn's quality was now well known to a wide circle of important people; Sir Robert Peel, for one, admired his ability, integrity and loyalty, and knew him to be a disciple of his own dictum that, 'if any national weakness be laid open and examined with true wisdom, it is more than half redressed'. Not surprising, therefore, when Peel's moment came after the tory victory in the general election of 1841, that Cockburn who had been elected for Ripon, should join the Earl of Haddington, the new First Lord at the Admiralty, as First Naval Lord.

It was a rigorous undertaking for a man of 69, but Cockburn carried his years lightly and was still both mentally and physically strong. It could be argued that no man of that of that age should accept the responsibilities of high office – particularly since the tempo of Admiralty work had increased significantly after its 1832 reorganisation. But Cockburn, unrivalled in experience, was the obvious man to deal with policy and strategy. All those in senior appointments were just as old, and though he, himself, had been responsible for a scheme for promoting younger men on merit, it had not yet taken effect. Had Cockburn been over-sensitive perhaps he would have been hurt by a member's proposal during the 1842 naval estimates' debate in the House of Commons that 'the gallant chiefs who led them to victory should be replaced by efficient and younger men, who can follow in their glorious track in the vigour of life'. In fact, the barb arose over the appointment of Admiral Sir E Owen, then in his middle-70s, to command the Mediterranean station and no slight was intended.

In August of that year the young Queen Victoria, accompanied by Prince Albert, was about to visit Scotland for the first time. Her diary records 'there was a large crowd to see us embark. Lord Haddington and Sir George Cockburn were present in full uniform. Sir George handed me into the barge. I annex a list of our squadron – the ship *Pique*, the sloop *Daphne*, and the steam vessels *Salamander*, *Rhadamanthus*, *Monkey*, *Shearwater*, *Black Eagle*, *Lightning* and *Fearless*'.

The presence of seven steam vessels – including the *Rhadamanthus*, Cockburn's old friend on the West Indies station – illustrates the increasing use of steam to replace sail. Cockburn considered that steamships would become of great importance in naval warfare and improve on their current role of 'assisting sailing ships by towing them in and out of action and employing their long range guns to good effect,' as he expressed it in Parliament.[11]

The 1840s coincided with a transition in the building of warships; while sailing men-of-war were being brought to the pitch of perfection in a newly-formed Experimental Squadron, advances were taking place in the construction of steam vessels eventually to replace them. Wood was slowly giving way to iron, and the newly-invented screw was showing its advantages over the paddle for propulsion.

The complex problems required both a deep understanding and a wise head at the helm. The part played by Cockburn in these developments was considerable but appears to have been underestimated by historians. He supported tests to prove the virtues of the screw, notably the well-documented occasion when a screwship, the *Rattler*, raced against a paddle steamer of similar size, the *Alecto*, and won handsomely over an 80-mile course; the *Rattler* confirmed her success against another paddle steamer, the *Vesuvius*, over a 20-mile course, this time round the Bass Rock.

Cockburn encouraged steamship design and was closely connected with the building of the largest experimental steam warship of the time, the *Terrible*.[12] Of 1847 tons and carrying 20 guns, she provided a platform for later developments. She was the first of her kind to carry guns on her main deck to supplement the broadside guns on her upper deck. The *Terrible's* large engines still drove paddles but with the advent of the screw, allowing machinery to be placed below the waterline, Cockburn was persuaded that there was no limit to future improvement. As things turned out, this reached its watershed 15 years later with the building of the first ironclad, the *Warrior.*

Despite the burden of administration he carried, Cockburn volunteered to rewrite the Sea Service Regulations, unamended since 1833. Admiralty management now demanded a clear-thinking, analytical brain; Cockburn's experience in drafting wartime orders allowing no room for ambiguity made him particularly suitable for a job which others might have delegated. Nevertheless, it was a remarkable undertaking and, even after two years' usage, no errors in the revised regulations were detected.

Undoubtedly he was taking too much upon himself for a man of his years. He became ill in 1843 and strained his heart. Among the many letters received from well-wishers was one from Captain Badcock who had commanded the *Brune* under him in the Chesapeake. The reply shows the same indomitable spirit, 'March 15, 1843, Admiralty. I ought to have sooner thanked you for your obliging letter of the 10th instant but I am still restricted by my medical advisers as to the number of hours I am permitted to write, and each day brings me many more letters than the allowed time will enable me to answer. I am, thank you, daily regaining strength but am not yet permitted to return to general official duties, and I am still confined to my house and one floor of it, and restricted to low diet. The medical gentlemen, however, give me reason to hope that by following their advice on those points a little longer, I shall get perfectly well again'. Sir John Barrow, the Permanent Secretary at the Admiralty, wrote, 'the Admiralty had the good fortune once more to reap the advantages of the splendid and unexampled talents of the Right Honourable Sir George Cockburn whose zeal for the service and whose indefatigable labours in the multifarious duties of the office of the Admiralty, it is much to be feared, have proved injurious to his health.'

Multifarious his duties certainly were; he wrote copiously on a wide range of subjects – to Gladstone at the Board of Trade, for example, proffering advice to the Shipwreck Committee then investigating ways and means of reducing the huge loss of life caused by shipwreck in the mercantile marine. The letters are a model of help-fulness and sound commonsense.

A continuous correspondence was maintained with his commanders-in-chief, notably with Admiral Sir William Parker on the China Station, where the first opium war had strained naval resources. When trade reopened there was a lingering problem with the British plenipotentiary – Sir Henry Pottinger – who upset the naval administration by an autocratic operational control of Parker's ships, even to the extent of hoisting a Lord High Admiral's flag when embarked, and demanding the equivalent salute. Anti-Pottinger feelings ran high even after Parker's relief by Admiral Sir Thomas Cochrane, as can be judged by Cockburn's private letter. 'Dear Sir Thomas – I quite concur with you over the injustice done to the lead-ers of our army and navy in China by the vaunting and constant public notice of Sir Henry Pottinger . . . How much more will such feeling be increased when you read about the Grand Dinners given to him, also the Freedom of the City and Service of Plate from Liver-pool. In short, the merchants seem to have become quite mad upon the subject, while Sir William Parker's arrival in London is wholly unnoticed by them, though the success of the contest was princi-pally, if not wholly his.'[13]

Britain's expanding far eastern trade necessitated the develop-ment of Hong Kong and Trincomalee as naval bases; Cockburn's views on every aspect were constantly in demand and, even today, provide evidence of his wise counsel.

Naval domestic affairs understandably absorbed much of his time. Having helped reduce the inflated lists of flag officers and lieutenants, he turned his attention in 1845 to captains. The idea was to award the title of rear-admiral coupled with a financial induce-ment to those prepared to forego active service, and thereby make way for younger promising captains. When introduced by Order in Council it had a marked and beneficial effect. Supplementing all these calls on his time was the need to attend regularly in the House of Commons – in aggregate a most demanding routine for a septuagenarian.

Peel's proposal in 1846 to abolish the Corn Laws, and thus over-come famine in Ireland, foreshadowed a change of government. If the whigs gained office, Cockburn could bow out gracefully – and with relief. He wrote to his friend Admiral Sir William Parker, now commanding the Mediterranean station and his most likely successor, warning him of events at home. The selection of Parker would be the universal choice for, as one lord had expressed it, 'with the exception of Sir George Cockburn there is no one admiral with whom you can compare him as a commander'.[14] But Parker thought differently, knowing full well that the drudgery of the Admiralty office would be a poor substitute for his present command. 'None can place me in a more satisfactory position than my duties here,' was his reply. When the official invitation arrived, he turned it down.

Sir George continued until Sir Robert Peel's resignation in mid-July. Throughout Lord Haddington's administration Cockburn's contribution over a particularly difficult period of the navy's development had been outstanding. His advice, backed by solid professional experience over a vast range of subjects, notably the construction of warships, exploration and surveying, and the manning of the fleet, was invaluable. Never the reactionary that some sources, mistakenly, have made him out to be, much of the navy's later development originated in decisions taken during those important transitional years. Admiral Parker's sentiments are typical of those Cockburn received from his many friends. 'Although your former letters and the extraordinary sensation produced by the late political measures, in a great degree prepared one for a change of administration, it has at last come upon us rather suddenly ... and concluding that you are now on the wing for a little repose from the labours of office, I lose not a moment in repeating to you my warmest thanks for all your friendly kindness to myself, and my cordial good wishes for your health and happiness.'

Sir George retired to Wallsgrove House, High Beech, where he lived quietly but not forgotten. In 1847 he had conferred upon him the ancient title of Rear-Admiral of the United Kingdom–an honourable and highly-valued professional distinction. In 1849 came the naval General Service medal, a long delayed reward from the queen to all officers and men who had played their part in the notable actions and sea battles of the Napoleonic Wars. Clasps were awarded for those actions which qualified: seven being the most received by any one person. Cockburn came a close second with six – a fine collection reflecting an outstanding war service.

The ultimate honour came in 1851 when Queen Victoria approved Sir George's promotion to Admiral of the Fleet which would keep him on the navy's active list until his death. 'So marked, and so just a compliment to his brilliant course of professional duty, will be regarded with great honour and favour throughout the service,' was how one of his contemporaries saw it.

Only one event marred his retirement: his brother James died in February, 1852 when Sir George succeeded to the family baronetcy.

• **Admiral of the Fleet Sir George Cockburn in his later years but still a youthful-looking figure (RN Museum, Portsmouth)**

Epilogue

AT THE END OF JUNE 1853, *The Courier,* the weekly journal of Leamington Spa, announced the arrival, among other distinguished guests, of Admiral of the Fleet Sir George Cockburn with Lady Cockburn and their daughter Miss Augusta Cockburn at the Clarendon Hotel – then a fashionable venue for those taking the waters of the Royal Spa. The small Warwickshire town with its saline springs, pump rooms, baths, and pleasant gardens now served so conveniently by the railway, had grown rapidly from an 18th-century village of no importance into a centre of Georgian elegance. In 1838, having been granted the privilege to call itself 'royal', its future as a regular visiting place by the *haute monde* was assured.

Sir George, now 82, had been in failing health for some while, a bare seven years having elapsed since his retirement as First Naval Lord. In the comfort of the Clarendon Hotel he had leisure to reflect on the service which he loved so much: of the navy of sail in which he had advanced from captain's servant to supremo in a career spanning more than 60 years.

He had arrived from his home at High Beech in the hope of restoring his health. Friends of his were already there – Admiral Bigland and Captain Hoseason, the latter in due course to marry Augusta, his daughter. Lord and Lady Raglan were expected together with the United States Ambassador, also his brother William Cockburn, Dean of York and his wife.

On August 19 the Admiral suffered a major heart attack. The death of so distinguished a visitor upset the town, not least the proprietor of the Clarendon Hotel who had to receive hastily-summoned relatives. Arrangements to return the body by rail for burial in the family vaults of London's Kensal Rise cemetery were put in hand, and on the morning of the 27th *The Courier* reported that 'the mortal remains of the gallant Admiral will be removed this day from his late residence at the Clarendon Hotel to the railway for London, Admiral Bigland and other naval officers at present in Leamington being in attendance with the immediate relatives of the deceased'. *The Courier* referred to Cockburn as the 'Wellington of the Navy', a soubriquet which would have pleased Sir George as the two of them had worked so much in tandem. Cockburn's memorialist added that his services ashore fully equalled his achievements afloat and, whether employed as sailor, soldier, diplomat or statesman, he showed all the qualities which characterized a great man.

Sir George's services were enumerated; when as a young post captain he served in Nelson's squadron in the Mediterranean and was honoured by that officer's friendship and confidence; of his daring achievements in the American War of 1812 where he helped to re-establish the naval supremacy of Great Britain 'which had been all but too successfully called into question by our trans-Atlantic brethren'; and of his selection to escort the ex-Emperor Napoleon into exile at St Helena. He possessed, said *The Courier*, an indomitable self-reliance 'thereby infusing into his subordinates that confidence which is the guarantee of success, and was extremely popular with those he commanded; he was intrepid without being rash, and bold without being indiscreet'. The obituary concluded, 'Sir George served in the important post of senior Naval Lord to the great benefit of the navy, and for 14 years he was in Parliament where he was considered one of the most able debaters of the day'.

On arrival in London, his body was taken to the house of his nephew, Sir Alexander Cockburn, in Mayfair and the funeral took place a week later. Among the naval pall-bearers was Captain James Scott who, 39 years before, had been by his side at the burning of Washington.

To his everlasting regret Sir George was not gifted with a male heir so the vacant baronetcy of Langton passed first to his brother William, Dean of York, and from him to their nephew Alexander, Lord Chief Justice of England, after which it became extinct.

But no one could have been more true to the family motto on his coat of arms than Sir George – *Vigilans et Audax*.

Notes on manuscript sources

The manuscripts of Admiral of the Fleet Sir George Cockburn are lodged in the archives of the Library of Congress, Washington DC, in 18 containers. With great foresight they were bought for the American nation from the catalogue of Karl Hiersemann, Leipzig, Germany in 1909, followed by a second purchase from Francis Edwards of London in 1912. Some 82 volumes span 60 years of Cockburn's life and include log books, journals, correspondence, fleet orders and a miscellany on special subjects.

The log books provide an uninterrupted record of Cockburn's sea service and throw light on three periods in particular – the early years of the Napoleonic Wars when Cockburn sailed in company with Nelson in the Mediterranean; services in the Chesapeake during the 1812 war between Britain and America; and the long sea voyage to St Helena in the *Northumberland* conveying Napoleon into final captivity. Twelve volumes of fleet orders, three of Admiralty in-and-out letters and six of private letters, support the ships' logs and include information on such esoteric incidents as the attempt to free King Ferdinand of Spain from the hands of Napoleon.

The papers are strongly flavoured with a diplomatic thread – for example, accounts of Cockburn's trips as envoy to Cadiz and Mexico, and his negotiations with the Spanish government on the independence of the South American colonies. They also reveal that the decision to attack Washington was undertaken on Cockburn's initiative and his alone; some histories leave the point in doubt. His later years, spent in Admiralty office and political life, are reflected in papers from 1844 to 1847.

The Cockburn papers form the primary source of information in this book and their availability on microfilm has largely replaced the need to refer to the Admiralty series of papers in the Public Record Office, London. That office, nevertheless, has provided valuable back-up information. Much detail has also been confirmed by the accounts given in Captain James Scott's *Recollections of a Naval Life* in three volumes published in 1834. By good fortune Scott's career started in 1803 under Cockburn's patronage, and his story provides an intimate insight of the admiral's character over a long period.

NOTES AND BIBLIOGRAPHY

(The initials CP indicate Cockburn Papers, NRS indicates Navy Records Society)

Chapter 1
1 Scott *Recollections of a Naval Life* vol III, p 291
2 Walter Lord *The Dawn's Early Light* p 123
3 Scott *ibid* vol III, p 308

Chapter 2
1 Genealogy drawn from *The House of Cockburn of that Ilk* by T H Cockburn-Hood and *The Records of the Cockburn Family* by R and H Cockburn
2 Ralfe *Historical Memoirs of Admiral Sir George Cockburn* vol III pp 257-8

Chapter 3
1 Ralfe *ibid* pp 257-260
2 Navy Records Society *The Sandwich Papers* vol III (1936) p 245
3 Cockburn to Goodall, Sep 17, 1794 *CP*
4 Cockburn to Hotham, Jan 6, 1795 *CP*
5 Nelson to Cockburn, July 19, 1795 *CP*
6 Nelson to Hotham, July 22, 1795 *CP*
7 Cockburn to Hotham, Aug 7, 1795 *CP*
8 NRS *Nelson's Letters to his Wife* (1958) p 217
9 Nelson to Cockburn, Aug 26, 1795 *CP*
10 Ralfe *ibid* p 261
11 Nicolas *Dispatches and Letters of Lord Nelson* vol II p 180
12 Jervis to Cockburn, Aug 6, 1796 *CP*

Chapter 4
1 Marquis Joseph de Silva to Cockburn, Sep 21, 1796 *CP*
2 Nicolas *Dispatches and Letters of Lord Nelson* vol II, p 270
3 Nelson to Cockburn, Oct 2, 1796 *CP*
4 *ibid* Oct 4, 1796 *CP*
5 For a full account of the Admiral Man debacle see Mahan *Life of Nelson* vol I, p 246
6 Cockburn to M Belleville, Oct 20, 1796 *CP*
7 Jervis to Cockburn, Oct 21, 1796 *CP*
8 Many accounts have been given of this fierce engagement cf Mahan *Life of Nelson,* Kennedy *Nelson's Band of Brothers* and Laird Clowes *The Royal Navy*
9 Nicolas, *ibid* vol II p 317
10 *ibid* vol II p 444

Chapter 5
1 A widely reported event by Mahan, Kennedy and Laird Clowes as above
2 Ralfe *ibid* p 266
3 Fleet Order, March 5, 1797 *CP*
4 See also *Mariner's Mirror* vol 45 (1959) p 208
5 Log of the *Minerve CP*
6 Cockburn to St Vincent Nov 7, 1797 *CP*
7 Ralfe *ibid* vol III, p 268
8 Cockburn to Danish Consul, Gibraltar, Nov 9, 1797 *CP*

Chapter 6
1 Cockburn to Admiralty, Aug 8, 1798 *CP*
2 NRS *Nelson's Letters to his Wife* (1958) p 450
3 Keith to Cockburn, June 23, 1799 *CP*
4 Cockburn to Duckworth, Jan 21, 1800 *CP*
5 Cockburn to Keith March 20, 1801 *CP*
6 Ralfe *ibid* vol III p 274

Chapter 7
1 James T Flexner *Washington the Indispensable Man*
2 Scott, *ibid* vol I, p 30
3 *ibid* p 33
4 Ralfe *ibid* vol III p 275
5 Merry to Cockburn, Dec 30, 1803 *CP*
6 Scott, *ibid* vol I p 85
7 A J Pack *Nelson's Blood* p 50

Chapter 8
1 Marsden to Cockburn, Aug 12, 1806 *CP*
2 Cockburn to Ramsey, East India House, Feb 22, 1807 *CP*
3 Kirkpatrick to Cockburn, March 7, 1807 *CP*
4 Scott, vol II, p 64
5 *ibid* p 83
6 Fleet Order Cochrane to Cockburn, Oct 30, 1808 *CP*
7 Scott, vol II, p 122
8 Articles of Capitulation *London Gazette* (1809), p 483
9 Cochrane to Admiralty Feb 25, 1809 *London Gazette* (1809), p 488

Chapter 9
1 Scott, *ibid* vol II, p 179
2 Articles of Capitulation *London Gazette* (1809), p 1328
3 James *Naval History of Great Britain* vol V, pp 137-140
4 Ralfe *ibid* vol III, p 280
5 Secret Dispatches, March 2 – May 21, 1810 *CP*

Chapter 10
1 Keats to Cockburn, Aug 26, 1810 *CP*
2 Ralfe *ibid* vol III, p 283
3 RM Corps Historian *Globe and Laurel* Oct 1964
4 Scott, *ibid* vol III, p 39

Chapter 11
1 Scott, *ibid* vol III, p 57
2 Cockburn to Martin, Nov 13, 1812 *CP*
3 James *Naval History of Great Britain* vol VI, p 224
4 R Horsman *The War of 1812* p 59
5 BJ Lohnes, British Naval Problems at Halifax during the War of 1812, *Mariner's Mirror* vol 59 (1973) p 319
6 Warren to Cockburn, Feb 15, 1813 *CP*
7 Cockburn to Warren, March 23, 1813 *CP*
8 Daschkoff to Cockburn (in French) April 2, 1813 *CP*
9 Brenton *Naval History of Great Britain*, vol V (1813) p 125
10 Cockburn to Warren *Naval Chronicle* vol XXX, pp 163-4
11 *ibid* p 165
12 *ibid* pp 167, 168
13 Cockburn to Warren June 16, 1813 *CP*
14 *ibid* June 17, 1813 *CP*
15 Scott *ibid* vol III pp 156, 157
16 *ibid* p 164

Chapter 12
1 Monroe to Cockburn, Jan 19, 1814 *CP*
2 Cochrane to Cockburn, April 24, 1814 *CP*
3 Barclay to Cockburn, March 11, 1814 *CP*
4 Scott, vol III, p 229 et seq
5 Cockburn to Barrie, June 3, 1814 *CP*
6 Barrie to Cockburn, June 19, 1814 *CP*
7 Badcock Lovell Papers *Narrative of Events in the Patuxent*
8 Cockburn to Cochrane secret dispatch, July 17, 1814 *CP*
9 *ibid* Aug 13, 1814 *CP*

Chapter 13
1 Walter Lord *ibid* p 27
2 Badcock Lovell papers *Plan of the Patuxent River* Captain Badcock was commanding the *Brune* at the time
3 Badcock Lovell papers
4 Cockburn to Cochrane *Naval Chronicle* vol XXXII, pp 344-5

Chapter 14
1 US Capitol Historical Society *We, the People*
2 *Map of Virginia and Maryland* 75005.1626 British Museum Map Room
3 Scott, *ibid* vol III, p 313
4 Cockburn to Ewell, Feb 5, 1815 *CP*
5 Scott, vol III, p 301

Chapter 16
1 Cochrane to Bathurst, Aug 28, 1814 PRO WO1/141 and Cochrane to Melville, Sep 3, 1814 *Cochrane Papers* 2345
2 Scott, *ibid* vol III, p 326
3 *ibid* p 334
4 *ibid* p 336 et seq
5 Cockburn to Brooke, Oct 25, 1814 *CP*
6 Cockburn to Croker, Jan 28, 1815 *CP*
7 Cockburn to Pinckney, March 2, 1815 *CP*

Chapter 17
1 Cockburn to Croker, Aug 9, 1815 *CP*
2 *Bonaparte's Voyage to St Helena* Extracts from the diary of Sir George Cockburn
3 *The Times* Oct 18, 1815 refers to the popularity of cards in Bonaparte's party
4 Bathurst to Admiralty, July 30, 1815 *CP*

Chapter 18
1 Cockburn to Croker, Oct 22, 1815 *CP*
2 Cockburn to Bathurst, Nov 11, 1815 *CP*
3 Cockburn to Poppleton, Dec 11, 1815 *CP*
4 Cockburn to Montholon, Dec 22, 1815 *CP*
5 Ralfe *ibid* vol III, p 306

Chapter 19
1 MA Rolleston *An English History Note Book*
2 Navy Lists of the period include this definition
3 See also Hansard *Navy Estimates Debate* (1821) pp 523-4, 873-4
4 Full report contained in *Proceedings of the 1820 Election of Members to serve in Parliament* and *Official Poll Book* of March 9, 1820, in the Record Office, Portsmouth, Hampshire, England
5 Reports of the Parliamentary Select Committee

Chapter 20
1 Navy List 1820 (corrected to the end of June) p 121
2 Cockburn to Bouverie, Dec 23, 1833 *CP*
3 Cockburn to Graham, March 1, 1833 *CP*
4 *Ibid* Nov 5, 1833 *CP*
5 Cockburn to King, May 8, 1834 *CP*
6 Samuel Cunard & Co was a merchant company operating from Halifax and engaged in contracts for the supply of mailboats in 1833
7 Cockburn to Beaufort, Sep 14, 1833 . . . 'You know full well how entirely I approve of small war vessels being employed during peace on surveying duty in every ocean.'
8 Scott's close association with Cockburn had endured for nearly 30 years
9 Cockburn to Parker, Aug 10, 1835 *CP*
10 *Autobiographical Memoir of Sir John Barrow* p 442
11 Cockburn to Captain Arthur RN, Jan 26, 1835 *CP*
12 Cockburn to Lord Bishop Gilpin, March 4, 1835 *CP*

Chapter 21
1 Hansard *Navy Estimates Debate* Feb 22, 1822 p 642
2 Norman Gash *Lord Liverpool* pp 178-9
3 Hansard *Her Late Majesty's Funeral* (1822) p 935 et seq
4 NAM Rodger *The Admiralty* pp 94-5
5 Muriel Wellesley *Wellington in Civil Life* p 105
6 J Briggs *Naval Administrations* pp 11, 13
7 Seamen's Register, introduced in 1835
8 Hansard *Navy Estimates* Feb 12, 1827 p 441 et seq and May 16, 1828, p 732 et seq
9 Cockburn to The Duke of Sussex, ms headed Admiralty Sep 10, 1826
10 J Briggs *Ibid* p 19
11 Hansard debates relating to steamers, screw v paddle etc, 1842 p 1232 and *Navy Estimates* for 1842, p 472
12 Hansard *State of the Navy* Feb 13, 1844 pp 413-4
13 Cockburn to Thomas Cochrane, Dec 6, 1844 *CP*
14 Lord Ellenborough in the House of Lords, June 1845
15 P Ziegler *King William IV* Collin's, 1971. A full account of the disagreement between the Duke of Clarence as Lord High Admiral and Cockburn is given pp 134-140

Printed Sources (General)
Briggs, Sir J *Naval Administrations* Sampson Low, 1897
Broadley & Bartelot *Three Dorset Captains* Murray, 1906
Caffrey, K *The Lion and the Union* Deutsch, 1978

Castelot, A *Napoleon Buonaparte* Harper, 1971
Churchill, WS *A History of the English Speaking Peoples* vols III & IV, Cassell, 1958
Cockburn, R & H *The Cockburn Family Records* 1913
Cockburn-Hood, TH *The House of Cockburn of that Ilk* 1918
Duff, D *Queen Victoria's Highland Journals* Webb & Bower
Field, C, *Britain's Sea Soldiers* vol II, Lyceum Press, 1924
Flexner, JT *Washington – The Indispensable Man,* Collins, 1976
Forester, CS *The Naval War of 1812* M Joseph, 1957
Gardiner, L *The British Admiralty* Wm Blackwood, 1968
Gash, Norman *Lord Liverpool* Weidenfeld, 1984
Hampshire, AC *Royal Sailors* Kimber, 1971
Horsman, R *The War of 1812* Eyre and Spottiswood, 1969
Kennedy, Ludovic *Nelson's Band of Brothers* Odhams, 1951
Lewis, M *Social History of the Navy* Allen & Unwin, 1960
Lewis, M *The Navy in Transition* Hodder & Stoughton, 1965
Lloyd, Christopher *Mr Barrow of the Admiralty* Collins, 1970
Lloyd, Christopher *St Vincent and Camperdown* Batsford, 1965
Lord, Walter *The Dawn's Early Light* WW Norton, 1972
Lovell, WS Vice-Admiral *Personal Narrative of Events 1799-1815* Wm Allen & Co, 1879
Mahan, AT *The Influence of Sea Power upon the French Revolution and Empire* 1898
Mahan, AT *The Life of Nelson* vols I & II, 1897
Mahan, AT *Sea Power in Relation to the War of 1812* 1905
Martineau, Gilbert *Napoleon's St Helena* Murray, 1968
Nicolas, PH *Historical Record of the RM Forces* vol II, Boone, 1845
Phillimore, Admiral, *The Life of Sir William Parker,* Harrison, 1891
Reilly, R *The British at the Gates* Cassell, 1974
Rodger, NAM *The Admiralty* Dalton, 1979
Scott, Captain James *Recollections of a Naval Life* vols I-III, Richard Bentley, 1834
Somerset, A *The Life and Times of William the Fourth* Weidenfeld, 1980
Stirling, AMW *Pages and Portraits from the Past – The Private Papers of Sir Wm Hotham*
Herbert Jenkins, 1919
Wellesley, M *Wellington in Civil Life* Constable, 1939

Standard works on naval history and biography

Allen, J *Battles of the British Navy* vols I & II, Bell, 1883
Brenton *The Naval History of Great Britain* C Rice, 1823
Clowes, W Laird *The Royal Navy* Sampson, Low, 1897-1903
Dillon, Sir Wm *A Narrative of my Professional Adventures* (NRS), edited by MA Lewis, Vol I (1953), Vol II (1956)
James *Naval History of Great Britain* R Bentley, 1886
Laughton, JK and Perrin, WG *Naval Miscellany* vols II and III, (NRS)
Marshall, J *Royal Naval Biography* vol I part II
Martin, Sir T Byam *The Journals and Letters of Admiral Sir Byam Martin,* vols I-III, (NRS)
Naish, GPB *Nelson's Letters to his Wife,* (NRS) 1958
Nicolas *Despatches and Letters of Lord Nelson* vols II & III H Colburn, 1845
O'Byrne *Naval Biographical Dictionary* Murray 1849
Ralfe, J *Historical Memoirs of Admiral Sir George Cockburn GCB* 1828

Papers and other sources

Badcock, Lovell Papers in the West Sussex Record Office
Burke's Peerage, 1881
Cockburn Papers in the National Maritime Museum (Presented by Mr Travers Buxton 1941)
Diary of Sir George Cockburn – Bonaparte's Voyage to St Helena (Original ms in the Library of Congress)
Dictionary of National Biography
Gentleman's Magazine 1853
Illustrated London News vol XXIII 1853
Leamington Courier June and July, 1853
London Gazette
Naval and Military Chronicle
Naval and Military Gazette
Naval Chronicle vol XXX 1813, vol XXXI 1813-1814 and vol XXXII 1814
Navy Lists 1815-1846
Parliamentary Debates – Reports of Proceedings in the House of Commons 1820-1845 Hansard
Proceedings of the 1820 Election of Members to serve in Parliament in the Portsmouth City Record Office
Stokoe, (ex Surgeon HMS *Conqueror*) *With Napoleon at St Helena* Lane, 1902
The Times, Aug 2-4, Oct 18-19, Nov 7 and Dec 5, 1815 on Bonaparte's movements
Warden, Wm, Surgeon, *Letters written onboard HMS Northumberland* Brussels, Parkin, 1817

Index

285

286